MEDIEVAL CLASSICS

GENERAL EDITORS
V. H. Galbraith and R. A. B. Mynors

FREDEGARII
CHRONICORVM LIBER QUARTVS
CVM CONTINVATIONIBVS

THE FOURTH BOOK OF
THE CHRONICLE OF FREDEGAR
AND CONTINUATIONS

Fredegarii Chronicorum Liber Quartus

cum Continuationibus

The Fourth Book
of the
Chronicle of Fredegar

with its continuations

Translated from the Latin
with Introduction and Notes by
J. M. Wallace-Hadrill
Professor of Medieval History in the University of
Manchester

GREENWOOD PRESS, PUBLISHERS
WESTPORT, CONNECTICUT

Library of Congress Cataloging in Publication Data

Fredegarii chronicon. English & Latin.
    The fourth book of the Chronicle of Fredegar,
with its continuations.

    Latin and English on opposite pages numbered in
duplicate; added t.p.: Fredegarii chronicorum liber
quartus, cum continuationibus,
    Reprint of the ed. published by T. Nelson,
London, in series: Medieval classics.
    Includes bibliographical references and index.
    1. Franks--History--To 768--Sources. 2. France
--History--To 987--Sources. I. Wallace-Hadrill,
John Michael. II. Title. III. Series: Medieval
classics (London)
[DC64.F7813 1981]   944'.01   80-28086
ISBN 0-313-22741-1 (lib. bdg.)

Reprinted by arrangement with Oxford University Press.

Reprinted in 1981 by Greenwood Press
A division of Congressional Information Service, Inc.
88 Post Road West, Westport, Connecticut 06881

Printed in the United States of America

10 9 8 7 6 5 4 3 2 1

CONTENTS

Introduction   ix

    I   The Chronicle   ix
    II   Authorship and Composition   xiv
    III   Language   xxviii
    IV   Manuscripts   xlvi
    V   The Present Text   lvii
    VI   Previous Editions   lxii
    VII   Biographical Note   lxiii

Latin Text   *verso* 1–121

English Translation   *recto* 1–121

Genealogies

    I   The Merovingians   122
    II   The Arnulfings or Carolingians   123

Index   125

Plate showing beginning of Prologue in MS.
    Paris, Bibl. Nat. fonds lat. 10910   *facing page* xlvi

PREFACE

THE debts incurred in editing a text of this sort can never adequately be recorded or recalled, since they range from help obtained from passing conversations through occasional correspondence to what amounts to virtual collaboration; but to the following, at least, I am in no doubt of the nature of what I owe : Professor Bernhard Bischoff, Dr. C. E. Wright and M. Delaissé, for advice on manuscripts ; Mr Philip Grierson, Professor Christopher Brooke and Professor W. H. Semple, for help with the translation, and Mr A. P. Douglas for a stimulating revision ; Professor E. Ewert and Mr F. J. Barnett for guidance in linguistic matters ; Mr George Morrison, Dr J. A. Boyle, Professor W. B. Henning, Professor H. H. Plaskett, Professor F. L. Ganshof, Mr C. E. Stevens and Mr D. A. Bullough, for advice on particular points ; and Professor R. A. B. Mynors, whose time and scholarship have always been at my disposal. Of her kindness, my mother typed and re-typed the entire book ; while my wife time and again has helped to clarify Fredegar's meaning and my own.

J. M. W-H.

INTRODUCTION

I

THE CHRONICLE

THE Chronicle attributed to Fredegar occupies a vital position in the history of Frankish Gaul, and thus of France as a whole. It does so for two reasons : first, because of the intrinsic importance of the information it contains ; and secondly, because it is the only source of any significance for much of the period it covers. Together with the *Libri Historiarum* of Gregory of Tours and the Neustrian chronicle known as the *Liber Historiae Francorum*, it constitutes a nearly continuous history of Gaul from the end of Roman rule to the establishment of the Carolingians, a period of three centuries. But for these, we should have to reconstruct our history entirely from the *Lives* of the Merovingian saints and such correspondence, charters and official documents as happen to survive ; and we should certainly find ourselves in greater difficulties than would the historians of Anglo-Saxon England, were they placed in such a predicament. However, our three narrative sources are not exactly alike in execution or design, intimately though they are associated. Gregory is more than a chronicler ; he is an historian, second only to Bede in his age, able to handle large masses of material and to fuse them into a vivid, coherent narrative. Furthermore, for all his disclaimers, his feet are firmly planted in the Roman past ; he may not write Classical Latin, but at least it is recognizable as Latin. Fredegar (I leave aside the question of identity for the moment) is a chronicler, not an historian. I do not mean so much that he lacks the gifts, and perhaps the opportunities, of Gregory, as that he is content to be bound more closely by the annalistic arrangement of much of the material that he uses, and also that he is readier to follow where his material leads him. This is why his story moves so disconcertingly from one Frankish court to another and is punctuated with strange passages of happenings from a wider world that he cannot fully grasp ; they are often important to us, but they break the narrative. Some years, again, are fully chronicled while others are bare or ignored ; here we may find a straightforward record of Merovingian politics, and next to it, without warning, a long account of a private feud or a tale of some expedition in Spain or mission to Byzantium. Like Gregory, Fredegar knows that the golden age lies behind, and the end of the world not so far ahead, and he knows that his Latin is bad ; but I doubt if he knew that what he wrote was by traditional standards scarcely Latin at all. Values, literary and other, were hard to determine in his world and consequently he groped with uncertainties that Gregory did not have to face. Fredegar has done his best, putting all that he could discover in his ' record of the years,' especially of the deeds of kings and great men ; and what he has left us is a great deal more intelligible, and intelligent, than is sometimes made out. The Neustrian chronicle, the *Liber Historiae Francorum*, a monastic compilation from the Paris region, is best discussed in relation to the borrowings from it made by the continuators of Fredegar in the eighth century.

The manuscript tradition of the chronicle of Fredegar does not make it easy to decide upon the order of its contents ; nor, indeed, have the contents themselves been beyond discussion till comparatively recent times. The summary description of them that follows is based on the text of the oldest manuscript (Paris, Bibl. Nat. Lat. 10910) :—

1. The so-called *Liber Generationis* of Hippolytus, with additions.

2. The *Supputatio Eusebii Hieronimi*, a computation from Adam to the first year of the reign of Sigebert II (613).

3. A list of popes to the accession of Theodore (642), later completed to the sixteenth year of Hadrian I (788).

4. The beginning of the chronicle of Isidore of Seville, dealing with the creation of the world.

5. Lists of patriarchs, kings and emperors, stopping at the thirty-first year of Heraclius I (640/1).

6. Interpolated extracts from the chronicle of Eusebius-Jerome.

7. Interpolated extracts from the chronicle of Hydatius (itself a continuation of Jerome).

8. A résumé or *Historia Epitomata* of Books i-vi of the *Libri Historiarum* of Gregory of Tours in 93 chapters, stopping at 584.

9. An original chronicle in 90 chapters from the twenty-fourth year of Guntramn, King of Burgundy (584) to the death of Flaochad, mayor of the palace in Burgundy (642).

10. Extracts from the chronicle of Isidore, with an *explicit* dated the fortieth year of the reign of Chlotar II (623/4).

For the present, it need only be said that the chronological material comprised by Jerome, Hydatius, Isidore and the *Liber Generationis* forms a hand-book of world chronology of a kind that commonly acts as preface to the chronicles of the early Middle Ages. From its sure foundation the local chronicler would build his own little structure of events. This is what happens in the case of Fredegar, whose story only narrows to the Frankish world with Gregory of Tours and his own times. However, Fredegar is no mere copyist. He is always inserting material of his own, gathered from hearsay and from what he has read. Here, as examples, are four characteristically different insertions that are important to historians :

(*a*) The earliest reference to the Trojan origin of the Franks (Book iii, chap. 2 and Book ii, chaps. 4-8 as printed in Krusch's edition). This legend, which is quite without historical substance, became popular among French writers and has given rise to much critical literature in recent years. The explanation of Edmond Faral (*La Légende Arthurienne*, 1, 1929, appendix 1) is that the chronicler misunderstood the text of Gregory, where it is reported that the Franks *primum quidem litora Rheni omnes incoluisse, dehinc, transacto Rheno, Thoringiam transmeasse*, supposed or pretended that *Thoringia* was a city, and transformed it into *Trogia*. But I am not entirely convinced. More than one Rhenish town was known as Troy in the Middle Ages, and we must reckon with the possibility that Fredegar's Trojan story, invention though it is, was already widely diffused when he heard it. It appears, I think quite independently, in the *Liber Historiae Francorum*.

(*b*) Fredegar is the first to add to Gregory's account of the baptism of Clovis the information that it took place at Rheims (Book III, chap. 21). Despite many attempts to disprove it, there is no serious reason to question the accuracy of the tradition here reported. It also appears, at about the same time, in the *Vita Vedastis* (ed. B. Krusch, *M.G.H. Script. Rer. Mero.* III, p. 419). Since he also reports that the famous vase of the Soissons incident recorded by Gregory of Tours (*Hist.* II, chap. 27) came from Rheims (Book III, chap. 16), he may quite possibly have had access to the records of the church of St Rémi.

(*c*) In Book II, chap. 40, following St Jerome's allusion to the Alamannic attacks in the West, Fredegar adds that *uastatum Auenticum praeuencione Wibili cuinomento*, the Alamans made for Italy. Here is the foreshadowing of Wifflisburg, the local name for the Roman city of Avenches, which can only just have been coming into use at the time the chronicle was written. (The point is discussed by Krusch in 'Die Chronicae des sogenannten Fredegar,' p. 450).

(*d*) In Book II, chap. 62, we have the earliest version of the medieval Belisarius Romance, a fantastic tale of the marriage of Belisarius and of his friend Justinian to two Amazon sisters, of intrigue in Byzantium, and of the part subsequently played by Antonina, the wife of Belisarius, in the latter's Vandalic campaign. Yet something of the tale can be shown to rest on fact. R. Salmon suggests Byzantine diplomatic contacts with Austrasia as a likely source for the story that reached Fredegar (*Byzantinische Zeitschrift*, xxx, 1929-30, pp. 102-10).

Additional material of this order lends special significance to the non-Fredegarian books of the chronicle and emphasizes the necessity of regarding the chronicle as an indissoluble whole.

The original chronicle, from 584, begins by being little more than a transcription of local Burgundian annals but becomes progressively fuller as it proceeds. It is from the year 603 that the reader is unmistakably aware that he has before him the words of a writer or writers who lived at the time of the events described ; and this holds good to the end of the chronicle, as we now have it, in the year 642. It is quite possible that the chronicler intended to go on beyond that year, for the present chap. 90 of Book IV does not seem to make a natural conclusion.

In some manuscripts, though not the oldest, there is a continuation of the chronicle from 642 to 768, of which the first part (642-721) is a version of the originally Neustrian *Liber Historiae Francorum*. Thereafter it becomes an original chronicle, very different in style and in point of view from the work of Fredegar.

The present edition covers only a part of the full chronicle of Fredegar as outlined above ; and enough has been said to suggest that in arbitrarily cutting off one limb of the whole a grave injustice is done to the compilator and peculiar risks are run by those who are led to mistake the part for the whole. Here we are not concerned with the first three Books of the chronicle but only with Book IV and the continuation. Yet there is some excuse for this act of amputation. Almost all of the first three Books is taken from other sources that are available independently in print (though not, of course, the valuable and sometimes lengthy additions of which examples have been given), whereas Book IV and the continuation comprise, for the most part, an original chronicle covering the whole of the seventh and half of the eighth centuries. For many years of this long period it is a unique source for the history of Frankish Gaul, carrying on the story of the Merovingian dynasty from the point at which Gregory of Tours stopped [1] to the day of its eclipse—and beyond, to the end of the reign of the first Carolingian king and the succession of his sons, Carloman and Charles the Great. Its vivid picture of the sacking of the Midi is one to which economic historians have paid too little attention. Moreover, it is a vital source for linguists whose business it is to trace the development of modern French from its roots in the Latin of Roman Gaul. This is an additional reason why, at the risk of being pedantic, special thought must be taken before discarding any linguistic usage of Fredegar that does not easily make sense. For English students, for whom this edition is primarily intended, it is a commonplace that Bede alone of the writers of the Dark Ages could write Latin and think like an historian. Fredegar may help them to see for themselves just how great Bede was ; but in making the necessary comparison it may also strike them that Fredegar was himself neither negligible nor dull.

II

AUTHORSHIP AND COMPOSITION

A characteristic of most medieval chronicles is their anonymity. Their authorship was not revealed, except by accident, and was plainly considered to be no concern of the reader. The present chronicle falls into this class. Any scholar who

---

[1] Fredegar, like others, used a copy of Gregory's *History* that lacked the last four Books. These should be read in conjunction with the opening chapters of Fredegar's independent narrative.

attempts to probe beneath this anonymity will find that, as with peeling an onion, each skin that is identified and removed simply reveals another skin. Whether or not one can give him a name, what exactly does one mean by the *author* of the chronicle ? He starts, it is clear, with a collection of much earlier chronicles, which he may or may not have put together himself or re-arranged or added to. To this collection he appends his own story ; but linguistic and other discrepancies will at once cause the careful reader to enquire how this story was set down, whether year by year or in blocks of several years at a time ; whether the story was corrected by its author ; whether the blocks were the work of different authors writing possibly in different places ; whether, finally, the writer or writers who continued the work in the Carolingian interest, after an obvious gap, did not revise the whole. Which of all these candidates is the *author*, anonymous or not ? If we may suppose (as is true) that the Carolingian continuators did not in fact seriously revise (though they may have re-arranged) the Merovingian chronicle that they found, then we can say that the author was the last man to shape and contribute to that chronicle ; but he was not the original author of the greater part of it and did not pretend to be so, for in his prologue he enumerates the authors and the chronicles that he has drawn upon. In fact, he was a compilator, an editor and a continuator who never regarded the work beneath his hand as a whole, but always as a collection of separate and identifiable pieces to which he and others might add.

Fredegar is a genuine, if uncommon, Frankish name ; but it was not demonstrably the name of any of the authors of the present chronicle ; this has long been known, and has given rise to the clumsy and pedantic ' Pseudo-Fredegar,' which it is as well to discard. The name was not attached to the chronicle earlier than the sixteenth century, when it appears as an annotation in a humanist hand in Saint-Omer MS. 706, fol. 118; this reads *Putemque esse Fredegarium archidiaconum*, and a photo-

graph of it was published by Krusch in his article on
' Fredegarius—Oudarius ' ; and again several times, in
Claude Fauchet's *Recueil des Antiquitez Gauloises et Françoises*
(Paris 1579) though in the French form, *Frédégaire*. No reason
for this ascription was advanced by Fauchet, nor has subsequent
investigation solved the problem. We do not known why the
sixteenth century decided to ascribe the chronicle to Fredegar,
but it would be foolish to abandon so convenient an attribution
at this late hour. The author has also been described as
Scholasticus, scholar or schoolmaster, but the title seems to go no
further back than 1572, when it was employed by Papire
Masson. The author has even borne the name Oudarius, for
which no better authority can be cited than a misreading of
Udacius (*sc.* Hydatius) by Beatus Rhenanus in 1531.

Whatever we call the chronicler, his identity is a small
matter in comparison with the fundamental problem of how
much of his chronicle he was responsible for. The battle
between the protagonists of multiple authorship and those of
single authorship has been long and bitter, and is still un-
decided. It may be as well to set out briefly the course that
it has followed :

1. The traditional view, at least from the seventeenth century,
was that the whole chronicle was the work of a single author,
and as late as 1878 so distinguished a scholar as Gabriel Monod
did not find it necessary to justify this view.

2. It was attacked at great length and with a wealth of detail
by Bruno Krusch in an article, ' Die Chronicae des sogenannten
Fredegar,' published in *Neues Archiv*, vii, in 1883. This article,
together with Krusch's edition of Fredegar in *M.G.H. Script.
Rer. Mero.* ii, 1888, forms the basis of all modern criticism of
the text. Its conclusions were bitterly assailed and as bitterly
defended by Krusch ; yet, whatever the outcome of the
debate, the distinction of placing the criticism of Fredegar on
an entirely new basis belongs to Krusch alone. It is interesting

that Monod, who in 1885 had published without comment the text of Fredegar preserved in the oldest manuscript (Bibl. Nat. Lat. 10910) as Part Two of his projected *Études critiques sur les sources de l'histoire mérovingienne*, proceeded no further.

Krusch's conclusion was that the chronicle of Fredegar was the work of three writers, whom he labelled *A*, *B* and *C*.[1] The first two were Burgundians from the district of Avenches, and the third an Austrasian. *A* was responsible for putting together the *Liber Generationis* (with chronological additions to 613), the extracts from the chronicles of St Jerome and Hydatius (with additions) and an original Burgundian chronicle covering the period 584-613. *B* added to this collection the résumé of Gregory of Tours and continued the Burgundian chronicle from 613 to 642. He also continued the chronological lists of popes (to 642) and of kings (to 640/1). *C*, who worked about 660, revised the collections of *A* and *B*, interpolated chaps. 48, 81-2, 84 (end)-88 inclusive, and refashioned the prologue of the original chronicle. Finally, Krusch argued that the chronicle of Isidore was introduced after *C*'s time and the prologue revised to include reference to it. Krusch's reasons for substituting three authors for one were in part linguistic and in part historical. Unremitting attention to the manuscripts persuaded him that he could detect three distinct styles ; and even at a first reading it must be clear that the shifts of interest in the chronicle do either betray the work of different writers or else need to be accounted for on other grounds.

Krusch's general position was accepted by Mommsen, Schnürer and Halphen, though Schnürer moved the end of *A*'s work from 613 to 616/17 and Halphen to 614.[2]

3. In 1914, the *Revue Historique* published in vol. 115 a detailed refutation of Krusch's article ('Encore la Chronique du

---

[1] *A* had in fact been anticipated by H. Brosien in 1868 (see Bibliography).

[2] Krusch later accepted Halphen's date.

B

Pseudo-Frédégaire ') by Ferdinand Lot, who claimed that Krusch's distinction between *A* and *B* was chimerical on linguistic grounds, while on historical grounds Krusch himself had shown that their interests were so close as to be identical. No particular importance was to be attached to the date 613 : ' la date de 613, l'auteur . . . l'a trouvée dans un livret composé à cette date en Bourgogne, livret renfermant les extraits interpolés de Jérôme, d'Idace, du *Liber Generationis* '—in just such a book, in fact, as Berlin MS 127 (discussed by Mommsen, *M.G.H. Auct. Ant.*, IX, p. 78). The author copied and completed the Burgundian book at the date fixed by Krusch for the completion of Book IV of the chronicle as it now stands ; and the special Austrasian interests of the last part of the Book could be explained away. Lot was not entirely happy about removing Krusch's Austrasian *C*, but he believed that it could be done.

4. Fourteen years later, in 1928, Lot's article received support from Marcel Baudot (in *Le Moyen Age*, XXIX), who went even further in championing the unity of the chronicle. He examined the twelve most notable instances of Carolingian glorification, such as seemed to point to an ultimate revision in Austrasia, and argued that these were mostly concerned with events so important as to be perfectly well-known anywhere in France ; the so-called Austrasian outlook of the end of the chronicle merely revealed the kind of information generally available and not the special interests of the writer. He detected three periods, not in the writing of the chronicle but in the collecting of material that led to its composition *circa* 660 : (*a*) 603-614, at the Burgundian court of Theuderic II, (*b*) 614-625, still the Burgundian court at Chalon, but under the direction of the mayor, Warnachar, (*c*) 627-642, the Neustrian court of Chlotar II. He concluded that the author was a native of the *Pagus Ultraiuranus* who held office at court first under Theuderic II and later under Chlotar II, and who

was present when Flaochad attacked Willebad in 642 ; he was a man whose heart remained Burgundian even when his sources of information were Neustrian ; and he did not compose his chronicle until 659/660 (the last sentence of Book IV chap. 81 can only have been written after 658) and plainly intended to continue after the Flaochad-Willebad episode of 642 (chap. 90). He left the lists of popes and kings as he found them in the Burgundian collection that formed the chronological introduction to his own composition. Finally, Baudot sought to identify Fredegar. His candidate was a layman, Count Berthar, the only secondary figure mentioned thrice in the chronicle, each time with a good deal of circumstantial detail.

5. Léon Levillain also came to the help of Lot and Baudot in a critical review of Krusch (*Bibliothèque de l'École des Chartes*, LXXXIX, 1928). Without going quite so far as to accept Baudot's identification of Fredegar, he fully accepted the principle of single authorship and 659/660 as the date of composition. He further insisted on acceptance of the prologue as irrefutable evidence of what the chronicle, as left in 660, actually contained ; Isidore was not to be treated as a later interpolation.

6. S. Hellmann ('Das Fredegarproblem,' *Hist. Vierteljahrschr.* XXIX, 1934) returned to the theory of multiple authorship, though he saw two authors where Krusch saw three ; *A* remained, if in somewhat reduced state, while *B* (who, if anyone, deserved to be called the author of the chronicle) grew at the expense of *A* and entirely absorbed the rôle of Krusch's *C*. *A* (a Burgundian) stopped after the wars of 613/14 ; then came a decade of scrappy notes, which, with the remainder of the chronicle and its final revision, was the work of *B* (another Burgundian). Apart from a difference in choice of material that in his view reflected two outlooks and not merely two sources of information, Hellmann also distinguished two styles ; and the greater part of his article is devoted to

making this distinction. The most notable difference lies in *B*'s stronger tendency to anacoluthon. But if Hellmann succeeds in destroying the theories of Lot and Baudot, he also points out how Krusch was led into error by failing to observe that events were not noted down year by year, as they happened, nor necessarily by the same system of dating or the regnal years of the same kingdom. In fact, *B* probably found *A*'s chronicle (604-613) already attached to the Burgundian annals and the excerpts from the older chronicles, but did not start revising any part of *A*'s collection or adding his own chronicle before 624/5. His method was to add sections to his own work and to revise *A*'s work as and when opportunity afforded ; sometimes, as after the account of the death of Dagobert I, he would put down his pen for a year or more. The result, as he left it *circa* 660, was an unfinished chronicle, the material still not cast into final form. Even so, Hellmann rightly judged *B* to be a chronicler of real stature. His chapters from Jerome and Hydatius are no mere *scarpsum*, as the man who later drew up the list of chapters described them ; they are a carefully edited selection designed to show how Jewish, Assyrian and other events all point towards the emergence of the Christian polity, and how this in its turn is the framework for the victory of the Frankish people who, like the Roman people, are descended from the fleeing Trojans. This is already foreshadowed in an interpolation in the *Liber Generationis* : *Trociane, Frigiiae* (chap. 5). The interesting interpolations in all the earlier Books seem to fall into a scheme devised by a single mind, and there are good stylistic reasons for holding that it was the mind of *B*.

7. We come finally to the view of Wilhelm Levison, as expressed in his revision of Wattenbach's *Deutschlands Geschichtsquellen* (1952). This is a reversion to the theory of triple authorship : *A* (a Burgundian) puts together Jerome, Hydatius, the *Liber Generationis* and his own material in 613 ;

B (another Burgundian) adds Gregory of Tours and continues the chronicle to 642, interpolating the whole with his own additions ; *circa* 658 *C* (an Austrasian) adds Isidore and inserts the chapters dealing with non-Frankish affairs and the specifically Austrasian parts of the last six chapters. In brief, *C* is a reviser rather than a chronicler.

This brief survey of the chief stages in the criticism of Fredegar omits many important arguments and takes no account of the smaller, but sometimes significant, contributions of other scholars. At least it will serve as a basis for the views advanced below.

The critics of multiple authorship have done a service in emphasizing how unsafe it is to assume that each shift of interest in this or any chronicle reveals a change of author. Material was always hard to come by, and we must imagine Fredegar happy enough in the main to incorporate information from whatever source. Omission of (to us) important facts may be deliberate, but it may also be the result of ignorance ; while inclusion of stories in praise of a particular man or of his family may be the expected return for patronage or innocent repetition of commonplaces about the famous. All the same, it cannot reasonably be questioned that the bulk of the chronicle is too consistently well-informed about the affairs of Burgundy to derive from any other part of Frankish Gaul. Further than this it would be hazardous to go, except where shifts in interest seem to coincide with already-established changes in style.

For it is stylistically that the multiple authorship of the chronicle can best be supported ; and here it seems to me that the researches of Krusch and Hellmann have yielded unassailable evidence, and the attacks of French scholars proved, in general, unavailing. I accept, in brief, Krusch's *A* and *B*, as modified by Hellmann, and abandon *C*, with reluctance and with certain reservations. (The stylistic differences between *A* and *B* will be noticed below, in the section on Language.) I reconstruct the composition of the chronicle as follows :

1. The first compilator, *A*, was a Burgundian ; this I infer from his interests and from the material available to him. There seems insufficient reason to assign him to any particular region of Burgundy. Avenches, Chalon, Geneva and Lyons all have something to be said for them, in descending order of probability, but there is nothing compelling about any one of them. *A* either finds or puts together a handbook of excerpts from four chronicles, namely the *Liber Generationis*, Isidore, Jerome and Hydatius (probably in that order). He also finds Burgundian annals for the period ?584-604, perhaps already attached to the handbook. He makes additions to the chronological lists in his collection that bring them up to date and he adds an original chronicle covering the period 604-613. The assumption is that he finished his work in 613/14. There is no reason for suspecting that he moved in the court circle or had any official encouragement in his undertaking.

2. For the same reasons, *B* also was a Burgundian, though again I cannot tie him to any particular region. Unlike *A*, *B* clearly had access to official documents, was able to interview envoys from foreign parts and had personal knowledge of, and feelings about, the great men of his world. It would not be surprising if he were a layman and a man of standing in the Burgundian court ; but again, there is no sense in which his writing can be considered official or officially-inspired. *A*'s collection is the foundation of *B*'s work, and we may picture *B* consulting it, correcting it and adding to it spasmodically over a period of many years. The decade of scrappy notes for the period 614-624 may or may not have been the work of *B* ; he certainly revised and added to them extensively ; but his own un-inhibited writing starts at 625, and it is likely enough that his labours as a chronicler and a reviser only began in that year.

To *A*'s four chronicles, duly interpolated, he added a fifth (the revised epitome of Gregory's *History* to 584, though this would have meant the excision of any pre-584 part of *A*'s annals, if such a part existed) ; and *A*'s own work, which he now determined to continue, he probably regarded as a sixth. *B* did not add to his chronicle on a year to year basis. When he had the material he would add a section covering several years, or would insert a chapter in the earlier material, or alter a fact ; and this he was doing until about the year 660. Even so, he cannot have considered his work as finished. He had already composed a preface to the whole work, where he explained how and why he had gone about it and what other writings he had drawn upon. Yet the work still stood in need of revision and can never have been planned to finish abruptly with the story of Flaochad and Willebad in 642. If our hypothesis is correct, *B* must have been an elderly man by 660, and it would have been natural if death had taken him suddenly. On the other hand, he may have written more that is now lost to us.

3. With *C* as a possible chronicler I do not think we have to reckon ; there is no linguistic evidence of his existence ; though the case for positing *C* as a final reviser is rather more serious. If it could be shown that our oldest manuscript (see below) was Austrasian and not Burgundian, then the time between 660 and the writing of that manuscript would be so very short—a generation, approximately—that I should be inclined to wonder whether *B* himself might not have taken his work to Austrasia and started revising it there in the light of easily accessible information. It is not, after all, the notoriety of the information about the Austrasian mayors that is striking but its detail and quality ; it seems to me to be derived less from hearsay than from written sources—and these were never easy to come by outside the place of their origin. On balance, however, I think the probability is that

B added his Austrasian material from sources available to him in Burgundy. But the possibility remains that *B* or *C* did this work in Austrasia, at a centre such as Metz where information of all sorts must have been readily available. If this is what happened, it still does not mean that either *B* or *C* was, so to say, in Carolingian pay. *B*, to my mind, was the effective compiler of the chronicle as we now have it and its most considerable contributor. Speculation about his identity cannot be carried far ; and for our purposes *B*, and *B* alone, deserves to be known as Fredegar.

Not *B* but some later hand decided that the simple arrangement of the compilation into six chronicles was not good enough ; these must be arranged into Books, and further, the sixth chronicle must be sub-divided into chapters after the fashion no doubt of Gregory's *History* (it seems reasonable to attribute both pieces of re-editing to the same mind, though it cannot be proved). The result was probably as follows :

Book i	*Liber Generationis* (1st chronicle)
Book ii	Isidore (2nd chronicle)
Book iii	Jerome (3rd chronicle)
„	Hydatius (4th chronicle)
Book iv	Gregory (5th chronicle)
„	Fredegar (6th chronicle)

I here follow Baudot, and not Levillain who prefers to put Isidore after Jerome/Hydatius and to regard Fredegar as originally a distinct Book V. Levillain was misled by the words *INCIPIT LIBER III CRONECORVM* at the head of Isidore in the oldest manuscript ; this does not mean that Isidore was originally Book iii of the whole compilation but only that he was the third book of the chronological lists in the compilation, the *Liber Generationis* being the first and the beginning of Isidore (on the Creation) together with the lists of patriarchs, kings and emperors, the second. (In the list of

contents of the oldest manuscript these would be respectively
I, IV +V, and X).

The sub-division into chapters is a clumsy piece of work that
often breaks the narrative at absurd points and occasionally even
in the middle of a sentence. In the oldest manuscript we can
see approximately how the text must have looked to Fredegar
without chapters or paragraphs. (The chapter-numbers have
been added by a later hand.) However, it is convenient for
reference to retain the chapters, the obvious absurdities having
been corrected. The tables of chapter-contents are incomplete
and inexact résumés of the chapters, modelled, no doubt, on
the tables in Gregory's *History*; they have no authority even
though they appear in the oldest manuscript. They are
omitted from the present edition.

In most of the manuscripts, though not in the oldest, the
chronicle is followed by a continuation to A.D. 768.

The first continuator, as Krusch has shown, was an
unconscious contributor to our chronicle. He continued, that
is to say, not the chronicle of Fredegar but the *Liber Historiae
Francorum*, a Neustrian chronicle put together perhaps at Saint-
Denis or Rouen in 727. What is known as the B version of
this chronicle is Austrasian, and its continuation, completed in
736,[1] is what was finally appropriated as the link between
Fredegar and the second continuation. This first, un-
intentional, continuation is full of interest for the way in which
it modifies the text of the *Liber* from the Austrasian point of
view ; the continuator occasionally failed to understand the
text before him, but it was hard to turn a Neustrian into an
Austrasian story. His own original chapters (11-17) contain
much valuable information.

The second continuation was carried out under more
obvious supervision ; in chap. 34 (which survives in one

---

[1] Established by (1) the chronological computation in chapter 16, and
(2) the end of chapter 10, which was written while Theuderic IV was alive :
he died in 737.

manuscript only) the scribe states that, up to that point (751), this *historiam uel gesta Francorum* had been written under the orders of Count Childebrand, and thereafter the authority is that of his son, Nibelung. He is referring not simply to the second contribution (736-751, chaps. 18-33) but to that of which it now became a continuation, namely a revised text of Fredegar (the *Liber Generationis* is omitted in favour of Hilarian's *De Cursu Temporum,* and a large part of Dares Phrygius' *De Origine Francorum* on the Trojan origin of the Franks is added to Jerome) together with the augmented Austrasian version of the *Liber Historiae Francorum* (642-736).

Count Childebrand must be held responsible for what was done in his name in 751/2 : a text of Fredegar is found and revised (presumably in Austrasia) to suit his taste ; to it is added enough of the local version of the *Liber* to take the story of the Franks to the point where his own employees can continue. But in 751/2 we must suppose that Childebrand died, and the family-chronicle is continued for his son, Nibelung.

Very little is known of the Nibelungs of history, as opposed to those of poetic tradition. Childebrand himself was half-brother to Charles Martel (their mother was the lady Alpaida) and thus uncle of Pippin III, and it is clear from the present chronicle that the Nibelungs actively assisted the Arnulfings in the critical years of their rise to power and no doubt reaped their reward. A charter dated 14 August 791 gives a decision of the royal *missi* in favour of the Abbot of Saint-Vincent and Saint-Germain against Count Autbert, who had unjustly taken possession of the woodland known as Mons Adraldus in the *pagus* of Melun, formerly held by Count Hildebrand (Childebrand) and his son Nevelongus (Nibelung), and thereafter given by Charlemagne to the abbey of Saint-Germain (*Recueil des chartes de Saint-Germain-des-Prés,* ed. R. Poupardin, I, p. 36, nº. 22). In addition to this property near Melun, we know also that the family had interests in the neighbourhood of

Autun, in Burgundy. However, there is no evidence that Childebrand's continuation was written at Autun or anywhere near it.

The second continuation is not all the work of one hand. Krusch showed that, on stylistic grounds, a break in authorship occurred after chapter 21.

The third continuation, undertaken for Count Nibelung and completed after the death of Pippin III, is from chapter 34 to the end (chap. 54).

The task of distinguishing the various hands that contributed to the three continuations is more difficult than for the chronicle proper, because they are writing even nearer each other in time and are stylistically close enough to cause two scholars (Monod and Hahn) to believe in a single hand [1] ; it is also less important, since the undertaking gave little scope for scribal initiative at any point : it was a family-chronicle over which we may be sure that Childebrand and Nibelung kept control. Thus it is more profitable to think in terms of continuations than of continuators in the post-Fredegarian section of the chronicle. They provide us with the first official record of the doings of the Carolingians, from whose viewpoint all events are seen. If, on the one hand, this narrows our line of vision and ensures a story from which, for example, much that is creditable to the last Merovingians is excluded, it does, on the other hand, present us with authoritative details about the one dynasty that was changing the face of Frankish politics. The scribes had no lack of information ; does a directive from above best explain the silence of the continuation on the disturbances caused by Grifo, son of Charles Martel, or on the great career of St Boniface ? Secular, and particularly military, matters are the concern of the continuations. Yet their authors express or imply a view of kingship and its duties that Fredegar himself would have thought anything but secular. They express the feeling, not necessarily derived from

[1] Two other scholars (Ruinart and Breysig) believed in four hands.

Boniface, common to the circle of Childebrand, Pippin and their advisers, that a Frankish king should have about him certain of the qualities of an Old Testament king. He should be a *novus David*. The Books of Joshua and Samuel come alive again. Without this feeling no appeal to the papacy would ever have been made. All the continuations bear traces of it.[1]

III
LANGUAGE [2]

The language of Fredegar is not a language with a future ; it is far removed from the Classical Latin from which it derived, far removed also from Romance, the parent of modern French. Hence it must strike any reader unacquainted with seventh-century writings as irretrievably barbaric, though anyone who is acquainted with the formularies or inscriptions of the period will see that, while it is less barbaric than they, it follows the same pattern of linguistic development.[3] All that can be attempted here is a sketch of the main features of Fredegar's Latin (not of barbaric Latin in general) with some indication of the differences that enable us to distinguish between the various contributors to the chronicle and its continuations. The historian may reasonably expect to be forewarned how, if not why, their Latin differs from Classical Latin. Three words of caution should be added : first, that the language of Fredegar is a written not a spoken language, that still strives

---

[1] See the important paper of E. Ewig, ' Zum christlichen Königsgedanken im Frühmittelalter ' (*Das Königtum*, Konstanz 1956, pp. 7-73, and especially pp. 51 ff.).

[2] This section, based largely on the work of Krusch, Haag and Hellmann, has been extensively revised by Mr F. J. Barnett and condensed by Dr Gweneth Whitteridge. However, I take responsibility for it as it stands.

[3] The only narrative writings exactly contemporary with Fredegar are *Lives* of Saints, such as those of Leudegarius, Radegundis and Praejectus ; but these mostly survive in later manuscripts.

to follow classical usages fast becoming meaningless, while at the same time it is heavily contaminated by the usages of vulgar speech ; secondly, that only one manuscript stands sufficiently near in date to the author to preserve as a matter of course the linguistic forms of his own day. As will be explained later, this is why readings of that manuscript, although at first glance they may look nonsensical, have often been retained in this edition. Thirdly, the comparative study of barbaric Latin is still in its infancy ; forms that now strike us as haphazard blundering may yet be shown to have linguistic justification.

GENERAL CHARACTERISTICS

On reading the chronicle of Fredegar one is immediately struck by the gulf which separates its language from Classical Latin. It is a gulf so wide that anyone can see that to dismiss this barbaric Latin as ' wrong ' and to ' correct ' it by classical standards would be certainly superficial and probably absurd. We are dealing with a language that had other tasks than those assigned to Classical Latin and for which new weapons needed to be forged. At such a time we should expect to find, and do find, confusion. Thus it sometimes happens that the spelling of the chronicle would seem chaotic by any standard. What, for example, are we to make of the spelling of proper names ? All the variations of one name that can be found on a single page cannot be put down to ' errors ' in transcription ; they are variations made by the author or copyist who was not troubled by their diversity. It is linguistically interesting that to him there should be no ' correct ' form of a proper name, Latin or Germanic in origin, while in the spelling of other words he takes great care to observe forms that are consistent, if barbaric. But chaos is by no means the dominant feature of the spelling of the chronicle. What we find is a persistent, if erratic, attempt to represent new sounds by new spellings, in many of which Old French is adumbrated. Because a

Classical Latin word was being pronounced in a new way, a new spelling was attempted to represent that change ; though it need scarcely be said that the immediate result was confusion, for alongside these new spellings the traditional ones are also found.

While reading the short survey that follows, it may be as well to bear in mind the main features of the movement from Latin to Romance. As a result of sound changes, the forms of words were modified ; and in consequence of this, the forms of the declensions and conjugations of Classical Latin were upset, and, because of this resulting confusion, new syntactical expressions had to be evolved. During this period there was a slow change in the character of Latin from a synthetic to an analytic language.

Phonology

Vowels

The following brief survey mentions only some of the chief sound changes which were occurring during the period of Vulgar Latin.

The Classical Latin vowels $\bar{\imath}$, $\breve{e}$, $\breve{a}$, $\breve{o}$, $\bar{u}$ continued to remain distinct. But as a qualitative change occurred in the pronunciation of $\breve{\imath}$ and $\bar{e}$, and of $\breve{u}$ and $\bar{o}$, the vowels came to be pronounced alike with the result that uncertainty and confusion in spelling ensued. Both $\breve{\imath}$ and $\bar{e}$ became closed e, and $\breve{u}$ and $\bar{o}$ became closed o. Of the Classical Latin diphthongs $au > o$, $ae > e$ and $oe > e$. As a result of the strong expiratory stress, characteristic of Germanic pronunciation, vowels in unstressed or weakly stressed syllables (this includes final syllables) tended either to disappear (syncope and apocope) or to lose their character, thus making their spelling uncertain. As a result of these sound changes much diversity of spelling ensued. The writer could use, and quite frequently does, the traditional Classical Latin spelling which no longer represented

the sound of the word ; or he could attempt a new representation of the sound. It frequently happens, however, that the
new spelling is written in the wrong place where it does not
represent either Classical Latin or the sound of the spoken
language. These ' reverse graphies ' add considerably to the
confusion of the language and are common in Merovingian
Latin.

Consonants

All trace of aspiration had probably disappeared from Latin
by this date, but it tended to re-appear under the influence of
Germanic pronunciation. It is frequently misused in spelling:
cf. *astarum* (19), *husus* (61).

Single unvoiced intervocalic consonants become voiced
$c > g$, $p > b$, $t > d$. This sound change is reflected in spelling,
and because of uncertainty of representation reverse graphies
also occur : cf. *pagandum* (90), *congrecare* (90) ; *recibebant* (69),
Aripertum (51) ; *idemque* (68) ; *gratum* (27).

g before *e* or *i* loses its plosive quality and becomes *yod*.
The group *di* likewise becomes *yod* and much confusion in
graphy results from these changes : *colliens* (55), *madio* (38).

As a result also of contact with the palatal vowel *i*, *ci* and
ti are confused : *audatiam* (43), *amicicias* (69).

The semivowel *ṳ*. Probably before the end of the Empire
the semivowel *ṳ* when initial of a word or syllable had become
the bilabial fricative *β*. At the same time *b* intervocalic, or
followed by *r*, had likewise become *β*. Consequently there
was much confusion of graphy between *b* and *u*.

The Germanic *w* initial of a word can be represented either
by *u* or *qu*, cf. *Villebadum* (89), *Quintrio* (14).

When following *k* and preceding *o* or *u*, *u* disappeared :
secuntur (64).

Nasal consonants disappear at the end of a word and as a
result may be omitted where they should occur or be wrongly
introduced where they do not belong. *n* disappears from the

group *ns* but may be introduced without reason, cf. *trasactis* (prologue) and *occansionebus* (77).

Consonantal groups were for the most part reduced by assimilation. All double consonants become single in pronunciation and the graphies may correspond, or double consonants may occur when Classical Latin uses only a single consonant : cf. *sepelitur* written *sepellitur* (56), and conversely, *uellint* written *uelint* (76).

The confusion of *r* and *l* in speech is a phenomenon of widespread occurrence. In words in which *r* occurs twice the first may dissimilate to *l* : *cerebrum* written *caelebrum* (38) (cf. *peregrinum* > Fr. *pèlerin*). Likewise in words in which *l* is followed by *r*, the *l* can assimilate to *r* : cf. *Bulgarus* written *Burgarus* (72) but possibly this was the original form. However, the phenomenon is not unknown elsewhere, cf. *ulmum* > Fr. *orme*.

Morphology and Syntax

Consequent upon the sound changes noted in the previous section, havoc was wrought in the characteristic endings of declensions and forms of verbs. Further to confuse the state of affairs the unorthodox spellings which prevailed at this period often make it impossible to decide whether the reader is faced with a significant new form or merely with a peculiar spelling of a traditional one.

Declensions

The five declensions of Classical Latin were, during the period of Vulgar Latin, reduced to three. The 5th declension was assimilated to the 1st, and the 4th declension was absorbed by the 2nd. Singular neuter nouns of the 2nd and 4th declensions became masculines of the 2nd declension. Singular neuter nouns of the 3rd declension sometimes became masculines of the same declension. Some neuter plurals ending in -*a* lost their plural meaning and became singular feminine nouns of the 1st declension. Masculine and feminine nouns on the whole retained their Classical Latin gender but there was a tendency for abstract nouns in -*orem* to become feminine : *ea pavore* (55), cf. Fr. *la peur*.

The confusion of case endings and the growing use of prepositions, all of which in due course came to govern the oblique or accusative case, are both characteristic of Vulgar Latin and are fully exemplified in the chronicle. The first declension defended itself best against phonetic erosion. The loss of the final -*m* of the accusative singular made nouns of this declension end in -*a* in both the nominative and accusative singular. Feminine plurals of the 3rd declension ended in -*es* in both these cases and consequently the nominative plural of the 1st declension was remade analogically to bring it into line with the accusative plural and both cases ended in -*as* : *ut omnes . . . vicinas gentes . . . de ipso . . . canerent* (1). As a result also of the loss of the final *m* of the accusative singular, accusative and ablative forms sounded identical and are consequently misused. The reduction of *ae* to *e* has already been noticed.

The confusion of graphy between *u* and *o* led to the production of outlandish forms in the declension of 2nd and 4th declension nouns of which few are philologically significant. The nominative singular -*us* appears as -*os* and the accusative plural -*os* as -*us* : *frater suos* (3) ; *cumtus* for *cunctos* (89). The loss of the final -*m* permitted the accusative -*um* to be written -*o* and caused confusion with the dative and ablative in -*o* which is frequently written -*um*. The accusative -*um* can also be spelt -*om* : *tuom* (64).

Confusion of graphy between *i* and *e* can result in the graphy -*es* for the dative and ablative plural -*is* : *propries* (64) ; *alies* (68).

Fourth declension nouns sometimes keep their characteristic endings and sometimes adopt those of the 2nd declension.

c

The phrases *cum exercito* and *maior domi* are common, but *domus* as the form of the genitive singular is also found.

Endings of nouns of the 3rd declension suffer seriously from the confusion of graphy between *e* and *i*. The nominative and genitive singular ending *-is* is confused in spelling with the nominative and accusative plural *-es* and vice versa. So *omnes* (66), *bonetates* (61) are singulars while *regis* (31), *princepis* (66) are plural. The loss of final *-m* accounts for the spelling *-e* of the accusative singular : *limite* (20), while confusion of *e* and *i* explains the accusative singular forms : *regi* (50), *comiti* (83), *patri* (90). The use of *-i* for *-e* as the ending of the ablative singular may be due to confusion of graphy or to uncertainty with regard to the correct termination : *duci* (24). The dative singular can end in *-e* instead of *-i* : *dicione* (78).

The replacement of the characteristic 3rd declension genitive singular *-is* by *-i* may perhaps be explained by confusion with the genitive of the 2nd declension : *Dagoberti regi* (78).

When all allowance has been made for the confusion of the forms of the declensions, it is none the less evident that cases are frequently misused in this chronicle. Uncertainty as to the precise meaning of case is characteristic of Vulgar Latin and is one of the causes for the increase in the use of prepositions.

Pronouns

Apart from *hic* and *qui*, pronouns are, as a rule, correctly inflected, even when pronunciation could easily lead to error. The forms of *hic* show considerable doubt as to its declension. It was one of the pronouns which was in process of disappearing from the language.

The relative pronoun *qui, quae, quod* also shows a certain variation in the forms used. For the accusative feminine singular *quam* the masculine *quem* can be written : *rigina . . . quem* (80) ; for the ablative feminine singular *qua* may be substituted the masculine or neuter *quo* : *ipsa diae quo* (22).

The neuter plural nominative *quae* is sometimes written *qua* : *sacramenta qua* (70). As is to be expected the neuter plural accusative *quae* is supplanted by the accusative feminine plural form *quas* : *milia . . . quas* (45). For the ablative plural form *quibus* may be substituted the accusative plural *quos* : *quos . . . conlocatis* (8).

Although the forms of the pronouns present little difficulty for their understanding, the use of the various demonstrative pronouns is frequently not in accordance with Classical Latin. As *is* tended to disappear from the spoken language it is not surprising to find it replaced by other pronouns :

by *hic* : *imperium huius qui* (64)

by *idem* : *eadem instetucionem* (79)

Ille and *ipse* both evolved into the definite article in Romance. This evolution is foreshadowed in the following examples :

iube illum hominem, qui . . . nunciauit, armare (51)

ut Bulgarus illus . . . interficerint . . . nec quisquam ex illis remansit Bulgaris (72)

si . . . conspecto Chlothariae presentatur, ipsum regem uellet interficere (54)

Other uses of *ipse* in this text differ from Classical Latin practice :

it may be used in place of *ille* : *odium contra ipsam* (42)

it may be used in place of *se* : *ducem super ipsos . . . instituunt* (21)

it may be used in place of *idem* : *ipso anno* (6)

Whereas in Classical Latin the possessive adjective *suus* was used for singular and plural alike in the 3rd person, there was a growing tendency in Vulgar Latin to replace it in the plural by the genitive plural of *is* or *ille* : *eorum studio . . . spondent* (74) (cf. Fr. *leur* < *illorum*).

Verbs

Three main tendencies are to be distinguished in considering the forms of verbs found in Vulgar Latin texts. The analytical tendency of the spoken language occasioned the invention of periphrases which replaced Classical Latin forms. The disintegrating effects of sound change resulted in disrupting the harmony of the conjugations as it did that of the declensions, but was in some measure countered by analogical influences which strove to re-establish this harmony. As with the forms of the declensions, so with the forms of verbs in the chronicle of Fredegar : it is not always possible to say whether a variant form represents a significant new development or is merely a misspelling of a traditional one.

With the exception of the past participle the passive voice disappeared during the course of Vulgar Latin. Uncertainty in its use is therefore to be expected in this chronicle. The weakening of the final syllable made confusion of the active and passive infinitives inevitable, and active forms are used with passive meaning : *armare* (51), *aperire* (66), *furmam . . . laudare dignasti, stratus tui iobe subiungere* (51). Occasional examples of the use of a passive for an active form are also found and seem to indicate still further the uncertainty in the use of this voice : *espunsalias has . . . fiunter* (89), *certamene conflige debuerant* (90), *fiaetur* (35).

To convey the idea of the passive, new periphrastic tenses were created by the use of the past participle compounded with various forms of *esse*. The Classical Latin passive perfect was used as the passive present, and the passive pluperfect as the passive imperfect. A new passive perfect and pluperfect were made by compounding the past participle with *fui* and *fueram* respectively : *speciale conuenencia . . . fuit conuentum ut* (7), *cernens genitorem suum fuisse defunctum* (56).

Deponent and semi-deponent verbs were given active forms : *adgredebat* (39), *conabat* (27), *dignarit* (52).

The characteristic personal endings of the tenses of verbs

persist, but owing to the confusion of graphy between *i* and *e* there is considerable uncertainty as to which is the correct vowel to precede the ending. So a verb ending in Classical Latin in *-et* may here be written *-it*, and vice versa ; *-ent* may be written *-int*, *-aret* as *-arit*, *-eret* as *-erit*, etc. Similarly among the subjunctive endings *-em* may be written *-im*, and *-imus* as *-emus*, etc.

In consequence of the doubt as to the spelling of the unstressed final vowel already mentioned, it should be noted that the ending of the 3rd person plural present indicative of the 3rd conjugation is written *-ent* instead of *-unt*: *aient* (36), *iungent* (90). The spelling *facint* (85) is probably due to the same cause.

Three new periphrastic tenses were created during this period by combining the past participle of the verb with the present, imperfect and perfect tenses of *habeo* respectively. The first of these tenses conveyed the idea of an action begun in the past but continuing into the present, the second of a continuous past action, and the third of a completed past action. Examples of these periphrastic tenses found in this chronicle are : *habent indultum* (74), *habuerat disponsatam* (34). This latter phrase is a legal formula.

The replacement of the simple future tense by a periphrasis is also characteristic in Vulgar Latin. It was made by compounding the infinitive of the verb with the present, imperfect or even pluperfect tenses of either *habeo*, *debeo* or *uelle* : *conuenerat ut . . . debuissimus confligere* (64).

The future and past infinitives ceased to be commonly used. For *pollicetur se esse impleturum*, the chronicle has *pollicetur esset implere* (40).

A certain hesitation as to the correct use of tenses is also discernible in the chronicle.

In so far as it is possible to make any general statement concerning the syntax of subordinate clauses in Vulgar Latin it is perhaps true to say that the elimination of the more artificial constructions of Classical Latin is one of its chief features. As a result, many of the subtle distinctions of Classical Latin were lost to the language, but new subtleties in time arose in their stead.

With the disappearance of many of the Classical Latin subordinating conjunctions, there is less simple attraction of the verb in the subordinate clause into the subjunctive mood. But on the other hand there is a growing appreciation of the value of the subjunctive as a mood, and it is frequently used to make distinction between conception and reality. An example of this is to be seen in the treatment of indirect questions and statements. The accusative and infinitive construction of Classical Latin is frequently replaced by a clause introduced by *quod*, *quia* or *quoniam*, and the mood of the verb which follows may be either indicative or subjunctive according as to whether the statement related is true or false, or may be put into the subjunctive as being merely the verb in a subordinate clause.

There are, as is shown below, usages peculiar to one or other of the authors of the chronicle ; but the foregoing examples may for the most part be taken to be their common stock-in-trade. These were the usages of Frankish and Burgundian writers who had had whatever education was available in seventh-century Gaul. Perhaps it was rather more than is sometimes thought ; they had an ear for the *purissimus fons largiter fluenta manantes* of the prologue, and despite their solecisms and their infelicities they were not entirely at sea with their grammar, which surprisingly often proves to be good Latin. But where this failed to satisfy their needs or proved beyond their reach, they followed the path already mapped out by Gregory of Tours and others. Most noticeably they adapted their spelling of Latin to current ways of speech and resigned themselves to simplified forms of inflexion. Seldom, if ever, did they commit the ultimate barbarism of writing nonsense according to their own usage.

Individual Styles

At first glance it might well seem that the entire ninety chapters of the original chronicle are the work of one man, allowance being made for such obvious borrowings as the annalistic material and the *Vita Columbani*. The following examples illustrate how easily the stylistic peculiarities of one part of the chronicle may be paralleled in another :

(a) *eclesiam beati Marcelli, ubi ipsi praeciosus requiescit in corpore* (1).

(b) *sepultusque est in ecclesia sancti Dionensis, quam ipse prius condigne . . . ornauerat. . . . patrocinium ipsius precioso expetens* (79).

(a) *Eo anno Richarid rex Gotorum diuino amplectens amore prius secrecius baptizatur* (8).

(b) *Meroeus secrecius iusso Chlothariae in Neptrico perducetur, eodem amplectens amore quod ipso de sancto excepisset lauacrum* (42).

(a) *Eo anno quinto Kal. Aprilis ipse rex moritur. Sepultus est in ecclesia sancti Marcelli in monasterio quem ipse construxerat* (14).

(b) *(Flaochadus) . . . undecemo diae post Willibadi interetum amisit spiritum, sepultusque est in ecclesia sancti Benigni suburbano Diuioninse* (90).

(a) *Chlotharius oppressus, uellit nollit, per pactiones uinculum firmauit* (20).

(b) *Sed has pacciones Austrasiae, terrorem Dagoberti quoacti uelint nonlint firmasse uisi sunt* (76).

(a) *Nos duo singulare certamen . . . reliqua multetudine procul suspinsa, iungamus ad prilium* (25).

(b) *petit, ut hii duo imperatores singulare certamine coniungerent, suspensa procul uterque exercitus multitudinem* (64).

(a) *precedamus chetheris* (25).

(b) *Bertoaldus cum nimis citeris precessisset . . . interficetur* (26).

(c) *eo quod Bertharius nimium reliquis precessisset, uolneratur graueter* (90).

(a) *plures ciuitates ab imperio Romano . . . abstulit et usque funda-*
    mentum destruxit (33).
(b) *Murus ciuitatebus supscriptis usque ad fundamento distruens* (71).

(a) *Quo uerbo quem legati nunciant probauit euentus* (38).
(b) *sed huius rei uicissitudinem probauit aeuentus* (56).

(a) *reddensque ei soledatum quod aspexerat ad regnum Austrasiorum,*
    . . . (53).
(b) *ut Neptreco et Burgundia soledato ordene ad regnum Chlodouiae*
    post Dagoberti discessum aspecerit (76).

(a) *tanta . . . iudicabat iusticiam ut creditur omnino fuisset Deo*
    placebile (58).
(b) *tanta in suo tempore pacem sectans fuit ut Deum esset placebelem*
    (84).

These ten examples contain much that is of the common
stock of chronicles. If they seem to point to single authorship
throughout the original chronicle, what can be urged against
this ?

In the first place, certain characteristics of the style of the
first forty-two chapters (which takes the story to the end of the
political upheaval that cost Brunechildis her life and gave
Chlotar II undisputed rule over Francia) are not to be found
thereafter ; while characteristics of the style of the subsequent
chapters will not be found in the earlier part, except in places
where later revision may reasonably be allowed. For the
present, let it be accepted that we are dealing with two authors,
A (chaps. 1-42) and B (chaps. 43-90) and that the break
between them comes at the end of chapter 42.[1] The tendency
of the age towards anacoluthon has not escaped either of our
authors, but it is more strongly marked in B. There is nothing
in the earlier chapters that at all resembles *Aostrasiae uero cum*
ad castro Wogastisburc ubi plurima manus forcium Venedorum

---

[1] Chaps. 43-7 covering the period 614-24, are scrappy in content and
composition, but stylistically it seems safer to ascribe them to B than to A.

inmurauerant circumdantes, triduo priliantes pluris ibidem de exercito Dagoberti gladio trucidantur (68), or *Cumque Erchynoaldus et Flaochadus maiores domi inter se quasi unum inissint consilium, consencientes ab inuicem, hunc gradus honorum, alterutrum solatium prebentes disponent habere felicetur* (89). Again, both like to introduce a subordinate, but logically connected, idea into the structure of a sentence ; but they do it in a slightly different way. *A*, for example, writes *Cum Brunechildis nepotem suum Teudericum integra adsiduetate monerit ut contra Teudebertum mouerit exercitum, dicens quasi Theudebertus non esset filius Childeberti nisi cuiusdam ortolanum, et Protadius ipsoque consilio adsistens, tandem iusso Teuderici mouetur exercitus* (27) ; the disposing of the main and subsidiary matter may be contrasted with that of the following, from *B*'s section : *Cumque regnum Chlothariae tam Neptreco quam Burgundias ad Dagobertum fuisset preoccupatum captis thinsauris et suae dicione redactis, tandem miserecordia mutus consilio sapientibus usus, citra Legere et limitem Spaniae quod ponitur partibus Wasconiae seu et montis Parenei pagus et ciuitates, quod fratri suo Gairiberto ad transagendum ad instar priuato habeto cum uiuendum potuisset sufficere nuscetur concessisse* (57). In the first, the break occurs near the end, at *adsistens/tandem*, whereas in the second it falls much nearer the beginning, at *redactis/tandem* ; and this holds true as a general distinction between the two styles. Again, obsolescent constructions, like relative clauses, the ablative absolute and participles in apposition, come more naturally to *A* than to *B*, while *B* employs the aorist participle as a matter of course where *A* seems to shun it. Quantitative adjectives, and adjectives of feeling and sensation, are about twice as numerous in *B* as in *A* ; stereotyped adverbs are common in *A*'s work, less common in *B*'s. *A*'s adverbs are far less frequently used in conjunction with adjectives than are *B*'s. In their choice of vocabulary the distinction is equally clear. For example, *plurus* and *plurimis* are found only in *B*, with one exception (37) ; *dicio* occurs twelve times in *B*, once in *A* ; and the case is much the same in the use of *intentio* and *discessus*, for *B*'s mind is a good deal more abstract than *A*'s. Though *uideri* is used as an auxiliary verb by both, *nosci* is used only by *B*. In short, the second part of the original chronicle is not only more lively and vivid in execution than the first, it is also remoter from the syntactical and other usages of Late Antiquity, such as are still common in the writings of Gregory of Tours. *B* is not simply a different man from *A* : he belongs to a later generation.

Krusch's arguments for a third (Austrasian) author, *C*, were as follows : the uncertain chronology of the last part, its characteristic linguistic usages, the Austrasian dating of chapters 87 and 88 as against the Neustrian-Burgundian dating of the preceding and following chapters, and finally, the lively interest in Austrasian doings and, above all, in the personality of Pippin's son, Grimoald. He attributed to him only chapters 81 and 82 of non-Frankish history and chapters 84 (end) to 88 of Frankish history, together with chapter 48 (Samo), and left open the matter of possible smaller additions. But neither uncertain chronology nor Austrasian dating need point to an independent author, as reference to Gregory of Tours will show. A chronicler will often leave attached to a freshly-acquired series of annals the regnal years of the place from which they were derived. Still less do Arnulfing interests betray Austrasian origin.

Admiration for the Arnulfings, as well as for Chlotar II and Dagobert, characterizes the whole section of the chronicle that begins at 613. Yet there is no particular affection for the Austrasians. The Austrasian defeat at Wogastisburg (when the Alamans and Lombards at least were victorious) is attributed to their *dementacio* (68) ; the Neustrians resume control of the duchy of Dentelin, *quod ab Austrasius iniquiter abstultus fuerat* (76) ; the Austrasian attack on the Thuringian Radulf *sine consilio initum est* (87). And why should an Austrasian admirer have known so little about the circum-stances of Pippin's death as to have been content with *Post fertur anni circolo Pippinus moretur* (85) ? Neither chronology nor subject-matter suggests an Austrasian chronicler, nor is the case much stronger for an Austrasian reviser of the chronicle. Linguistically, Krusch's only solid reason for the existence of *C* is the use of *fertur* in chapters 81, 82 and 85 and nowhere else. But the similarity between, for example, chapters 85, 86 and the beginning of chapter 90 is even more striking : the phrase *eumque dispicere conaretur* is found in chapters 86 and 90 and nowhere else. Yet chapter 90 is of exclusively Neustrian-Burgundian interest. This coincides with the observation of Ferdinand Lot that chapter 84, where Erchinoald's character is described, contains the sentence *tanta in suo tempore pacem sectans fuit ut Deum esse placebelem*, which cannot have been written before Erchinoald's death in 657 and must therefore have been the work of *C*, whether or not *C* was to be identified with *B* ; but yet it has no Austrasian interest. On every ground, therefore, we can dispense with Krusch's *C* and leave *A* and *B*, both Burgundians, in possession of the field.

THE CONTINUATIONS

It is not proposed to subject the language of the continuations to the scrutiny accorded to the main chronicle, but merely to indicate how differences in style enable us to distinguish between the continuators.

The style of the first continuator (*C.1*), who revised the *Liber Historiae Francorum* and continued it from (in the present edition) chapter 11 to the end of chapter 17, is marked by a love of subordinate clauses ; e.g. *Eodone . . . recedente, quo conperto . . . Carlus princeps commoto exercito Liger fluuium transiens, ipso duce Eodone fugato praeda multa sublata bis eo anno ab his hostibus populata iterum remeatur ad propria* (13). There is nothing like this in the section written by *C.2*, the first author of the second continuation (chap. 18 to the end of chap. 21) : his syntactical preference is for co-ordination, not subordination, e.g. *Carlus . . . fluuium . . . transiit, Gotorum fines penetrauit, usque Narbonensem Galliam peraccessit, ipsam urbem . . . obsedit, . . . munitionem . . . instruxit, regem . . . reclusit castraque metatus est undique* (20) ; and he seems more accustomed than the other continuators to the use of the relative clause. He is, further, very fond of using superlatives : *Saxonis paganissimis* (19), *regione illa dirissima cede uastauit* (ibid.), *gentemque illam seuissimam* (ibid.), *urbem munitissimam* (20), *munitissimam ciuitatem* (ibid.), *urbem celeberrimam* (ibid.), *urbes famosissimas* (ibid.), *tutissimis rupibus* (21), and so forth.

The distinction between the language of *C.3*, the author of the second continuation (22 to 33, inclusive) and *C.4*, the last continuator (34 to 54 inclusive), is less strongly marked [1] ; their outlook is much the same and the opportunities for exercising choice in the matter of vocabulary are few indeed. However, there are certain significant differences to be noticed. *C.4* correctly uses *castra* for 'encampment' or 'fortified position' (*castra metatus est, castra diripuit*), but for 'fortress' uses *castrus* (*ipse castrus*) ; and he likes the expression *ad castro*. *C.3* uses *castrum* once only, and then correctly (25) ; and *C.1* also once only (15). Again, the normal phrase in which *C.4* records the act of surrender of a conquered people to the Frankish king is *dictione sue facere*. It occurs several times, but never in the early continuations. *C.3* prefers *dicione se subdere* or *iure se submittere*.

C.1 and *C.4* have certain marked similarities of style. They share, for example, a liking for the word *partibus* ; but *C.4* will use it not only of places but also of persons : *partibus rege Pippino dedit* (38), *fideles partibus regis* (51), and elsewhere. *C.1* uses it only of places. *C.3* uses it once in the manner of *C.4*. When referring to previous events, *C.4* will often employ *dudum* as a catchword, in the classical sense of ' a few days ago ' but also of ' several years ago.' He is the only continuator who makes

---

[1] The language of chapter 31 is quite strikingly like that of the last continuator ; it may be the work of his youth or, alternatively, the model on which he later decided to found his style.

any use of the word, though *C.3* in particular gives himself several opportunities to do so.

C.4 is by far the least literate of the continuators, and it is perhaps of some interest that he should have been the best man available to so influential a person as Count Nibelung. His writing is more heavily influenced by current speech ; his cases are more hopelessly mixed, his verbal forms incorrect, his accusative absolutes and sentences without a main verb commoner. He allows himself duplicated objects, e.g. *Hec Pippinus rex cum per internuncios hoc audisset* (38), and *Haec omnia Waiofarius . . . hoc totum facere contempsit* (41) ; his adverbial usages may be illustrated by *ut amplius numquam . . . contumax esse non debeat* (38) and *iterum de Sellus castro cum paucis ad persequendum Waiofarium eo anno iterum perrexit* (52). The earlier continuators, and especially *C.1*, do occasionally permit themselves duplicated objects and verbs, but only *C.4* could write *usque Hisandonem ueniens unde maxima parte Aquitaniae plurimum uinearum erat coepit ac uastauit unde pene omni Aquitania, tam ecclesias quam monasteria, diuites et pauperes uina habere consuerunt, omnia uastauit et coepit* (47). He has a particular liking for relative clauses though his use of them is often ungrammatical. Relative pronouns occur some fifty times, and of these the commonest is *quod* ; it is employed, incorrectly, for *qui, quem, quam, quos, quas* and *quae*. Another favourite pronoun is *qui*. This might suggest that *C.4* was a native of the Midi, particularly when one recalls his sympathy for the Aquitanian vine-growers and his knowledge that the Gascons were known as *Vaceti*.

The case for multiple authorship of the continuations is thus a fairly strong one on linguistic grounds. It is impossible to envisage the decline of *C.3* to the depths touched by *C.4* ; one cannot unlearn the correct use of the relative clause and pronoun. Nor is the case much less strong for distinguishing *C.3* from *C.2*, and *C.2* from *C.1*. That they have much in common was only to be expected.

IV

MANUSCRIPTS

The chronicle survives in some thirty-four manuscripts. These have been described, in some cases exhaustively, by Krusch in the first part of his study, ' Die Chronicae des sogenannten Fredegar ' (*Neues Archiv* vii, 1882), and again, more summarily, in the introduction to his *Monumenta* edition of the chronicle published in 1888. It would here be superfluous to cover the same ground, and for this, as for much else, the reader must refer to that great man's work. Krusch did not personally examine all the manuscripts but he established the groups into which they fall. I have myself examined the greater part of them and have not omitted any that, being accessible, I judged could be in any way of value to me. I list below all the manuscripts, giving Krusch's numeration for convenience of reference, and confine detailed descriptions to those manuscripts that are of particular importance here.

The contents of the five groups of manuscripts may be distinguished as follows :—

GROUP I	GROUP II	GROUP III	GROUP IV	GROUP V
1. *Liber Generationis*	1. *Liber Generationis*	1. *Liber Generationis* to chap. 23	1. Hilarian, *De Cursu Temp.*	
2. Jerome and Hydatius	2. Jerome and Hydatius	2. Jerome and Hydatius	2. Jerome and Hydatius (with Dares Phrygius)	
		3. Hilarian, *De Cursu Temp.*		
3. Gregory, *Hist. Epit.*	3. Gregory, *Hist. Epit.*	4. Gregory, *Hist. Epit.*	3. Gregory, *Hist. Epit.*	1. Gregory, *Hist. Franc.* to x, 28.
4. Chron. to chap. 90	4. Chron. to chap. 9	5. Chron. to chap. 90	4. Chron. to chap. 90 and all conts.	2. Chron. to chap. 90 and conts. to chap. 24
5. Isidore				

Beginning of prologue
in MS Paris Bibl. Nat. fonds lat. 10910, fol. 124 *verso*
(*Reduction one-third*)

The first group is represented by two manuscripts only :

1 *Paris, Bibl. Nat. fonds lat. 10910 :* written in a rapid, not very expert uncial, late 7th or early 8th century, provenance unknown. It once belonged to the College of Clermont at Paris,[1] and, before that, to Sirmond, but there is no indication of how he acquired it. Krusch has pointed out that the earliest associations of the chronicle appear to be with Metz, and it is not impossible that this manuscript came originally from St Arnulf's, Metz. E. A. Lowe, however, describes it as ' perhaps . . . Burgundian ' (*Codices Latini Antiquiores,* v, no. 608) but by inference does so, as Professor Bischoff first pointed out to me, on historical rather than on palaeographical grounds.

The date at which it is written is probably, but not certainly, revealed in the following computation, written in uncial mixed with Merovingian cursive, on the last folio (184^r) :

> † INVENIT LVCERIOS PRESBETER MONACOS DOM
> TVM A . . PER ISTA CRONECA ET PER ALIA CRONE
> SV . QVOD SEPTOAGENTA ET QVATTVOR ANN
> . . . . . . V . AVID QVOD SEXTVS MILIARIOS
> . . . . ESSE EXPLITOS CONPOTAVIT IPSOS . .
> AN . S X IN INDICCIONE EXSIENTE TE . . . . .
> . O QVARTO DAGOBERTO RIGNANTE

Accepting Krusch's emendations, this would read : *inuenit Lucerios presbeter monachos dom/tum a . . per ista croneca et per alia crone(ca) su. quod septoagenta et quattuor ann(i ab ista comp)utauid quod sextus miliarios . . (docit) esse explitos, conpotauit ipsos (ann. LXXIIII et) an(o)s X in indiccione exsiente te(rtia decimo ann)o quarto Dagoberto rignante.* This can be rendered ' the priest and monk Lucerius of the house of . . . has found the following from this chronicle and another chronicle ; he reckoned 74 years from the end of this chronicle and calculated the

---

[1] Not to Clermont itself, as W. M. Lindsay thought (*Notae Latinae,* p. 474), thus misleading Lesne and others.

completion of the sixth millenium as 74 + 10 years to the end of the 13th indiction, in Dagobert's 4th year.'

Nothing is known of the presbyter Lucerius ; but it is clear that if we can determine to which Dagobert he here refers, we shall have a date for the writing of the manuscript. Even if, as is possible, Lucerius was not the scribe of the whole manuscript, nor perhaps the scribe of the computation, at least he is near enough in age to that scribe to make the lapse of time between them unimportant. Dagobert I died in 638 and figures prominently in the chronicle : he must certainly be excluded ; Dagobert II, whose fourth regnal year was 676/7, seems to be excluded by the computation itself ; and this leaves Dagobert III, whose fourth regnal year was 714/5 ; and this year does in fact fit the computation, as Krusch has shown. However, this cannot exclude a slightly earlier date for the writing of the manuscript itself : Delisle (*Cabinet des Manuscrits*, III, 218) did not hesitate to assign it to the 7th century. Whether we follow Delisle or Krusch, we have here a manuscript of the chronicle written within a generation of its composition, and perhaps in the same generation. On the other hand, it contains errors that reveal it as no more than a bad copy, or a copy at more than one remove, of the manuscript of Fredegar himself. The copyist cannot, in the first place, read the cursive script that must have been before his eyes ; he confuses s with r, t with e, t with c, n with u, ci with a ; he often blunders over cursive contractions, sometimes makes unfortunate corrections and introduces punctuation that casts grave doubt on his ability to understand the text. Further, he seems to have made his copy with a special end in view ; and the result has been called a clerical ' Lesebuch.' Two drawings appear in this manuscript and not elsewhere (though spaces were left for them in both manuscripts of the second group) : one, on fol. 75 verso, in the middle of Book II, chapter 58, is the figure of a woman, identified by Monod with St Helena ; and the other, on fol. 23 verso, opposite chapter 26 of the *Liber*

Generationis, is of two men, again identified by Monod with Eusebius and Jerome.[1] Both may have been found by the scribe of Paris 10910 in his original. When we have allowed that Paris 10910 may give a very imperfect idea of the chronicle as left by Fredegar, it stills remains uniquely important because of its early date ; the more so if, with Krusch, we hold that all other extant manuscripts are descended from it. But this it is difficult to do, for although Paris 10910, bad as it is, contains many better readings than do the remaining manuscripts, it yet makes a few significant blunders that are not repeated by the others. This can only mean that they derive not from Paris 10910 but from another manuscript, admittedly very like Paris 10910, that had avoided these blunders. The crucial blunder occurs in the prologue, where the chronicler wrote (and every manuscript but Paris 10910 repeats) : *etiam et uidendo cuncta que certeficatus cognoui huius libelli uolumine scribere non silui.* Paris 10910 has *solui* for *silui*, and Krusch defends it thus : ' *soluere pro* rumpere, intermittere, *ut* soluere ieiunium '. But this will not do, particularly since the chronicler uses the phrase a second time in chapter 81 (*scribere non selebo*). I am no more able than was Hellmann to imagine that the scribe of the manuscript from which all but our group 1 manuscripts descend could have corrected *solui* to *silui* and yet allowed numerous other solecisms that would have been much easier to correct. Again, in the long excerpted chapter from the *Vita Columbani* (chap. 36), there are three places where other manuscripts have the correct reading and Paris 10910 the incorrect ; but this might be explained on other grounds if we did not already have the mistake in the prologue before our eyes. The conclusion can only be that Paris 10910 is not the parent of any extant manuscript of the chronicle, although it

---

[1] The drawings are discussed by E. H. Zimmermann, *Vorkarolingische Miniaturen*, pp. 74 and 178 ff. He thinks that they are influenced by Corbie and Luxeuil but executed at some out-of-the-way scriptorium ; both are illustrated on plate 74.

D

stands very near to them and is, in general, their superior.[1] It was published by Monod ('La Compilation dite de Frédégaire,' *Bibliothèque de l'École des Hautes Études*, fasc. 63) in 1885, and formed the basis of Krusch's *Monumenta* edition in 1888. I have collated the manuscript afresh and find that where the two scholars disagree on a reading, I am usually in agreement with Krusch. I indicate in the text where I have preferred a reading of Monod.

1[x] *Metz, 134:* 8th/9th century, from St Arnulf's, Metz. Parts only of Books I and II, copied not from Paris 10910 but from a collateral. The manuscript was destroyed in 1944 (E. A. Lowe, *Cod. Lat. Ant.* VI, no. 788).

The second group, which is of little importance for the present edition since it stops short in the middle of Book IV, chapter 9, nonetheless descends from an intermediary or intermediaries between itself and the original.

2a *Berne, 318:* 9th century; on f. 130, HAECPERTVS ME FECIT; QVI ISTVM LIBRVM LEGIT ORAT PRO HECPERTO SCRIPTORE SI $\overline{\text{DM}}$ HABEAT ADIVTOREM ET DEFENSOREM.

2b *British Museum, Harleian 5251:* late 9th century, French, in the opinion of Professor Bischoff. It must have been a direct copy of the same manuscript as 2a, to which it is very closely related. Mommsen (M.G.H., *Auct. Antiq.* XI, 399) thought it a copy of 1.

The third group, which descends not from 2a and 2b but from a collateral of their immediate parent, is represented by three manuscripts which contain the whole of our main chronicle (Book IV) and the *Liber Historiae Francorum*.

3[1] *Leiden, Voss. Lat. 5* + 3[2] *Vatican, Reg. 713*, are two parts of the same manuscript: 8th/9th century, from the Saint-Gall-Reichenau-Mehrerau area, written in German pre-Caroline minuscule (*Cod. Lat. Ant.* I, no. 108). The break occurs in the *incipit* of

---

[1] We may recall the warning of Professor Laistner : 'That all extant manuscripts of an author go back to a single archetype was a favourite dogma of many nineteenth-century editors, which has so often been disproved that it arouses extreme scepticism' (*Speculum*, XXVIII, 1953, p. 559).

Gregory's *Historia Epitomata*, and thus the part that is relevant to the present edition lies wholly in the Vatican MS.

From 3^1+3^2, probably through an intermediary, derive :

a *Vienna, 482 :* 9th century, from Mehrerau, and

b *Augsburg, 223 :* 15th century, on paper, also from Mehrerau.

The fourth group is more numerous and more complicated. It derives from a parent that must have been copied from the same manuscript as was 3^1+3^2 ; but the extant manuscripts· of the group, which fall into three sub-groups, are none of them direct copies of that parent ; nor do any of the three manuscripts, from which the sub-groups obtain their characteristic variants, survive.

a *Vatican, Reg. lat. 213 :* 9th/10th century (Wilmart, *Cat. Bibl. Vat., Cod. Reg. Lat.* i, pp. 502-4), from the monastery of St Rémi, Rheims, where it was probably written ; and 9th century it must surely be, if all the manuscripts of group v are derived from it, and if it was one of the books given by Manno of Saint-Oyan to the monastery of Saint-Claude (E. Lesne, *Histoire de la propriété ecclésiastique en France,* iv, *Les Livres,* p. 116, n. 2). It lacks chapters 51-90.

* *Troyes, 802 :* 9th/10th cent., from Lorsch, was copied from the same manuscript as was 4a.

1 *Milan, Bibl. della Basilica di S. Ambrogio, M. 13 :* late 9th century.

2 *British Museum, Harleian 3771* [1] *:* mid-9th century, apparently written in western Germany, perhaps at Cologne [Professor Bischoff, in a letter to the present editor]. This provenance, and, it may be, origin, is confirmed by an inscription at the top of fol. 2 (first leaf of the text) now erased, which according to the *Catalogue of Ancient Manuscripts in the British Museum,* pt. ii, Latin, 1884, p. 85, read *Liber Sancti Panthaleonis in Colonia,* in a 15th century hand. (It may be relevant that Harleian MS 2767, which does not contain the text of Fredegar and lacks an inscription, has, on a blank leaf (fol. 145^v), the name

[1] 3671, in Krusch's edition, p. 12, is a misprint.

' Goderamnus prepositus,' which the Catalogue identifies with the *prepositus* of that name at the Abbey of St Pantaleon at Cologne, who was afterwards (1022-30) first abbot of Hildes- heim.) Krusch, who did not see the manuscript, accepted it as 10th century. The new dating, and the suggested provenance, gives it more authority within the group than it enjoyed before ; and I have occasionally included, either in the text or in the apparatus, readings from it that Krusch wrongly assumed to be identical with those of $4b^{2x}$. Between $4b^2+4b^{2x}$ and the manuscript from which $4b^1$ was copied there would appear to have stood an intermediary. And we must further infer several intermediaries between our extant $4b$ group as a whole and their parent (4).

$4b^{2x}$ *Munich, Lat. 4352 :* 15th century, on paper, from the monastery of St Ulrich, Augsburg. Copied from the same manuscript as was $4b^2$. Krusch gave considerable weight to its variants, by no means all of which he noticed.

$4c^1$ *Montpellier, Schol. med. 158 :* 10th century, once belonged to Bouhier in Dijon, but further provenance undetermined.

$4c^2$ *Paris, Bibl. Nat. lat. 4883 A :* 11th century, from the monastery of Arnac-Pompadour, between Brives and Limoges, in which neighbourhood Krusch judged it to have been written. The scribe stops in chapter 44 of the continuation with the words, *Non repperio plus. Sufficiat igitur hoc.*

$4c^3$ *Leiden, Voss. Lat. 20 :* 10th century fragments of Book II only, in a composite manuscript.

A special sub-group (of no importance for the present edition) includes Book II, chapters 57-62 under the general heading *Gesta Theoderici regis*, in addition to the ' A ' text of the *Liber Historiae Francorum*. These are :

$4z^1$ *Vatican, Reg. lat. 549 :* 12th century.

$4z^2$ *Karlsruhe :* 12th century.

$4z^3$ *Vienna, univ. 3334 :* 15th century, on paper.

$4z^4$ *Graz, univ. fol. 42/59 :* 12th century, written in the monastery of St Lambert at Liège.

z^{4x} *Graz, univ. quart. 33/52 :* 15th century, on paper ; a copy of $4z^4$.

z^5 *Vienna, 428 :* 13th century.

The fifth, and most numerous, class (important for its text of Gregory of Tours) derives from 4a, though certain readings that it shares only with 4c make it probable that it was revised from a copy of 4c.

5a *Heidelberg univ. Palat. Lat. 864 :* 9th century, written at Lorsch.

a^x *Paris, Bibl. Nat. lat. 5921 :* 11th century, apparently a copy made at, or for, St Arnulf's, Metz, of 5a.

^{x}a *Berlin, Lat. quart. 266 :* 10th century fragment, derived from 5a.

5b *Paris, Bibl. Nat. lat. 9765 :* 9th/10th century.

5c *Saint-Omer, 706 :* 10th/11th century, written at St Bertin. In the humanistic marginalia of this manuscript Krusch found what he took to be the earliest reference to Fredegar.

c^x *Brussels, 6439-51 :* 11th century, a copy made perhaps at Lobbes or at St Vaast of 5c.

5d *Namur, Société Archéologique, 11 :* 9th century, from St Hubert ; contains Bede's *Historia Ecclesiastica* in addition to Gregory and Fredegar.[1]

5e *Brussels, 9361-67 :* 12th century, written in the monastery of St Laurence, Liège.

5f *Vienna, 473 :* late 9th century ; contains only the continuations ; corrected from 5b, or from a manuscript very like 5b. Chapters 10-24 of the continuations are added to the *Liber Historiae Francorum* in the following :

x^1 *Leningrad, λ. F. Otd. IV :* 10th century (*Script. Rer. Mero.* VII, 772).

x^2 *Paris, Bibl. Nat. lat. 10911 :* 9th century, from Liège.

^{2x} *Giessen, univ. 254a :* 18th century copy of $5x^2$.

$_x$^{3} *Saint-Gall, 547 :* 11th/12th century, or 12th/13th century and of Saint-Gall provenance according to Bruckner, *Scriptoria medii aevi Helvetica*, III (1938) p. 107 ; also contains Orosius, Eusebius, Paul the Deacon, Bede and Einhard. This manuscript deserves study as an historical collection.

Professor Mynors kindly examined this manuscript for me.

The relationship of the manuscripts may be expressed in the following stemma based on that of Krusch (hypothetical links in brackets) :—

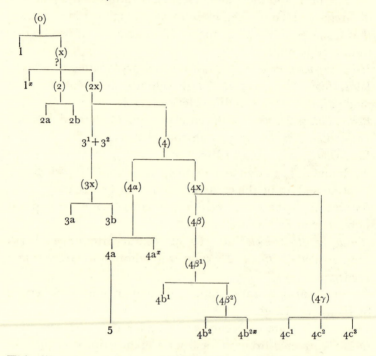

This, like every stemma of its kind, ignores the vital factors of date and origin of manuscripts, and thus obscures for the historian the true story of the dissemination of the chronicle. We know little of the provenance, let alone the original homes, of the manuscripts, and their dating is not in every case certain ; but still we should be able to see enough to justify an attempt at an historical reassessment of what happened to the chronicle during the Middle Ages, while omitting the subsidiary story of how it influenced or contaminated other narrative material (e.g. the Carolingian annals).[1]

---

[1] The continuations were used at Lorsch *c.* 786, and slightly later at Moissac (819), Metz and St Wandrille.

Fredegar must have had a single, unfinished manuscript (o) of his chronicle when he last added to it (*c.* 660) ; nor is there any reason to suppose that it would have been known about, let alone sought after, outside the private circle of his Burgundian friends. Some fifty years later, or possibly less, it was copied out, in a somewhat garbled form, by an un-intelligent Burgundian cleric (Paris 10910), and at some time between then and the middle of the 8th century a second copy reached Austrasia. From this second copy (x), whether directly or through lost intermediaries, all subsequent manu-scripts are descended. One copy of (x) may have been Metz 134, though there are no means of checking this. At least we can see that it is from the 9th century, and not earlier, that something like general interest was aroused in the chronicle (Austrasian version) and the dissemination of copies began. We have 9th century manuscripts of four of the five groups (group I being represented only by Paris 10910) with some indication that they were most sought after in the area of the Rhineland and Northern France. Group II (Haecpert's copy and Harleian 5251) are both 9th century but there is no evidence on which to determine provenance. Group III, which, if anything, is older than group II is confined to the Lake Constance area : it could be called the Mehrerau group. Group IV is also basically 9th century. It appears to start in the Rhineland : one may suppose that (4) or, more likely, (2x) was copied in Metz for a Rhenish monastery. Hence we get Harleian 3771 (? Cologne) in the mid-9th century, with the Ambrosian manuscript (origin unknown) and the Lorsch manuscript (Troyes 802) a generation or so later ; and at the same time we get an extension of interest westward into Austrasia with the Rheims manuscript (Vat. Reg. 213). A late flowering of the group from the 12th century (sub-group z) cannot be localized : it might have been in the Upper Rhine-land. It is associated with interest in the *Liber Historiae Francorum* in its Neustrian form, but this may have been coincidence. Group v is very like group iv, except that it is associated with Gregory of Tours, Bede and Einhard instead of with the *Liber Historiae Francorum*. Again we start with 9th century interest in the Rhineland (the Lorsch manuscript, now Heidelberg 864) and Northern France (the Liège manuscript, now Paris 10911). One would dearly like to know the origin, or at least the provenance, of two other 9th century manuscripts of the group, Vienna 473 and Paris 9765. From the following century we find a distinct northern group (St Bertin, St Vaast, St Hubert, Liège) that might almost be called the Ardennes group. Thereafter come some interesting manuscripts at Metz (Paris 5921) and Saint-Gall (547). All this leaves out of account manuscripts that cannot be placed at all, and our picture may in consequence be misleading. But, as it stands, it serves to emphasize the point that though group v derives from group iv, and iv and iii from ii, there are group v manuscripts that are older than some group iv manuscripts, and manuscripts of both that are as old as those of group ii. Furthermore, they come from houses that would have been able to secure good texts. Except, then, in the matter of verbal forms, where I think there is generally little to choose between any of these 9th century manuscripts, there is plainly a case for giving equal consideration to the readings of all five groups. It must finally be remembered that groups iv and v contain the continuations, in whole or in part. This leads one to the conclusion that (4), which is a more likely source for the continuations than (2x), must have been the manuscript of Count Childebrand's scribe, whose record reached the year 751. The scribe would have found his text of Fredegar in (2x), which must have been written in the early 8th century. Thus, all group iv and v manuscripts are descended from an official Carolingian text. It is hardly surprising that it should have evoked more interest than the obscure Burgundian text that is now Paris 10910.

V

THE PRESENT TEXT

My text of the main chronicle is based on a fresh collation of
MS Paris 10910, which I cite in my apparatus as ' 1 '. It will
be found to follow Krusch quite closely, except that the
punctuation and the paragraphing are frequently altered, and
the numbering of the chapters is not always the same. These
are not respects in which any authority attaches to 1, where
sheer nonsense often reigns. I have been tempted to go further
and entirely dispense with the traditional chaptering,
particularly for the earlier section, where strict annalistic
arrangement can be the only right one, and have refrained
only because I should have added to the difficulty of referring
back to Krusch's edition and the literature dependent upon it.
Moreover, mine is not an edition of the complete chronicle.
I have only altered chapters where the sense imperatively
required it, and have noted where this has been done. In some
cases I have been in doubt. For example, I have separated
chapters 43 and 44 where Krusch compromised with a comma ;
but I do so merely as a matter of convenience. I expand
contractions without notice. There are corrections in 1 by
several hands of various dates. Krusch admitted that a few of
these corrections were nearly contemporary with the original
hand; but Monod went further and, by incorporating some
of them into his text of 1, accepted them as by a contemporary,
if not by the scribe of 1 himself. This is a matter in which, on
the whole, I find myself with Monod. In a few instances, therefore, I have incorporated what I suspect is a contemporary
correction in the text.[1]

I have nowhere ' corrected ' the grammar or orthography
of 1 without noting it, and have never done so without anxious

---

[1] E. A. Lowe, *Cod. Lat. Ant.* v, no. 608, allows that there are
contemporary corrections but cites only one. He adds that there
are contemporary marginalia.

consideration. Readings such as *imperatores* for *imperatoris* (chap. 9) are not ' wrong,' for they were deliberately written ; nor, with a translation opposite, need they be misleading. Very occasionally the orthography of 1 may mislead the modern reader because it suggests to him an entirely different Latin word from the word intended by the scribe ; an example is *uero* (=*uiro*) in chapter 25. I change *uu* to *w* without warning: they represent the same sound.

It would be pointless to repeat the full apparatus of variant readings that is to be found in Krusch's edition, except where disagreement occurs. Mention has already been made of *solui* for *silui* in the prologue ; but Krusch prefers 1's *nemi*, in chapter 20, to the *nimis* of all other MSS, and to *nimis* I would give preference whether or not groups II, III, IV and V descended from I. Again, he reads *praecipit* in chapter 32, when 1 quite clearly has *precipit*, as Monod saw ; and 1 has equally clearly *ipsis* and not *ipis* in chapter 15. In chapter 31, all MSS except 1 have *inruerint ut*; their *ut* may be misplaced but must surely figure in the sentence. These are random examples of the kind of error into which Krusch allowed 1 to lead him. He would even allow 1 to provide a wrong date against every sort of opposition (chap. 56, death of Chlotar). Finally, he occasionally inserts capital letters where there is no change of writing in the manuscripts and puts arabic numerals where the texts have Roman. This last is an important matter, since a wrong numeral is more readily discernible in its original Roman shape than after conversion into modern guise. Except in very rare cases, I have not admitted into the text readings different from 1 for which there is no manuscript authority. Readings that I prefer to 1 come normally from 4a, 4b², and 5b. 3 is very occasionally useful.

We lack the overwhelming authority of 1 when we turn to the continuations. There is no longer any linguistic reason for preferring the readings of one manuscript to those of another, for we are dealing, by and large, with manuscripts of the same date. This is not to say that the Carolingian manuscripts lack any linguistic interest : 4a's *con* for *cum* in continuations chapter 47 is obviously worth retention ; but in general we are more free to take the reading that pleases us best, so long as we remember that orthography as much as grammar may reveal change in authorship or subsequent correction. Like Krusch, I consider 4a the best of the group IV manuscripts and hence the best text of the continuations, where I have often, though far less often than Krusch, preferred its readings to those of 4b and 4c. Of the 4b manuscripts, Krusch gave, to my mind, undue authority to 4b^{2x}, and to this I have preferred 4b^2 (Harleian 3771). 4b manuscripts do agree very closely, it is true ; but sometimes Krusch asserts that all 4b manuscripts give a reading that he found in 4b^{2x} when in fact 4b^2 gives a different reading. This is not enough to upset the classification of the manuscripts ; but it needs to be noted. For group V, I rely chiefly on 5b (Paris 9765), which is in some ways better than the 11th century copy (Paris 5921) of Heidelberg 864, which I have not seen. Where I have preferred a 4b, 4c or 5 reading to 4a I have noted the change, but only when I am not following Krusch. I do not note the minute variants of spelling within each sub-group of manuscripts.

Proper names, and to some extent place-names, are bound to exasperate the reader. I have made no attempt to standardize their spellings, though it would have been comparatively easy to do so. The reader must steel himself to Gunthram or Guntram, Chlotar or Clotar, Teudebert or Theudebert ; indeed, if he will turn to chapter 70 he can see at once what can happen to a single name in the space of a few lines. Why leave this confusion ? Because it is in the manuscripts and because, almost certainly, that is how Fredegar would have left things. To the Frank or Burgundian there was no one correct written form of a proper or place name, though there would have been one correct spoken form. The editor of any classical Latin text (and of certain classes of mediaeval texts) who left things thus would with justice be accused of pedantry. Here, it would be pedantry to standardize. The philologist will need no reassurance on this point. It is part of the civilization that the historian studies : he had better know the worst.

The difficulty of translating Fredegar is twofold. First, the chronicle is an uneasy marriage of rather gossipy narrative, perhaps best taken at a trot, with annalistic material, and in consequence the style of the translation must be adaptable to both ; and secondly, it is an isolated text, and often one feels the need of a text nearer in style and date than Gregory of Tours or the *Liber Historiae Francorum* with which to compare it. I have sometimes felt uncertain which of two possible meanings of a phrase or word to accept, and may have accepted the wrong one ; and more than once I have been hard put to it to extract any meaning whatever from what may not be the corruption we assume. Yet another difficulty lies in the translation of quite common words ; *leudes*, for example, seems to bear a technical meaning in some contexts but not in all. I have not striven after vain uniformity : Fredegar, of all authors, precludes it.

The general editors have been generous in the space they have allowed to historical footnotes. My aim has been to provide just enough geographical [1] and historical explanation to enable the English reader, unfamiliar with Frankish Gaul, to find his way about, and just sufficient reference to important publications of the last generation or so to enable him to interpret the material in the light of the best available opinion. Ability to use, and find, well-known foreign periodicals must be assumed ; for this is foreign history.

I have not thought it necessary to differentiate Fredegar's excerpts from other writers by printing them in italics, as is done by Krusch. Where great blocks of material have been

---

[1] Most small towns or villages are identified in the footnotes by their present départements (normally given in brackets).

taken, as from the *Vita Columbani* or the *Liber Historiae Francorum*, it is enough to indicate their extent in a footnote, and to draw attention to any significant addition to the original text ; minor textual changes that leave the original sense unaffected (e.g. *uenire* for *uenisse* in chap. 36) have not been noted. This method would be less justifiable in an edition of the earlier Books, where Fredegar's own additions need to be distinguished word by word from whatever is derivative. Biblical references are to the Authorized Version. Vulgate references, where they differ, are added in brackets. Readers will also detect frequent Biblical reminiscences, conscious or otherwise, to which attention has not been drawn, except in so far as they have been allowed to influence the translation.

A word must be added about chronology. I have placed in the margin of the main text the dates that Fredegar himself accepted. These are not always the dates accepted by modern scholarship ; Fredegar is sometimes a year or two out, as Krusch himself showed much virtuosity in proving. In such cases I have placed the true date in a footnote. The reason for retaining Fredegar's own dates is that they make sense of his chronicle and show that, once we understand his method of calculating regnal years, his plan grows in consistency. Fredegar always counts the last year of one king as the first year of his successor. This was noted by Schnürer long ago, but has only recently been subjected to careful demonstration by Courtois. We must suppose, either that all Burgundians of the 7th century did this, or that *B* (Fredegar proper) revised the work of *A* to fit in with his own chronological scheme. The chronology of the continuations is less thoughtfully worked out, and it seemed best to confine dates in this section entirely to the footnotes. They can often be found out from other sources where the text itself is vague. The continuations abound in what may be called conjunctive time-phrases of a deliberately vague nature. These were never meant to express any exact lapse of time but only to ensure that the right order of events was preserved. This makes them all the more trying to translate.

VI

PREVIOUS EDITIONS

The earliest editors of Fredegar used a manuscript of group v and thus confined themselves to Book iv, the continuations to chapter 24 and Gregory of Tours. Of these, the first was Flacius Illyricus, *Gregorii Turonici Historiae Francorum libri decem* (Basle 1568), where Fredegar and the continuations are edited from MS 5a under the title *Index libri XI seu appendicis ad Gregorium additae, quae nunc primum accessit.* Subsequent editions depend on Flacius until we reach Canisius' *Antiquae Lectiones* (Ingolstadt 1602), where the text of the whole chronicle is based on an insufficient collation of MSS 3b and $4b^{2x}$. MS $4a^x$ appears to have been used by Scaliger for the Fredegarian text of Hydatius in his *Thesaurus Temporum* (Leiden 1606). Freherus produced an edition of Books iii and iv with the continuations, partly from MS 5a, in his *Corpus Francicae historiae ueteris et sincerae* (Hanover 1613) ; and this was the first edition to which the name Fredegarius was adjoined. The first serious modern edition was that of Ruinart, *Gregorii Turonensis opera omnia necnon Fredegarii Scholastici Epitome et Chronicon cum suis Continuatoribus* (Paris 1699), who used MSS 1, $4c^1$, 5a and $5a^x$. On this edition depend the texts in Bouquet's *Recueil* (ii, 391-464, and v, 1-9) and in Migne, *Patrologia Latina* (lxxi, 573-704). Monod's text of 1 in the *Bibliothèque de l'École des Hautes Études* (1885) may be regarded as definitive, but it is not, of course, an edition of the chronicle. Krusch's edition for the *Monumenta Germaniae Historica* (1888) is the first edition that takes account of all the manuscripts. It has certain faults some of which the present edition has attempted to rectify, but it was a mighty undertaking, completed at a time when its editor, the greatest Merovingian scholar who has ever lived, was just reaching the height of his powers. Krusch's work is susceptible of correction but never of replacement.[1]

There have been several French translations of Book IV and the continuations, the earliest dating from 1610. The most serious, and the only one that I have found at all useful, was that of Guizot, first published in 1823 and revised (with useful appendices) by Alfred Jacobs in 1861. However, it proves to be more of a version than a translation whenever real difficulties crop up. The German translation by Otto Abel, *Die Chronik Fredegars und der Frankenkönige* (3rd edition, revised by Wattenbach, Leipzig 1888) is rather better. This is the first English translation.

VII

BIBLIOGRAPHICAL NOTE

The note that follows is designed to save space in the text and to give some guidance on general reading for the period covered by the chronicle. It is highly selective. I cite nothing that is not available in English libraries.

THE TEXT AND ITS CRITICISM

RUINART, TH. : *Gregorii Turonensis opera omnia necnon Fredegarii Scholastici Epitome et Chronicon cum suis Continuatoribus* (Paris 1699).

BREYSIG, T. : *De continuatione Fredegarii Scholastici* (Berlin 1849).

HAHN, A. : ' Einige Bemerkungen über Fredegar ' (*Archiv für deutsche Geschichtskunde*, XI, 1858).

MONOD, GABRIEL : ' Sur un texte de la compilation dite de Frédégaire relatif à l'établissement des Burgundions dans l'empire romain ' (*Bibliothèque de l'École des Hautes Études*, fasc. 35, 1878).

MONOD, GABRIEL : ' Du lieu d'origine de la chronique dite de Frédégaire ' (*Jahrbuch für schweiz. Geschichte*, III, 1878).

---

[1] I can find no trace of the projected edition by the late Léon Levillain (Calmette-Higounet, *Le Monde Féodal*, 1951, p. 38), despite a prolonged search among his papers in the Archives de la Seine and enquiries at the University of Caen and elsewhere.

KRUSCH, BRUNO : ' Die Chronicae des sogenannten Fredegar ' (*Neues Archiv*, VII, 1882, pp. 247-351, 421-516).

MONOD, GABRIEL : ' Études critiques sur les sources de l'histoire mérovingienne, pt. 2 : La compilation dite de Frédégaire ' (*Bibliothèque de l'École des Hautes Études*, fasc. 63, 1885). Text of MS 1 without commentary.

KRUSCH, BRUNO : ' Chronicarum quae dicuntur Fredegarii Scholastici Libri IV cum continuationibus ' (*Monumenta Germaniae Historica, Scriptorum Rerum Merovingicarum*, II, 1888). The standard edition and commentary, with a valuable though imperfect *Lexica* (Anglade has a list of omissions, but a full study of the vocabulary of Fredegar has still to be made).

SCHNÜRER, G. : ' Die Verfasser der sogenannten Fredegar-Chronik ' (*Collect. Friburg.*, fasc. IX, 1900).

HALPHEN, LOUIS : ' Une théorie récente sur la Chronique du Pseudo-Frédégaire ' (*Revue Historique*, LXXIX, 1902).

LOT, F. : ' Encore la Chronique du Pseudo-Frédégaire ' (*Revue Historique*, CXV, 1914). Reviewed by Krusch in *Neues Archiv*, XXXIX, 1914, pp. 548-9.

KRUSCH, BRUNO : ' Chronologica regum Francorum stirpis Merowingicae ' (*Monumenta Germaniae Historica, Scriptorum Rerum Merovingicarum*, VII, 1920, pp. 468-516). The essential chronological study.

KRUSCH, BRUNO : ' Fredegarius Scholasticus—Oudarius ? Neue Beiträge zur Fredegar-Kritik ' (*Nachr. der Gesellschaft der Wiss. zu Göttingen*, Philol.-hist. Cl., 1926, pt. 2).

BAUDOT, MARCEL : ' La question du Pseudo-Frédégaire ' (*Le Moyen Age*, XXIX, 1928).

LEVILLAIN, LÉON : critical review of Krusch (*Bibliothèque de l'École des Chartes*, LXXXIX, 1928, pp. 89-95).

LEVISON, W. : critical review of Baudot (*Jahresberichte der deut. Geschichte*, 1928, pp. 174 ff.).

KRUSCH, BRUNO : ' Die handschriftlichen Grundlagen der Historia Francorum Gregors von Tours ' (*Historische Vierteljahrschrift*, XXVIII, 1934, pp. 15-21). Returns to the problem of Fredegarius-Oudarius.

HELLMANN, S. : ' Das Fredegarproblem ' (*Historische Vierteljahrschrift*, XXIX, 1934).

WATTENBACH-LEVISON : *Deutschlands Geschichtsquellen* (Weimar 1952). I, 109-13 ; II, 161-3.

WALLACE-HADRILL, J. M. : ' Fredegar and the history of France ' (*Bulletin, John Rylands Library*, XL, 1957-8).

GEOGRAPHY

JACOBS, A. : *Géographie de Grégoire de Tours, de Frédégaire et de leurs continuateurs.* 2nd ed. (Paris 1861).

LONGNON, A. : *Géographie de la Gaule au VIe siècle* (Paris 1878). With volume of maps.

LINGUISTIC (mainly background)

BIELER, L. : *Libri Epistolarum S. Patricii Episcopi*, pt. 2, commentary (Dublin 1952).

BONNET, MAX : *Le Latin de Grégoire de Tours* (Paris 1890).

EWERT, A. : *The French Language* (2nd ed. London 1943).

HAAG, O. : ' Über die Latinität Fredegars ' (*Romanische Forschungen*, X, 1899). Reviewed by J. Anglade : *Revue de philologie française*, XIV, 1900, pp. 150-67.

LÖFSTEDT, E. : *Syntactica, Studien und Beiträge zur historischen Syntax des Lateins* (Lund, I², 1942 ; II, 1933).

LOT, F. : ' A quelle époque a-t-on cessé de parler latin ? ' (*Bulletin Du Cange*, VI, 1931, pp. 91-159).

MULLER, H. F. : ' A chronology of Vulgar Latin ' (*Zeitsch. f. roman. Philol.*, *Beiheft* LXXVIII, 1929).

MULLER, H. F. and TAYLOR, PAULINE : *A Chrestomathy of Vulgar Latin* (Boston 1932).

MULLER, H. F. : *L'Époque mérovingienne : essai de synthèse et d'histoire* (New York 1945).

NORBERG, D. : ' Ad epistulas varias Merovingici aevi adnotationes ' (*Eranos*, XXXV, 1937).

PALMER, L. R. : *The Latin Language* (London 1954).

PEI, MARIO : *The Language of the Eighth-century Texts in Northern France* (New York 1932).

PIRSON, J. : ' Le latin des formules mérovingiennes et carolingiennes ' (*Romanische Forschungen*, XXVI, 1909).

POPE, MILDRED K. : *From Latin to Modern French* (Manchester 1934).

SAS, LOUIS : *The Noun Declension System in Merovingian Latin* (Paris 1937).

TAYLOR, PAULINE : *The Latinity of the Liber Historiae Francorum* (New York 1924).

TIECHE, E. : ' Fredegars Notiz über die Schlacht bei Wangen : ein Beitrag zur Syntax des Mittellateins ' (*Museum Helveticum*, VI, 1949).

UDDHOLM, ALF : *Formulae Marculfi : études sur la langue et le style* (Uppsala 1953).

VIELLIARD, JEANNE : *La Langue des diplômes royaux et chartes privées de l'époque mérovingienne* (Paris 1927).

General reference may be made to the *Bulletin Du Cange*. Vol. XXV (1955) indexes its many valuable studies of Late Latin.

E

General

BREYSIG, T. : *Jahrbücher des fränkischen Reichs, 714-41* (Leipzig 1869).

BROSIEN, H. : *Kritische Untersuchungen der Quellen zur Geschichte des fränkischen Königs Dagobert I* (Göttingen 1868).

CHALOUPECKÝ, V. : ' Considérations sur Samon, le premier roi des Slavs ' (*Byzantinoslavica*, XI, 1950).

CHAMARD, DOM F. : ' L'Aquitaine sous les derniers Mérovingiens, aux VIIe et VIIIe siècles ' (*Rev. des Quest. Hist.*, XXXV, 1884).

CHAUME, M. : *Les Origines du duché de Bourgogne*, I : *Histoire politique* (Dijon 1925)

CHAUME, M. : *Recherches d'histoire* (Dijon 1947). Pp. 147-62.

COURTOIS, C. : ' L'avènement de Clovis II et les règles d'accession au trône chez les Mérovingiens ' (*Mélanges Louis Halphen*, Paris 1951).

DUCHESNE, L. : *Fastes épiscopaux de l'ancienne Gaule*, 3 vols. (2nd ed. Paris 1907-15).

DUPRAZ, L. : *Le Royaume des Francs et l'ascension politique des maires du palais au déclin du VIIᵉ siècle (656-680)* (Fribourg 1948).

EWIG, E. : *Die fränkischen Teilungen und Teilreiche (511-613)* (*Mainz. Akad. der Wissen.* Wiesbaden 1952).

EWIG, E. : *Die fränkische Teilreiche im 7. Jahrhundert (613-714)* (*Trierer Zeitschrift*, XXII, 1953).

FUSTEL DE COULANGES, N. D. : *Histoire des institutions politiques de l'ancienne France*, III, *La Monarchie Franque* (revised by C. Jullian, 3rd ed. Paris 1905). A classical study.

FUSTEL DE COULANGES, N. D. : *Recherches sur quelques problèmes d'histoire* (3rd ed. Paris 1913). Valuable for study of Merovingian judicial organization.

GOUBERT, P. : *Byzance avant l'Islam*, II, pt. 1, *Byzance et les Francs* (Paris 1956).

KERN, F. : *Gottesgnadentum und Widerstandsrecht im früheren Mittelalter* (revised by R. Buchner, Münster-Cologne 1954).

KURTH, G. : *Études franques*, 2 vols. (Paris-Brussels 1919). A classical defence of Brunechildis' reputation is in vol. I.

KURTH, G. : *Histoire poétique des Mérovingiens* (Paris 1893). Essential for epic background to Fredegar's stories, for some of which other explanations are preferable.

LESNE, E. : *Histoire de la propriété ecclésiastique en France aux époques romaine et mérovingienne*, I (Lille-Paris 1910) and IV (Lille-Paris 1938).

LEVILLAIN, L. : ' La succession d'Austrasie au VIIe siècle ' (*Revue Historique*, CXII, 1913).

LEVILLAIN, L. : ' Encore la succession d'Austrasie au VIIe siècle ' (*Bibliothèque de l'École des Chartes*, CV, 1946).

LEVILLAIN, L. : ' Les Nibelungen historiques et leurs alliances de famille ' (*Annales du Midi*, XLIX, 1937 ; L, 1938).

LEVILLAIN, L. : 'Campus Martius' (*Bibliothèque de l'École des Chartes*, CVII, 1948).

LEVISON, W. : *Aus Rheinischer und Fränkischer Frühzeit* (Düsseldorf 1948). A collection of his more important articles on Merovingian and other subjects.

LÖHLEIN, G. : 'Die Alpen- und Italienpolitik der Merowinger im 6. Jahrhundert' (*Erlanger Abhandlungen*, XVII, 1932).

LOT, F., PFISTER, CH. and GANSHOF, F. L. : *Les Destinées de l'empire en Occident*, pt. I (Paris 1940). The best modern survey.

MARTIN, P. E. : *Études critiques sur la Suisse à l'époque mérovingienne (534-715)* (Paris-Geneva 1910).

MAYER, TH. : 'Fredegars Bericht über die Slawen' (*Mitteilungen d. Öst. Inst. f. Gesch.* Ergbd. II, 1929, pp. 114-20).

MOLINIER, A. : *Les Sources de l'histoire de France*, I. Paris 1901. Pp. 63 ff.

OELSNER, L. : *Jahrbücher des fränkischen Reichs unter König Pippin* (Leipzig 1871).

RICHTER, G. : *Annalen des fränkischen Reichs im Zeitalter der Merovinger* (Halle 1873)

THOMPSON, J. W. : *The Dissolution of the Carolingian Fisc* (Berkeley, California 1935). Section on the Merovingian fisc.

VERLINDEN, CH. : 'Le Franc Samo' (*Revue belge de philologie et d'histoire*, XII, 1933).

WALLACE-HADRILL, J. M.: 'Frankish Gaul' (in Wallace-Hadrill, J. M. and McManners, J., *France, Government and Society*, London 1957).

ZÖLLNER, E. : 'Die Herkunft der Agilulfinger' (*Mitteilungen d. Inst. Öst. Gesch.* LIX, 1951).

ZÖLLNER, E. : *Die politische Stellung der Völker im Frankenreich* (Vienna 1950).

LATIN TEXT

and

ENGLISH TRANSLATION

FREDEGARII CHRONICA

INCIPIT PROLOGVS[a]

Cvm [1] aliquid unius uerbi proprietate non habeo quod proferam nisi prestitum ab Altissimo fuerit, et dum quero implere sentenciam, longo ambiatu uix breuis uiae spatium consummo, uernaculum linguae huius uerbi interpretatur absorde resonat ; si ob necessitate aliquid in ordine sermone mutauero, ab interpretis uideor officio recessisse. Itaque beati Hieronimi, Ydacii et cuiusdam sapientis, seo Hysidori immoque et Gregorii chronicis a mundi originem dilientissime percurrens, usque decedentem regnum Gunthramni, his quinque chronicis huius libelli nec plurima pretermissa siggyllatem congruentia stilo inserui, quod illi sollertissime absque reprehensionem condederunt.

Cum [2] haec ita se habebant, necessarium duxi uiretatem diligencius insequi, et ob id in priores his

[a] 2a, 2b, 3, 4a ; Prolocus 4b[2]. INCIPIT PROLOGVS CVIVSDAM SAPIENTIS 1. *Lot thinks the longer title probably displaced from the preface to the* Liber Generationis. *Hellmann more plausibly considers the shorter title original to this prologue, to which the scribe of* 1, *wishing to attribute the prologue to somebody, added* cuiusdam sapientis *from the text. The* sapiens *of the text is of course the author of the* Liber. *St Boniface refers to the writer of* Ecclesiasticus *as* sapiens quidam (*Letter* 34, *ed. M. Tangl,* S. Bonifatii et Lullii Epistolae, Berlin 1916, p. 58).

[1] St Jerome, *Chron.* : ' Significatum est aliquid unius uerbi proprietate : non habeo meum quo id efferam, et dum quaero implere sententiam, longo ambitu uix breuis uiae spatia consummo. Accedunt hyperbatorum anfractus, dissimilitudines casuum, uarietas figurarum, ipsum postremo suum et ut ita dicam uernaculum linguae genus. Si ad uerbum interpraetor

THE CHRONICLE OF FREDEGAR

HERE BEGINS THE PROLOGUE

UNLESS [1] the Almighty helps me, I cannot tell how I can express in one word the labour on which I am embarking and how, in striving to succeed, my long struggle devours days already too short. ' Translator ' in our own vernacular gives the wrong sense, for if I feel bound to change somewhat the order of words, I should appear not to abide by a translator's duty. I have most carefully read the chronicles of St Jerome, of Hydatius, of a certain wise man, of Isidore and of Gregory, from the beginning of the world to the decline of Guntramn's reign ; and I have reproduced successively in this little book, in suitable language and without many omissions, what these learned men have recounted at length in their five chronicles.

Further,[2] I have judged it necessary to be more thorough in my striving for accuracy, and so I have

---

absurde resonat ; si ob necessitatem aliquid in ordine, in sermone mutauero, ab interpraetis uidebor officio recessisse ' (ed. J. K. Fotheringham, Oxford 1923, p. 1).

   [2] ' Cum haec ita se habeant, necessarium duxi ueritatem diligentius persequi et ob id in priori libello quasi quandam materiam futuro operi omnium mihi regum tempora praenotaui. . . . In praesenti autem stilo eadem tempora contra se in uicem ponens et singularum gentium annos dinumerans, ut quid cuique coaetaneum fuit, ita curioso ordine coaptaui ' (ibid. pp. 6, 7).

chronicis quasi quandam[a] futuro opere omnium mihi regum[b] et tempora prenotaui. In praesenti autem stilo ea tempora ponens et[c] singularum gentium curiosissimo ordine que gesserant coaptaui, quo prudentissime uiri, quos supra memeni, cuius[d] chronicis (uerbo huius nomenis Grego, quod Latini interpretatur gesta temporum[1]) seuirissimi dictantes condiderunt uelut purissimus fons largiter fluenta manantes.[e] Optaueram et ego ut mihi subcumberit talia dicendi fagundia, ut uel paululum esset ad instar, sed carius[f] auritur ubi non est certa perennitas aque. Mundus iam seniscit,[2] ideoque prudenciae agumen in nobis tepiscit, ne quisquam potest huius tempore nec presumit oratoribus precedentes esse consimilis. Ego tamen, ut rusticitas et stremitas[g] sensus mei ualuit, studiosissime de hisdem libris breuiatem quantum plus potui aptare presumsi. Nec quisquam legens hic quicquam dubitet per uniuscuiusque libri nomen redeat ad auctorem, cuncta reperiat subsistere uiretatem. Trasactis namque Gregorii libri uolumine, temporum gesta que undique scripta potui repperire et mihi postea fuerunt cognita, acta regum et bella gentium quae gesserunt, legendo simul

[a] om. materiam   [b] regnum 1
[c] corr. in by scribe of 1   [d] ? his Krusch
[e] The phrase, which I translate with no conviction, is not classical. Father Grosjean has suggested to me that it derives stylistically from some Christian Latin introduction, dedicatory letter or preface of comparatively late date, though the immediate source may have been Flores or extracts, artes dictandi in their earlier shape. Professor M. L. W. Laistner has drawn my attention to purissima doctrinarum fluenta potavit, referring to St John, in St Jerome's prologue to his commentary on St Matthew (P.L. 26, col. 18b). Did Fredegar simply pile on words that he found in a glossary? The Abolita glossary (Glossaria Latina, edd. W. M. Lindsay et al., III, pp. 143-4) has manantia : fluentia. Abstrusa (ibid. pp. 55) has manat : fluit, and (p. 41) fluenta : aquae. In general, however, Fredegar's style does not suggest the use of glossaries.
[f] 4b[2] ; sarius 1. Again the phrase can hardly be original. The Abstrusa glossary (loc. cit. p. 44) has hauritur : bibitur, potatur.
[g] sc. extremitas ; strenuitas 4b[2]

noted in the above-mentioned chronicles, as it were a source of material for a future work, all the reigns of the kings and their chronology. I have brought together and put into order in these pages, as exactly as I can, this chronology and the doings of many peoples and have inserted them in the chronicles (a Greek word meaning in Latin the record of the years [1]) compiled by these wise men, chronicles that copiously gush like a spring most pure. I could have wished that I had the same command of language, or at least approached it ; but it is harder to draw from a spring that flows intermittently. And now the world grows old,[2] which is why the fine point of wisdom is lost to us. Nobody now is equal to the orators of past times, or could even pretend to equality. Thus I am compelled, so far as my rusticity and ignorance permit, to hand on as briefly as possible whatever I have learned from the books of which I have spoken ; and if any reader doubts me, he has only to turn to the same author to find that I have said nothing but the truth. At the end of Gregory's work I have not fallen silent but have continued on my own account with facts and deeds of later times, finding them wherever they were recorded, and relating of the deeds of

---

[1] Isidore, *Etymol. Lib.* v, 28, ' De chronicae uocabulo ' (ed. W. M. Lindsay, Oxford 1911)

[2] Sidonius Apollinaris, *Epist.* VIII, 6, ' namque uirtutes artium istarum saeculis potius priscis saeculorum rector ingenuit, quae per aetatem mundi iam senescentis ' (ed. P. Mohr, Teubner 1895, p. 178). E. R. Curtius, *European Literature and the Latin Middle Ages*, p. 28, looks to St Augustine for the seminal idea. Neither the growing-old of the world nor Fredegar's profession of rusticity need be taken too seriously (ibid. pp. 83-5), any more than the *mundus iam declinat* of his near contemporary St Columbanus (*Sancti Columbani Opera*, ed. G. S. M. Walker, p. 40) and similar passages in Gregory of Tours, *Hist.* IX, chaps. 39 and 42.

et audiendo etiam et uidendo cuncta que certeficatus cognoui huius libelli uolumine scribere non silui,[a] sed curiosissime quantum potui inseri studui de eodem incipiens tempore scribendum quo Gregori fines gesta cessauit et tacuit, cum Chilperici uitam finisse scripsit.

[a] solui 1, silui *all other MSS*

EXPLICIT PROLOGVS

kings and the wars of peoples all that I have read or heard or seen that I could vouch for. Here I have tried to put in all I could discover from that point at which Gregory stopped writing, that is, from the death of King Chilperic.

END OF PROLOGUE

IN NOMEN DOMINI NOSTRI IESV CHRISTI INCIPIT CHRONICA SEXTA[a]

I

Gunthramnus [1] rex Francorum cum iam anno xxiii [b] Burgundiae regnum bonitate plenus feliciter regebat, cum sacerdotibus utique sacerdus ad instar se ostendebat et cum leudis [2] erat aptissimus, aelymosinam pauperibus large tribuens, tante prosperetatis regnum tenuit ut omnes etiam uicinas gentes ad plinitudinem de ipso laudis canerent. Anno xxiiii regni sui deuino amore eclesiam beati Marcelli, ubi ipsi praeciosus requiescit in corpore, suborbanum Cabilonninsim, sed quidem tamen Sequanum est territurium,[3] merefice et sollerter aedificare iussit, ibique monachis congregatis monasterium condedit ipsamque ecclesiam rebus pluremis ditauit. Senodum xl episcoporum fieri precepit [4] et ad instar institucionis monasterii sanctorum Agaauninsium,[5] que temporibus Sigysmundi regis ab Avito et citeris episcopis ipso iobente princepi fuerat firmatum, idemque et huius senodi coniunctionem monasterium sancti [c] Marcelli Gunthramnus institucionem firmandam curauit.

584 (margin)
515 (margin)

---

[a] 1 ; *other MSS have* INCIPIT LIBER CHRONICE *with slight variations (see Introduction, p. xxiv).*

[b] *I have restored the roman numerals throughout which Krusch replaced by arabic.*

[c] Sancti *Krusch, who frequently gives initial and other capitals where the MSS have none. Hereafter, I amend without notice.*

[1] A genealogical table of the Merovingian dynasty is provided at the end of the book.

[2] The Merovingian *leudes* were the personal following, both official and military, of the kings. Their normal recompense for devoted service was land from the fiscal estates.

4

IN THE NAME OF OUR LORD JESUS CHRIST
HERE BEGINS THE SIXTH CHRONICLE

I

Guntramn,[1] king of the Franks, had been ruling happily over the kingdom of Burgundy for twenty-three years. He was full of goodness, and when with his bishops he conducted himself like one of them ; and he lived on the best of terms with his followers [2] and contributed generously to the relief of the poor. He ruled so wisely and so prosperously that all the neighbouring peoples sang his praises to the full. In the twenty-fourth year of 584 his reign, his love of God caused him to have built in the faubourg of Chalon (though in fact on land belonging to the territory of the Seine [3]) the sumptuous church of Saint Marcel, where the saint's precious body now rests. There, too, he brought together monks and founded a monastery and endowed its church with many possessions. He ordered the convening of a synod of forty bishops [4] and made it confirm the foundation of this house of Saint Marcel on the precedent of the confirming by Avitus and other bishops of the foundation of the house [5] dedicated to the saints at Agaune, made in the 515 days of King Sigismund and upon his orders.

---

[3] This may mean that the faubourg lay outside the diocese of Chalon, which extended only slowly over the old *territorium Sequanum*. See also Gregory of Tours, *Hist.* v, chap. 27. *Suburbanus* was a term without definite geographical meaning.

[4] Probably the synod of Valence (584)

[5] cf. Greg. *Hist.* iii, chap. 5. On the Burgundian cult of St Maurice and the Eastern origins of the liturgical practices of Agaune, see J. M. Theurillat, 'L'abbaye de Saint-Maurice d'Agaune' (*Vallesia*, Sion 1954).

2

584   Hoc anno Gundoaldus cum solatio Mummolo et Desiderio mense Nouembre [1] partem regni Gunthramni presumsit inuadere et ciuitates euertere. Gunthramnus Leudisclum comestaboli et Aeghylanem patricium [2] cum exercito contra ipsum direxit. Gundoaldus terga uertens Conbanem ciuitatem [3] latebram dedit. Exinde de rupe a Bosone [4] duci praecipetatus interiit.

3

585   Cumque Gunthramno perlatum fuisset, eo quod frater suos Chilpericus esset interfectus, festinans perrexit Parisius [5] ibique Fredegundem cum filio Chilperici Clothario ad se uenire precipit, quem Rioilo uilla [6] baptizare iobet, et eum de sancto lauacro excipiens in regnum patris firmauit.[7]

4

Anno xxv regnum Gontramni Mummolus Senuuia [8] iusso Gunthramni interfecetur. Vxorem eius Sidoniam [10] una cum omnes thinsauris eius Domnolus domesticus [9] et Wandalmarus camararius Gundramno presentant.

---

[1] cf. Greg. *Hist.* vii, chap. 11
[2] cf. Greg. *Hist.* vii, chap. 24 and viii, chap. 30
[3] Saint-Bertrand-de-Comminges (Haute-Garonne)
[4] cf. Greg. *Hist.* vii, chap. 38
[5] cf. Greg. *Hist.* vii, chap. 5 and viii, chap. 1
[6] Seine-et-Oise. cf. Greg. *Hist.* x, chap. 28.
[7] C. Courtois, ' L'avènement de Clovis et les règles d'accession au trône chez les Mérovingiens,' *Mélanges d'histoire du Moyen Age dédiés à la mémoire de Louis Halphen* (Paris 1951), p. 162, argues that Fredegar is right in associating the baptism of Chlotar with his elevation to the throne, but the year should be 591, not 584.

2

In November [1] of this year Gundoald, supported by 584
Mummolus and Desiderius, dared to invade part
of Guntramn's kingdom and to destroy his cities.
Guntramn sent to meet them an army under Leudegesil
the constable and Aegyla the patrician. [2] Gundoald took
to flight and sought refuge in the city of Comminges, [3]
whence Duke Boso [4] hurled him from the cliffs ; and
thus he died.

3

When the news that his brother Chilperic had been
killed reached him, Guntramn hastened to Paris [5] and
ordered Fredegundis and Chlotar, son of Chilperic, to
meet him there. He had Chlotar baptized at his villa
of Rueil, [6] himself standing godfather to him ; and he
established him over Chilperic's kingdom. [7]

4

In the twenty-fifth year of Guntramn's reign, Mummolus 585
was killed at Senuvia [8] on the king's orders. Domnolus
the domesticus [9] and Wandalmar the chamberlain
handed over his widow Sidonia [10] and all his treasure
to Guntramn.

---

[8] Possibly Chenôve, near Dijon (Côte-d'Or)
[9] A court official, employed by the king on any confidential business.
J. F. Niermeyer, *Mediae Latinitatis Lexicon Minus*, gives to *domesticus* in this
context the special sense of 'mayor of the palace': without justification, in
my view.
[10] cf. Greg. *Hist.* VII, chap. 40

5

Anno xxvi [1] regni sui exercitus Gunthramni Espanias
ingreditur, sed loci infirmitatis grauatus protenus ad
propria reuertur.[2]

Anno xxvii eiusdem regno Leudisclus a Gunthramno
patricius partibus Prouenciae ordenatur. Filius Childeberti regis Theodebertus natus fuisse nunciatur.[3]

6

Eo [a] anno nimia inundatio fluminum in Burgundias fuit,
ut eorum terminus nimium transcenderint. Ipsoque
anno Syagrius comex Constantinopole iusso Gunthramni
in legatione pergit ibique fraude patricius ordenatur.
Ceptum quidem, sed ad perfectione haec fraos non
peraccessit.[4] Eo anno signum apparuit in caelum,[5]
globus igneos decedens in terram cum scintellis et
rugeto. Ipsoque [b] anno Leubildus rex Spaniae moritur,
et obtenuit regnum Richarid filius eius.

7

Anno [c] xxviii [6] regni domni Gunthramni alius filius
Childeberti nomen Teudericus natus nunciatur.[7] Gunthramnus [d] se cum Childeberto pacem firmandum[e]

---

[a] *All MSS begin chap. 6 except* 1 *and* 4c². 2b *begins chap.* 7.
[b] *chap.* 6, 1 *and* 4c²   [c] *chap.* 7, 2a   [d] *chap.* 7, 1
[e] *Krusch's conjecture* ; firma(n)t dum *in MSS*

[1] All the events of chapter 5 belong to the twenty-fifth year of
Guntramn's reign, i.e. 585. The events of chapter 6 are dated by the death
of Leuvigild.
[2] cf. Greg. *Hist.* viii, chap. 30
[3] cf. Greg. *Hist.* viii, chap. 37
[4] Syagrius' mission, Guntramn's anxiety to reach agreement with the
Emperor Maurice, and Maurice's plans for the West are discussed by

5

In the twenty-sixth year [1] of Guntramn's reign, his army entered Spain but it returned forthwith, overcome by sickness contracted there. [2]

In the twenty-seventh year of the same reign, Guntramn appointed Leudegesil to be patrician in Burgundian Provence. News came that King Childebert had had a son, named Theudebert. [3]

6

In that same year there were great floods in Burgundy and the rivers overflowed their banks ; in that same year also, Count Syagrius went on a mission to Constantinople at Guntramn's order and there fraudulently was made patrician, though, in fact, the treachery thus hatched never achieved its object [4] ; and in the same year a phenomenon appeared in the sky [5]—a fiery globe that fell sparkling and glowing to earth. In the same year died Leuvigild king of Spain. His son Reccared succeeded him.

7

In the twenty-eighth [6] year of King Guntramn's reign came news that Childebert had had another son, named Theuderic. [7] Guntramn had a meeting with Childebert

---

P. Goubert, *Byzance avant l'Islam*, ii, pt. i, pp. 74-81. I see no evidence for his view that Maurice tried to make Syagrius a second Gundoald.

[5] cf. Greg. *Hist.* viii, chap. 42

[6] 587 should be the 27th year of Guntramn's reign by Fredegar's reckoning.

[7] cf. Greg. *Hist.* ix, chap. 4

F

Andelao [1] coniuncxit. Inibi mater et soror et coniux Childeberti regis pariterque fuerunt. Ibique speciale conuenencia inter domno Guntramno et Childeberto fuit conuentum, ut regnum Gunthramni post eius discessum Childebertus adsumerit.

8

Ipsoque tempore Rauchingus [2] et Boso Gunthramnus, Ursio et Bertefredus optematis Childeberti regis, eo quod eum tractauerant interficere ipso regi ordenante interfecti sunt. Sed et Leudefredus Alammannorum dux in offensam antedicti regis incidit, etiam et latebram dedit. Ordenatus est loco ipsius Vncelenus dux.

Eo anno Richarid rex Gotorum diuino amplectens amore prius secrecius baptizatur. Post haec omnes Gothus, dum Arrianam sectam tenebant, Toletum adhunare precepit et omnes libros Arrianos precepit ut presententur, quos in una domo conlocatis incendio concremare iussit et omnes Gothos ad christianam legem baptizare fecit.

9

Eo anno uxor Anaulfi [3] imperatores Persarum nomen Caesara uirum relinquens, cum quattuor pueris totidem puellis [4] ad beatum Iohannem episcopum Constantino-

---

[1] Near Langres (Haute-Marne). The text of this agreement is given in Greg. *Hist.* ix, chap. 20, and a detailed map of the resulting territorial divisions in A. Longnon, *Géographie.*

[2] cf. Greg. *Hist.* ix, chap. 9

[3] This story is also told, with certain differences, by Paul the Deacon, *Hist. Lang.* iv, chap. 50. Authentic tradition may underlie parts of it. Anaulf, for example, may be the Persian ruler Chosroes I (531-79), known to his people as Anōsharvān. He was indulgent to Christians, and his

at Andelot,[1] to reach an understanding with him ; and there were also present Childebert's mother, sister and wife. A special agreement was made between King Guntramn and Childebert, that after Guntramn's death Childebert should inherit his kingdom.

8

At this same time Rauching [2] and Guntramn Boso, Ursio and Bertefred, great men of the following of King Childebert, were executed on the king's orders because they had planned to assassinate him. Leudefred, duke of the Alamans, had also incurred the same king's displeasure ; but he escaped into hiding. Uncelen was made duke in his place.

In this year Reccared, king of the Goths, embraced the love of God, and was first baptized in private. Then he summoned before him at Toledo all Goths who were still Arians, and all Arian books were ordered to be surrendered to him. These books were collected together in one house and were burnt at his command. He compelled all the Goths to be baptized into the Christian faith.

9

In this year Caesara, wife of Anaulf,[3] the Persian emperor, left her husband and came with four male and four female servants [4] to the blessed John, bishop of

---

favourite wife was the Christian Shīrīn or Sira, whose name may lie behind Caesara, as suggested by P. Goubert, *Byzance avant l'Islam*, I, p. 174.

   [4] *cum paucis suis fidelibus* (Paul). *Puer* is sometimes used in Frankish Latin in the sense of ' military retainer,' but here, I think, rather as ' freedman,' or even ' slave.'

pule ueniens, se unam esse de populo [1] dixit et baptismi gratiam ad antedictum beatum Iohannem expetit. Cumque ab ipso pontifice fuisset baptizatus, agusta Maurici imperatores ea de [a] sancto suscepit lauacro. Quam cum uir suos imperatur Persarum per legationis sepius repetiret et Mauricius emperator uxorem ipsius esse nesciret, tunc agusta uidens eam pulcerrimam, suspicans ne ipsa esset quam legati quaerebant, dicensque eis : ' Mulier quedam de Persas hic uenit, dixit se unam esse de populo. Videte eam : forsitan [b] ipsa est quam queretis.' Quam legati uidentis proni in terram adora-uerunt, dicentes ipsam esse eorum domina quam querebant. Dicit ad eam agusta : ' Reddi illis respon-sum.' Tunc illa respondit : ' Ego cum istos non loquor, uitam illorum instar ad canis est. Si conuersi christiani sicut et ego sum efficiunter, tunc eis respondebo.' Legati uero animo libenti baptismi gratiam accipiunt, postea dicens ad eos Caesara : ' Se uir meus voluerit fieri christianus et baptismi gratiam accipere, libenter ad eum reuertam, nam paenitus aliter ad ipso non repedabo.' Legati imperatore Persarum nunciantes, statim ille legationem ad Mauricio imperatore misit, ut sanctus Iohannis uenerit Anciocam, ipso tradente baptismum uellet accipere. Tunc Mauricius imperator infinitissimum adparatum Anciocam fieri iussit, ubi imperator Persarum cum sexaginta milia Persus bapti-zatus est, et per duabus ebdomadis a Iohanne et reliquis episcopis Persas ad plenitudinem suprascripto [c] numero baptizantur. Emperatorem illum Gregorius episcopus Anciocam suscepit de lauacrum. Anaulfus imperator

---

[a] 4a ; eadē 1   [b] 4a ; forsitam 1   [c] 4a ; supra-scripto 1

[1] *privato habitu* (Paul the Deacon, ibid.)

Constantinople. She said she was a private person [1] and besought the blessed John to baptize her. She was baptized by the bishop himself, and the illustrious wife of the Emperor Maurice stood godmother to her. Her husband, the Persian emperor, on several occasions sent ambassadors to seek his wife, though the Emperor Maurice had no idea that that wife was Caesara ; but the empress then suspected that she could be the person the ambassadors were seeking, for she was very beautiful. So she said to them : ' A woman has arrived here from Persia, saying that she is a private person. There she is. Perhaps she is the person you want.' When the ambassadors saw her they prostrated themselves on the ground in adoration and declared her to be the mistress they sought. The empress said to her, ' Make some reply to them.' She replied : ' I shall not address these fellows. They live dogs' lives. I will answer them only if they will do as I have done, and become Christians.' The ambassadors received baptism with willing hearts ; after which Caesara said to them, ' If my husband is willing to become a Christian and to receive the grace of baptism, I will gladly return to him ; but I will return on no other condition.' The ambassadors reported these words to the Persian emperor, who at once sent a mission to the Emperor Maurice to request that the blessed John be despatched to Antioch, for he wished to be baptized by him. The Emperor Maurice thereupon ordered the most prodigious preparations to be made at Antioch. The Persian emperor was there baptized with sixty thousand of his subjects ; and it took John and other bishops two weeks to deal with the total number of Persians. Bishop Gregory of Antioch stood godfather to the Persian emperor himself.

Mauricio imperatore petens ut episcopus cum clero sufficiente eidem darit quos in Persas estabelirit, ut uniuersa Perseda baptismi gratiam adhiberint. Quod Mauricius libenti prestetit animo, summaque celeritate omnes Perseda ad Christi cultum baptizantur.

10

589 Anno xxviiii Gunthramni exercitus in Spaniam eiusdem iusso diregitur, sed negligenciam Bosone qui capud exercitus fuit, grauitur a Gotis exercitus ille trucidatur.[1]

11

590 Anno xxx regni suprascripti princepis tonica domini nostri Ihesu Christi, qui eidem in passionem sublata est et a militibus qui eum custodebant est sortita, de qua David propheta dixit : *Et super uestimenta mea posuerunt sortem*,[2] profetenti Symoni filio Zacob, discooperitur.[a] Per duabus ebdomadis multis cruciatibus adfectus, tandem profetetur ipsam tonicam[3] in ciuitatem Zafad procul[b] a Hyerusolima in arca marmorea posetam esse. Quam Gregorius Anthiocenus et Thomas Hyerusolimarum, Iohannis Constantinopolitanus episcopi, cum aliis multis episcopis triduanum facientes ieiunium, exinde condigni cum arca marmorea, leue effecta quasi ex ligno fuisset, ordine pedestro Hyerusolima cum deuocione sanctissema perduxerunt et eam in loco ubi crux Domini adoratur cum triumpho posuerunt.

[a] *Krusch's conjecture ;* dis. 1 [b] ? non procul
[1] cf. Greg. *Hist.* ix, chap. 31
[2] Psalm xxii. 18 (Vulg. Ps. xxi. 19)
[3] cf. Greg. *Liber in gloria martyrum*, chap. 7 (ed. Arndt and Krusch, *M.G.H. Script. Rer. Mero.* i, pp. 492-3)

The Emperor Anaulf begged the Emperor Maurice to give him bishops and sufficient clergy to be established in Persia, so that all Persians might receive the grace of baptism. Maurice gladly gave them ; and all Persia was speedily converted to Christianity.

10

In the twenty-ninth year of Guntramn's reign an army 589 marched into Spain on his orders, but it was cut to pieces by the Goths through the negligence of Boso, its commander.[1]

11

In the thirtieth year of the reign of the aforesaid prince, 590 our Lord's garment—the one taken from him during his Passion and drawn lots for by the soldiers guarding him, of which the prophet David said ' And they cast lots upon my vesture '[2]—this same garment[3] was discovered by the revelation of Simon, son of Jacob, who, after various tortures lasting a fortnight, finally confessed that it was in a marble receptacle in the town of Joppa, near Jerusalem. After fasting for three days, Gregory of Antioch, Thomas of Jerusalem, John of Constantinople and many other bishops carried the garment on foot and with all piety to Jerusalem, enclosed in its marble receptacle, which had become as light as wood. They placed it with due ceremony at the spot where our Lord's Cross was adored.

Eo anno luna obscurata est. Eo anno inter Francos et Brittanis super fluuio Vicinonia bellum est ortum.

12

Beppelenus dux Francorum factione Hebracharii idemque ducis a Brittanis interficetur. Vnde post Hebracharius ad plenitudinem paupertatis de rebus suis expoliatus peruenit.

13

Anno xxxi [1] regni Gunthramni Teudefredus [2] dux Vltraioranus moritur, cui successit Wandalmarus in honorem ducati. Ipsoque anno Ago [3] dux in Aetalia super Langobardus in regno sublimatur.

592

Anno xxxii regni Gunthramni ita a mane usque media diae sol minoratus est, ut tercia pars [a] ex ipso uix adpareret.

14

593 Anno xxxiii regni Gunthramni. Eo anno, quinto kalendas Aprilis ipse rex moritur. Sepultus est in ecclesia sancti Marcelli in monasterio quem ipse construxerat. Regnum eiusdem Childebertus adsumsit. Eodem anno Quintrio [4] dux Campanensim cum exercito

---

[a] 5b ; pras 1. *Confusion of* par *with* pra *and of* per *with* pre *is common in Frankish Latin ; cf. Anglade, Rev. de Philol. Franç.* xiv, 1900, p. 158.

[1] Incorrect, if Theudfrid did die in the year in which Agilulf became king of the Lombards. On this territory see Martin, *Études Critiques,* p. 371.

[2] Perhaps an early member of the Agilolfing dynasty (see Zöllner, ' Die Herkunft der Agilulfinger,' p. 251)

[3] It is of interest that Fredegar, like Paul the Deacon later (*Hist. Lang.* iv, chap. 1), should know the more intimate version of Agilulf's name.

In this year there was an eclipse of the moon ; and in the same year war broke out between the Franks and the Bretons on the banks of the river Vilaine.

12

Beppelen, duke of the Franks, was killed by the Bretons through the machinations of their duke, Ebrachar, though in the end Ebrachar lost everything and was reduced to the direst straits.

13

In the thirty-first year [1] of Guntramn's reign died Theudfrid, [2] duke of the territory east of the Jura. His successor in the ducal honour was Wandalmar. In the same year Duke Ago [3] was raised to the Lombard throne in Italy.

In the thirty-second year of Guntramn's reign the sun was in eclipse from dawn to midday to the extent that the third part was scarcely visible. 592

14

The thirty-third year of Guntramn's reign. On 28 March of this year the king died. He was buried in the church of Saint Marcel in the monastery that he had himself built. Childebert succeeded him. In this year Wintrio, [4] duke of Champagne, invaded in force the 593

---

[4] cf. Greg. *Hist.* VIII, chap. 18 and X, chap. 3. (Gregory himself died on 17 November, 593/4.)

in regno Clothariae ingreditur. Clotharius cum suis obuiam pergens hostiliter Quintrione in fugam uertit, sed utrasque exercitus nimium trucidatus est.

15

594 Anno secundo cum Childebertus regnum accepisset Burgundiae, exercitus Francorum et Brittanorum in inuicem proeliantes, uterque nimium gladio trucidantur.

595   Anno III Childeberto in Burgundia regnante, multa signa in caelo ostinsa sunt, apparuit stilla comitis.[1] Eo anno exercitus Childeberti cum Warnis [2] qui reuellare conauerant fortiter demicauit, et ita Warni trucidati uicti sunt ut parum ex ipsis remansisset.

16

596 Quarto anno post quod Childebertus regnum Gunthramni acciperat defunctus est,[3] regnumque eius filii sui Teudebertus et Teudericus adsumunt. Teudebertus sortitus est Auster sedem habens Mittensem, Teudericus accipit regnum Gunthramni in Burgundia [a] sedem habens Aurilianes.

---

[a] 4a ; Burgudia 1

[1] Krusch assigns the comet to the year 594 on the strength of W. J. Williams, *Observations of Comets* (London 1871), who reports a comet seen in China on 10 November 594. But Professor H. H. Plaskett assures me that the comet reported by Fredegar would be that also reported by Paul, *Hist. Lang.* IV, chap. 10 and assigned by him to January 595. The two comets were distinct.

[2] Thuringians

kingdom of Chlotar ; but the king and his warriors went to meet him and they put him to flight. Both sides suffered great losses.

15

In the second year after Childebert's accession in Burgundy, war broke out between the Franks and the Bretons. Many on both sides fell by the sword.   594

In the third year of Childebert's reign in Burgundy, many signs were seen in the sky. A comet was seen.[1] In that same year Childebert's army fought bravely against the Warni,[2] who had been trying to rise in rebellion. So many Warni fell in battle that few indeed of that people survived.   595

16

Childebert died [3] in the fourth year after succeeding to Guntramn's kingdom. His kingdom fell to his sons, Theudebert and Theuderic, of whom Theudebert obtained Austrasia with his seat at Metz and Theuderic succeeded Guntramn in Burgundy with his seat at Orleans.   596

---

[3] Poisoned *cum uxore propria*, according to Paul, *Hist. Lang.* iv, chap. 11.

17

596 Eo anno Fredegundis cum filio Clothario regi Parisius uel reliquas ciuitates rito barbaro [1] occupauit et contra filius Childeberti regis Teudeberto et Teuderico mouit exercitum loco nominante Latofao.[2] Castra uterque ex aduerso ponentes, Chlotharius cum suis super Theudebertum et Teudericum inruens eorumque exercito grauiter trucidauit.

597 Anno secundo regni Teuderici Fredegundis moritur.

18

598 Anno tercio regni Teudeberti [4] Wintrio dux instigante Brunechilde interficetur.[3]

599 Anno IIII regni Theuderici Quolenus genere Francus patricius ordenatur. Eo anno cladis glandolaria Marsilia et reliquas Prouinciae ciuitates grauiter uastauit. Eo anno aqua caledissima in laco Duninse,[5] quem Arola flumenis influit, sic ualidae aebulliuit ut multitudinem pissium coxisset. Eo anno Warnecharius maior domi Teuderici transiit, qui omnem facultatem suam in alimuniis pauperum distribuit.

19

599 Eo anno Brunechildis ab Austrasies eiecta est et in Arciacinsem campaniam a quidam homini paupero

---

[1] *rito barbaro*, here and in IV, chap. 37, may have a pejorative sense, i.e. they behaved barbarously. *Ritu* (sc. *modo*) *hostili* is used by St Patrick (Bieler, *Epist. Pat.* II, p. 193) and *tyrannico ritu* by Gildas (*De Excid.* chap. 66).
[2] near Soissons (Aisne)
[3] At Droizy near Soissons, according to *Liber Hist. Franc.* chap. 36 (ed. Krusch, *M.G.H. Script. Rer. Mero.* II, pp. 215-328).
[4] Theuderic ?
[5] Thunersee, near Berne

17

In this year Fredegundis and her son, King Chlotar, 596
took possession of Paris and other cities after the
barbarian fashion.[1]   To deal with Theudebert and
Theuderic, Childebert's sons, she despatched a force ✓
which reached a place called Laffaux.[2]   The forces
camped facing each other.   Chlotar and his men hurled
themselves upon Theudebert and Theuderic and made
great carnage among their forces.

Fredegundis died in the second year of Theuderic's 597
reign.

18

Duke Wintrio was assassinated [3] at the instigation of 598
Brunechildis in the third year of the reign of Theudebert.[4]

In the fourth year of Theuderic's reign, Quolen, by 599
birth a Frank, was made patrician.   In this year
Marseilles and other cities of Provence were devastated
by plague ; and in the same year the water of the Lake
of Thun,[5] into which flows the river Aar, became so
hot that it boiled and cooked shoals of fish.   Also in
this year died Warnachar, mayor of the palace to
Theuderic.   He distributed all his goods in alms to the
poor.

19

In this year Brunechildis was hunted out of Austrasia. 599
A poor man found her wandering alone near Arcis in

singula reperitur. Secundum eius peticionem ipsam ad Teuderico perduxit. Teudericus auiam suam Brune-childem libenter recipiens gloriose honorat. Huius uicissitudine meretum episcopatum Audicioderinsem faciente Brunechilde adsumpsit.[1]

20

600 Anno [a] v regni Teuderici iterum signa que anno superiore uisa fuerant globae igneae per caelum currentes et ad instar multitudinem astarum [2] igneum ad occidentem apparuerunt.

Ipsoque [b] anno Teudebertus et Teudericos reges contra Clotharium regem mouint exercitum et super fluuio Aroanna nec procul a Doromello uico [3] prilium confligentes iuncxerunt. Ibique exercitus Clothario grauissime trucidatus est. Ipsoque cum his qui reman-serunt in fuga uerso, pagus et ciuitates ripa Sigona qui se ad Clothario tradedirant, depopulant et uastant. Ciuitates ruptas, nimis [c] pluritas captiuorum ab exercito Theuderici et Theudeberti exinde ducetur. Chlotharius oppressus uellit nollit per pactiones uinculum firmauit, ut inter Segona et Legere usque mare Ocianum et Brittanorum limite pars [d] Teuderici haberit, et per Secona et Esera docatum integrum Denteleno [4] usque Ocianum mare Theudebertus reciperit. Duodicem tantum pagi inter Esara et Secona et mare litores Ociani Chlothario remanserunt.[5]

---

[a] *chap. 20, 3*   [b] *chap. 20,* 1
[c] nemi 1, nimis *all other MSS*
[d] 5b ; pras 1 (*see chap. 13, above*)

[1] This could only be St Desiderius, who became bishop of Auxerre in 605 ; but, according to local tradition, he was of royal blood (Duchesne, *Fastes Épiscopaux*, II, p. 447). Kurth, *Études franques*, I, p. 308, here sees legend at work to denigrate both the queen and a trusted friend.

Champagne and took her, at her request, to Theuderic who made his grandmother welcome and treated her with ceremony. Brunechildis had the poor man made bishop of Auxerre in return for the service he had done her.[1]

20

In the fifth year of Theuderic's reign the same signs were observed in the western skies that had been observed in the preceding year : fiery balls racing across the sky, and what looked like a great number of glowing spears.[2] 600

In the same year Kings Theudebert and Theuderic took the field against King Chlotar and brought him to battle on the banks of the river Orvanne, near Dormelles.[3] Chlotar's army was here massacred, but he himself took to flight with the remainder. Then they laid waste the towns and districts along the Seine that had gone over to Chlotar. The towns were razed and from them the army of Theudebert and Theuderic took a great number of prisoners. The defeated Chlotar had no option but to agree to terms, whereby Theuderic got all the land between the Seine and the Loire right to the Atlantic and the Breton frontier while Theudebert had the entire duchy of Dentelin [4] between the Seine and the Oise, to the Channel. All that remained to Chlotar were twelve cantons between the Seine, the Oise and the sea.[5]

---

[2] cf. Paul, *Hist. Lang.* iv, chap. 15
[3] near Montereau (Seine-et-Marne)
[4] The region bounded by the Oise, the Canche, the Channel and the Forêt Charbonnière. cf. chap. 76, below.
[5] Comprised within the territories of Beauvais, Amiens and Rouen.

601   Anno sexto regni Theuderici Cautinus dux Teudeberti interficetur.

21

602 Anno VII regni Theuderici de concubina filius nascitur
nomen Sigybertus, et Aegyla patricius nullis culpis
extantibus instigante Brunechilde legatus interficetur
nisi tantum cupiditatis instincto ut facultatem eius fiscus
adsumerit.

Eo anno Teudebertus et Teudericus exercitum
contra Wasconis dirigunt ipsoque Deo auxiliante
deiectus suae dominatione redegiunt et tributarius
faciunt. Ducem super ipsos nomen Geniale instituunt,
qui eos feliciter dominauit.

22

602 Eo anno corpus sancti Victoris, qui Salodero cum sancto
Vrsio passus fuerat, a beato Aeconio [1] pontifice Maurien-
nense inuenitur. Quadam nocte in suam ciuitatem
ei reuelatur in sompnium ut surgens protinus iret
ad eclesiam quam Sideleuba [2] regina suburbanum
Genauinse construxerat : in medium eclesia designatum
locum illum sanctum corpus adesset. Cumque Genaua
festinus perrexisset cum beatis Rusticio et Patricio [3]
episcopis, triduanum faciens ieiunium, lumen per
noctem ubi illum gloriosum et splendidum corpus erat

[1] Hiconius (Duchesne, *Fastes Épiscopaux*, I, p. 240)
[2] This cannot be the Sideleuba whom Fredegar earlier (III, chap. 18)
states to have been the sister of Chrotechildis, wife of Clovis I. Maurice
Chaume suggests that she may have been the sister not of Chrotechildis but
of Guntheuca, daughter or granddaughter of Godegisel and Theudelinda,
and thus heiress to her parents' Arian basilicas in this region (*Recherches
d'Histoire*, p. 156).

In the sixth year of Theuderic's reign Cautinus, one 601 of Theudebert's dukes, was killed.

21

In the seventh year of his reign, Theuderic had, by a 602 mistress, a son named Sigebert. Aegyla the patrician was bound and put to death, though innocent, at the instigation of Brunechildis for no other reason than her cupidity ; for his property would be taken by the fisc.

In the same year Theudebert and Theuderic sent an army against the Gascons and with God's help defeated them, subjected them to their overlordship and made them pay tribute. They appointed a duke named Genialis, who ruled them well.

22

In this year the blessed Aeconius,[1] bishop of Saint-Jean- 602 de-Maurienne, discovered the body of Saint Victor, who had been martyred at Solothurn with Saint Ours. One night, when he was in his city, it was revealed to him in a dream that he should get up at once and go to the church built by Queen Sideleuba [2] outside Geneva. He would be informed of the spot where, in the middle of the church, the saint's body lay. So he made all haste to Geneva with the blessed Bishops Rusticius and Patricius.[3] For three days he fasted and then, in the night, a light appeared over the spot where

---

[3] One of them must have been bishop of Geneva (Duchesne, *Fastes Épiscopaux*, I, p. 229).

G

apparuit. Quem cum selencio hii tres pontifecis cum lacrimis et orationibus, eleuato lapide, in arcam argentiam inuenerunt sepultum cuius faciem robentem quasi uiuum repperunt. Ibique princeps Theudericus presens aderat, multisque rebus huius eclesiae tribuens, maxemam partem facultates Warnacharii ibidem confirmauit.[1] Ad sepulchrum illum sanctum mirae uirtutes ex ipsa diae quo repertum est prestante Domino integra 602 adsiduaetate ostenduntur. Eo anno Aetherius episcopus Lugdunensis obiit : ordenatur loco ipsius Secundinus episcopus.

23

602 Eo anno Fogas dux et patricius reipublicae uictur a Persas rediens, Mauricio emperatore interfecit. In loco ipsius imperium adsumsit.

24

603 Anno VIII regni Teuderici de concubina nascitur ei filius nomen Childebertus, et senodus Cabillonno [2] collegitur. Desiderium Viennensem episcopum deieciunt, instigante Aridio Lugdunensi episcopo et Brunechilde, et subrogatus est loco ipsius sacerdotale officio Domnolus, Desiderius uero in insula quedam exilio retrudetur.[3] Eo anno sol obscuratus est. Eo quoque tempore Bertoaldus genere Francos maior domus palacii Teuderici erat, morebus mensuratus, sapiens et cautus, in prilio fortis, fidem cum omnibus seruans.

[1] see chap. 18, above.
[2] see Mansi, *Coll. Conc.* x, p. 493.
[3] see Sisebut's *Vita Desiderii* (ed. Krusch, *M.G.H. Script. Rer. Mero.* III, pp. 620-48). cf. chap. 32. Kurth, *Études franques*, I, pp. 323 ff., discusses the matter at length.

lay those glorious and illustrious remains. The three
bishops, praying and in tears, silently lifted a stone and
there found the body in a silver coffin. The saint's face
had the fresh complexion of a living man. King
Theuderic, who was present, made many gifts to the
church and on the spot confirmed it in possession of the
greater part of Warnachar's goods.[1] From the day of
that discovery astounding miracles were, by God's grace,
constantly performed at that blessed grave. In this year 602
died Aetherius, bishop of Lyons. Secundinus was consecrated in his place.

23

In this year Phocas, duke and Roman patrician, 602
returned victorious from Persia, slew the Emperor
Maurice and seized the empire.

24

In the eighth year of his reign Theuderic had, by a 603
mistress, a son called Childebert. A synod assembled
at Chalon,[2] which deposed Desiderius from the bishopric
of Vienne at the instigation of Bishop Aridius of Lyons
and of Brunechildis. The see was given to Domnolus.
Desiderius was exiled to an island.[3] This year, there
was an eclipse of the sun ; and this was when Bertoald,
by birth a Frank, was mayor of the palace to Theuderic.
He was a man of moderate ways, sensible and careful, but
brave in war and always true to his word.

604   Anno VIIII regni Teuderici nascitur ei de concubina filius nomen Corbus. Cum iam Protadius genere Romanus [1] uehementer in palacium ab omnibus ueneraretur et Brunechildis stubre gratiam eum uellit honoribus exaltare, defuncto Wandalmaro duci in pago Vltraiorano et Scotingorum [2] Protadius patricius ordenatur instigatione Brunechilde. Vt Bertoaldus pocius interiret, eum ripa Segona usque Ocianum mare per pagus et ciuitates fiscum inquerendum dirigunt. [3]

25

Bertoaldus a Teuderico directus, cum trecentus tantum uiros illis partibus properauit. Cumque Arelao uilla [4] uenisset et uenationem inibi exercerit, haec conperiens Clotharius, filium suum Maeroeum et Landericum maioris domus cum exercitum Bertoaldum opprimendum direxit et maximam partem inter Segona et Legere pagus et ciuitates de regno Theuderici presumpsit contra pactum peruadere. Bertoaldus haec audiens, cum sustenere non preualebat, terga uertens Aurilianes ingreditur ibique a uiro [a] beatissimo Austreno episcopo suscepetur. Landericus cum exercito Aurilianes circumdans, uocabat Bertoaldum ut exiret ad prilium. Bertoaldus de muro respondens : ' Nos duo singulare certamen, si me expectare deliberas, reliqua multetudine procul suspinsa, iungamus ad prilium, a Domino iudecemur.' Sed haec Landericus facere distulit.

---

[a] 4a ; uero 1

[1] i.e. a Gallo-Roman, which is the normal sense of the word when used of a native of Gaul.
[2] now Salins. The Scotingi were Alamans forcibly settled in this area in the fourth century.

In the ninth year of his reign Theuderic had, by a 604
mistress, a son called Corbus. Protadius, by birth a
Roman,[1] was held in high esteem in the palace and his
bedfellow, Brunechildis, wished to load him with
honours ; and at her instance he was appointed
patrician over the territory east of the Jura and of the
Scotingi [2] at the death of Duke Wandalmar. Bertoald
was sent to inspect the royal domains in the cantons and
cities along the banks of the Seine up to the Channel.
This was done the more easily to procure his death.[3]

25

Bertoald set out with a mere three hundred men for the
district to which Theuderic had sent him. He went
hunting when they reached the villa of Arèle.[4] Chlotar
got to hear of this and so sent a force under his son
Merovech, and Landri, mayor of his palace, to over-
power him. Flouting the agreement, this force dared
to storm through most of the towns and the countryside
lying between the Seine and the Loire which belonged
to Theuderic. On receiving this news Bertoald fled to
Orleans, for he lacked the means to resist. He was
received at Orleans by the blessed Bishop Austrenus.
Landri then invested the town with his men and called
on Bertoald to come out and fight, to which Bertoald
replied from the ramparts : ' If you are prepared to
await me and send your men some distance off, I will
come and do single combat with you and God shall be

---

[3] On the interpretation of this passage see F. Lot, *L'Impôt foncier et la
capitation personelle*, Paris 1928, p. 102.
[4] Probably a hunting-lodge in the Forêt de la Brotonne (Eure) on the
right bank of the Seine, opposite Caudebec.

Addens Bertoaldus dixit : 'Dum facere non audes, proximum temporis domini nostri pro ea que facetis iungent ad prilio. Induamur uterque ego et tu uestibus uermiclis, precedamus chetheris ubi congressus erit certamenis ; ibique tua et mea utilitas adparebit, promittentes ante Deum ab inuicem, promissionis huius ueritatem subsistere.'

26

Nov. 11 Cumque haec in diem festi sancti Martini antestites actum fuisset, Theudericus cum haec conperisset quod a Clothario pars regni sui contra pactum fuerat peruasum, natiuitate Domini protinus cum exercitum Stampas super fluuio Loa peruenit, ibique obuiam Meroeus filius Clotharii regis cum Landerico et magno exercito uenit. Cum esset artus peruius ille ubi Loa fluuius transmeatur, uix tercia pars exercitus Teuderici transiuerat, initum est prilium. Vbique Bertoaldus secundum placetum adgreditur, uocetans Landericum, sed Landericus non est ausus, ut promiserat, tantum [a] huius certaminis congressionem adire. Ibique Bertoaldus cum nimis citeris precessisset ab exercito Clothariae cum suis interficetur, nec uellens exinde euadere, dum senserat se de sui gradus honorem a Protadio degradandum. Ibique Meroeus filius Clothariae capetur, Landericus in fuga uersus est, nimia multitudo exercitus Clothariae in eo prilio gladio trucidatus est. Teudericus uictur Parisius ingreditur. Teudebertus pacem cum Clothario Conpendio uilla iniuit, et uterque exercitus eorum inlesus redit ad propriam.

[a] *sc.* ita

judge.' But Landri declined, and Bertoald added :
' You dare not ! But our masters will at once go to
war for what you have done. When the fighting starts,
let us both wear red and be well to the fore of our
men. Then we shall see what the two of us are made
of ! Swear with me before God to keep this promise.'

26

This challenge was made on the feast of the blessed Nov. 11
Bishop Martin. When Theuderic heard that Chlotar
had entered his territory contrary to their agreement,
he at once set out at Christmas with an army for Étampes
on the river Louet, where he encountered a great force
under Merovech, King Chlotar's son, and Landri. The
ford over the river was so narrow that scarcely a third
of Theuderic's army was over before the engagement
started. Bertoald kept his promise and advanced,
calling on Landri, who dared not thus face the duel to
which on the day of battle he was committed by oath.
But Bertoald had advanced too far. He and his men
were killed by Chlotar's force. He made no effort to
escape, knowing that Protadius planned his downfall.
Merovech, Chlotar's son, was there taken prisoner,
Landri was put to flight and very many of Chlotar's
following were cut down. Theuderic entered Paris in
triumph, Theudebert made peace with Chlotar at
Compiègne and their two armies got home unscathed.

27

605 Anno x regni Theuderici Protadius, instigante *a* Brunechilde, Teuderico iobente, maior domi substituetur.
Cum *b* esset nimium argutissimus et strenuus in cunctis
sed saeua illi fuit contra personas iniquitas, fiscum
nimium stringens, de rebus personarum ingeniose fisco
uellens implere et se ipsum ditare ; quoscumque de
gentem nobilem repperiret, totusque humiliare conabat,
ut nullus repperiretur qui gratum *c* quem adriperat
potuisset adsumere. Haec his et alies nimia sagatitate
uexatus, maximae cunctos in regno Burgundiae locratus *d*
est inimicus. Cum Brunechildis nepotem suum
Teudericum integra adsiduetate monerit *e* ut contra
Teudebertum mouerit exercitum, dicens quasi Theudebertus non esset filius Childeberti nisi cuiusdam
ortolanum,[1] et Protadius ipsoque consilio adsistens,
tandem iusso Teuderici mouetur exercitus. Quod cum
loco nomen Caratiaco [2] Teudericus cum exercito castra
metasset ortabatur a leudibus suis ut cum Theudeberto
pacem iniret. Protadius singulos ortabatur ut prilium
committeretur. Teudebertus nec procul exinde cum
exercito resedebat. Tunc omnes exercitus Teuderici
inuenta occasione supra Protagio inruunt, dicentes
melius esse uno hominem moriturum quam totum
exercitum in periculum missum. Protadius in tenturio
Teuderici regis cum Petro archyatro tabulam ludens
sedebat. Cum eum undique iam exercitus circumdasset
et Teudericum leudis suae tenebat ne illuc adgrederit,
misit Vncelenum ut suae iussionis uerbum nunciaret
exercitum ut se de insidias Protadiae remouerint.
Vncilenus protinus ad exercitum nuncians dixit : ' Sic

---

a instante 1, instigante *all other MSS*   *b* *chap.* 27, 1
c 1 ; gradum 4a   *d* *sc.* lucratus   *e* moneret 4a ; nonerit 1

27

In the tenth year of his reign and at the wish of 605 Brunechildis, Theuderic made Protadius mayor of the palace. In every way Protadius was as clever and as capable as a man could be ; but in certain cases he was monstrously cruel, extorting the last penny for the fisc and with ingenuity both filling the fisc and enriching himself at the expense of others. He set himself to undermine all those of noble birth, so that nobody could deprive him of the position he had acquired. In these and other ways his excessive cunning harassed everyone, and not least the Burgundians, every man of whom he made his enemy. Brunechildis was persistent in urging her grandson Theuderic to attack Theudebert ; he was a gardener's son, she declared, not Childebert's.[1] Protadius concurring with this advice, Theuderic at length gave orders to raise a force. While they were encamped at a place called Quierzy,[2] Theuderic's warriors begged him to come to terms with Theudebert, Protadius alone urging battle ; for Theudebert and his men were not far away. Thereupon all the warriors took their chance to set upon Protadius, a single death, in their view, being a great deal preferable to the endangering of a whole army. Protadius was sitting in King Theuderic's tent playing dice with Peter, the court physician. The warriors surrounded the tent and his men-at-arms detained Theuderic in case he should enter. However, the king sent Uncelen with orders that they should stop molesting Protadius. Uncelen,

---

[1] cf. Greg. *Hist.* VIII, chap. 37 and IX, chap. 4 : both Theudebert and Theuderic were sons of Childebert.
[2] on the Oise near Noyon (Aisne)

iobet domnus Theudericus, ut interficiatur Protadius.'
Inruentes super eum, tenturium regis gladio undique
incidentis, Protadium interficiunt. Teudericus confusus
et coactus cum fratri Teudeberto pacem iniuit et
inlesus uterque exercitus reuertit ad propriis sedibus.

28

606 Post discessum Protadiae, anno *a* xi regni Teuderici
subrogatur maior domus Claudius genere Romanus,
homo prudens, iocundus in fabolis, strenuus in cunctis,
pacienciae deditus, plenitudinem consiliae habundans,
litterum eruditus, fide plenus, amiciciam cum omnibus
sectans, priorum exempla metuens lenem se et paci-
entem huius gradi ascensus ostendit. Sed hoc tantum
inpedimentum habebat, quod saginam esset corpore
adgrauatus.

607 Anno xii regni Teuderici Vncelenus, qui ad mortem
Protadiae insidiose fuerat locutus, instigante Brunechilde pede truncatum de rebus expoliatus ad reuilli-
tatem perductus est.

29

Vulfos patricius, idemque Brunechilde instigante consilio
qui mortem Protadiae consenserat, Fauriniaco uilla [1]
iobente Teuderico occidetur, et in patriciatum eius
Ricomeris Romano generis subrogatur.

[a] *chap. 28*, 1
[1] near Luxeuil (Haute-Saône)

on the contrary, forthwith declared to the warriors :
' The Lord Theuderic orders Protadius' execution ! '
Accordingly they cut the royal tent to ribbons and
hurled themselves on Protadius and killed him.
Theuderic, now not knowing what he was doing, was
made to agree to terms with his brother Theudebert.
The two forces went home without a fight.

28

In the eleventh year of Theuderic's reign, after the death 606
of Protadius, Claudius was appointed mayor of the
palace. By birth a Roman, Claudius was an intelligent
man and a good storyteller, yet a man that got things
done, resolute and full of good advice, well-read,
absolutely trustworthy and the friend of all. He took
note of what had happened to his predecessors and
behaved quietly and kept his temper while he held this
office. But he had one disadvantage : his excessive
corpulence, the result of overeating.

In the twelfth year of Theuderic's reign, that 607
Uncelen whose cunning had brought about Protadius'
death had a foot cut off at the instigation of Brunechildis. He was stripped of his belongings and reduced
to the most pitiable circumstances.

29

The patrician Wulf, who had been a consenting party
to Protadius' death, was done to death at the villa of
Faverney [1] on Theuderic's orders—once again on the
advice of Brunechildis ; and the Roman Ricomer was
his successor as patrician.

607   Eodem anno natus est de concupina Teuderici filius nomen Meroeus, quem Clotharius de sancto lauacro suscepit.

30

607 Eodem anno Teudericus Aridium episcopum Lugduninsem, Rocconem et Aeborinum comestaboli ad Bettericum regem Spaniae direxit, qui exinde Ermenberta filia eius Teuderico matrimonio sociandam adducerint. Ibique datis sacramentis ut a Teudericum ne umquam a regno degradaretur,[a] ipsamque accipiunt et Teuderico Cabillonno presentant, quem ille gaudens diligenter suscepit. Eadem factionem auiae suae Brunechilde uirile coitum non cognouit. Instigantibus uerbis Brunechilde aua et Teudilane germana efficetur odiosa. Post anni circulum Theudericus Ermenbergam expoliatam a thinsauris Spaniam retransmisit.[1]

31

Bettericus haec indignans legationem ad Clothario direxit. Legatus Clothario cum Betterici legato [b] ad Teudebertum perrexit. Iterum Teudeberti legati cum Clothario et Betterico legataries ad Agonem regem Aetaliae accesserunt ut [c] unianimiter hii quattuor regis cum exercitum undique super Theudericum inruerint,[d] regnum eius auferrint et eum morte damnarint, eo quod tantam de ipso reuerentiam ducebant. Legatus uero Gothorum euicto nauale de Aetaliam per mare Spaniam reuertitur. Sed haec consilius diuino noto non

[a] degradatur 1, degraderetur *all other MSS*   [b] *om.* 1
[c] et *all MSS*   [d] 1, *all other MSS add* ut

In this same year Theuderic's mistress gave him a 607
son, called Merovech. Chlotar was his godfather.

30

In this year Theuderic sent Bishop Aridius of Lyons, 607
Rocco and the constable Eborin to Witteric, king of
Spain, to ask for the hand in marriage of his daughter,
Ermenberga. When the envoys had given their oath
that Theuderic would never depose her, she was
surrendered to them, and at Chalon was presented to
Theuderic, who received her delightedly. But his grandmother saw to it that Theuderic's marriage was never
consummated : the talk of Brunechildis his grandmother
and of his sister Theudila poisoned him against his bride.
After a year, Ermenberga was deprived of her dowry
and sent back to Spain.[1]

31

Witteric was furious. He sent to Chlotar an envoy who,
together with an envoy from Chlotar, made their way
to Theudebert. Then the envoys of Theudebert,
Chlotar and Witteric went to Agilulf, king of Italy.
The four kings agreed on a plan to attack Theuderic
from four different directions, then to depose him and
condemn him to death. Such was their fear of him.
In fact, the Gothic envoy embarked from Italy to return
by sea to Spain. But God willed that the design of these

---

[1] Kurth, and following him G. S. M. Walker (op. cit., p. xxi) have
doubted the complicity of Brunechildis on the ground that she too was a
Visigothic princess ; but this carries little conviction.

sortitur effectum. Quod cum Theuderico conpertum fuisset, fortissime ab eodem dispicetur.

32

607 Eo anno Teudericus consilio Aridio episcopo Lugduninse perfedum utens et per suasum auae suae Brunechilde, sanctum Desiderium [1] de exilium egressum lapidare precipit. Ad cuius sepulcrum mirae uirtutes a diae transitus sui Dominus integra adsiduaetate ostendere dignatur ; per quod credendum est pro hoc malum gestum regnum Theuderici et filiis suis fuisse distructum.

33

Eo anno, mortuo Betterico, Sisebodus [2] Spaniae successit in regno, uir sapiens et in totam Spaniam laudabelis ualde, pietate plenissemus. Nam et aduersus manum publecam fortiter demicauit, prouinciam Cantabriam Gothorum regno subaegit quam aliquando Franci [3] possederant. Dux Francio nomen,[4] qui Cantabriam in tempore Francorum egerat, tributa Francorum regibus multo tempore impleuerat. Sed cum parte imperiae fuerat Cantabria reuocata, a Gothis ut super legetur preoccupatur, et plures ciuitates ab imperio Romano Sisebodus litore maris abstulit et usque fundamentum destruxit. Cumque Romani [5] ab exercito Sisebodi trucidarentur, Sisebotus dicebat pietate plenus : ' Eu

---

[1] cf. chap. 24 above, and Jonas, *Vita Columbani*, i, chap. 27 (ed. Krusch, *M.G.H. in usum scholarum*, 1905)

[2] author of the life of St Desiderius, cited above. In fact, Witteric died in 610 and was succeeded by Gunthimar, who died in 612 and was succeeded by Sisebut.

[3] The Franks never held Cantabria.

kings should come to nothing. Theuderic got wind of
it but treated it with utter contempt.

32

In this year the blessed Desiderius [1] returned from 607
banishment. Theuderic followed the wicked advice of
Bishop Aridius of Lyons and of his grandmother
Brunechildis and ordered him to be stoned to death ;
and the Lord was pleased to show splendid miracles at
his tomb from the day of his death, which makes it
credible that this evil deed cost Theuderic and his sons
their kingdom.

33

In this year died Witteric. He was succeeded as king
of Spain by Sisebut, [2] a wise and most pious man, much
admired throughout Spain. He had fought bravely
against the Roman Empire and had won Cantabria,
previously held by the Franks, [3] for the Gothic kingdom.
A duke named Francio [4] had conquered Cantabria in
the days of the Franks and had long paid tribute to the
Frankish kings ; but when the province was once more
restored to the Empire the Goths, as I said above, took
possession of it. Sisebut captured several of the imperial
cities along the seaboard and razed them to the ground.
The slaughter of the Romans [5] by his men caused the
pious Sisebut to exclaim : ' Woe is me, that my reign

---

[4] The possibility that Francio was a Byzantine *magister militum* is
discussed by G. P. Bognetti, *Relazioni dello X° Congresso Int. di Sci. Stor.* III,
p. 41.
[5] i.e. Byzantine soldiers. Sisebut won most of the Byzantine possessions
in southern Spain from the Emperor Heraclius.

me misero, cuius tempore tante sanguis humanae effusio
fietur ! ' [1] Cuiuscumque potebat occurrere de morte
liberabat. Confirmatum est regnum Gothorum in
Spaniam per mare litora usque Paereneos montes.

34

Ago [2] rex Langobardorum accepit uxorem Grimoaldi et
Gundoaldi germanam nomen Teudelendae ex genere
Francorum,[3] quem Childebertus habuerat disponsatam.
Cum eam consilium Brunechilde postposuisset,
Gundoaldus cum omnibus rebus se cum germanam
Teudelende in Aetaliam transtulit et Teudelindae
matrimonium Agonem tradedit. Gundoaldus de gente
nobile Langobardorum accepit uxorem, de qua duos
filius habuit his nominibus, Gundeberto et Chairiberto.
Ago rex, filius [4] Authario rege, de Theudelindem habuit
filium nomen Adoaldo et filiam nomen Gundoberga.
Dum [a] Gundoald a Langobardis nimium dilegeretur,
factione Agone regi et Teudelindae, cum ipsum iam
zelum tenerint, ubi ad uentrem purgandum in faldaone
sedebat saggitta saucius moritur.

35

608 Anno XIII regni Teuderici cum Theudebertus Bili-
childem habebat uxorem, quam Brunechildis a negucia-
toribus mercauerat ; et esset Bilichildis utilis et a

---

[a] *sc.* cum

[1] This seems to be an echo from King Sisebut's correspondence (ed.
Gundlach, *M.G.H. Epist.* III, *Epist. Wisigothicae*, 4, p. 665).

[2] Agilulf (see chap. 13, above)

should witness so great a shedding of human blood ! ' [1]
He saved all whom he could from death. Gothic rule
in Spain was established from the sea to the Pyrenees.

34

The Lombard King Ago [2] took to wife a Frank named
Theudelinda,[3] a sister of Grimoald and Gundoald.
She had been betrothed to Childebert, who resigned her
on the advice of Brunechildis. So Gundoald took his
sister Theudelinda and all her belongings to Italy and
gave her in marriage to Ago. Gundoald himself took
to wife a noble Lombard, by whom he had two sons,
Gundebert and Charibert. King Ago, son [4] of King
Authari, had by Theudelinda a son named Adaloald
and a daughter named Gundeberga. Since Gundoald
was too popular with the Lombards, Ago and Theudelinda, already suspicious, caused him to be shot with an
arrow while he was relieving nature. Thus he died.

35

In the thirteenth year of Theuderic's reign, Theudebert 608
had as his wife Bilichildis, whom Brunechildis had
bought from merchants. Bilichildis was a woman of
spirit and much loved by all the Austrasians because she

---

[3] Theudelinda was certainly an Agilolfing princess, but whether her
family was native Bavarian, or Frankish as Fredegar here claims, or
Burgundian (see Zöllner, ' Die Herkunft der Agilulfinger,' p. 245) must
remain in doubt. Her mother may have been a Frank. Paul, *Hist. Lang.*
III, chaps. 30 and 35, explains that she was first the wife of the Lombard
King Authari but on his death, in 590, she married Agilulf. cf. chap. 51,
below.
[4] untrue

H

cunctis [a] Austransiis uehementer diligeretur, simplici-
tatem Teudeberti honeste conportans, nihil se menorem
a Brunechilde esse censirit sed sepius per legatus
Brunechilde dispicirit, dum ab ipsa increpabatur quod
ancilla Brunechilde fuisset, tandem his et aliis uerbis
legatis discurrentibus ab inuicem uexarentur, placetus
inter Colerinse et Sointense [1] fiaetur, ut has duas reginas
pro pacem inter Teudericum et Teudebertum coniun-
gerint conloquendum. Sed Bilichildis consilio Austrasiis
inibi uenire distulit.

36

609 Anno [2] XIIII regni Teuderici beatus Columbanus cre-
uerat [3] iam passim [b] fama is [c] in uniuersas Gallias
uel Germaniae prouincias, eratque omnium rimore [d]
laudabilis, omnium cultu uenerabelis; in tantum ut
Teudericus rex ad eum saepe Lossowio uenerit et
orationum suarum suffragio omni cum humilitate
poscerit. Ad quem saepissimae cum uenerit, coepit uir
Dei eum increpare, quur concubinarum adulteriis
misceretur et non pocius legetimi coniugii solamina
frueretur, ut regales prolexs ex honorabilem reginam
prodiret et non pocius ex lupinaribus uideretur emergi.
Cumque iam ad uiri Dei imperium regis sermo
obtemperaret et se omnibus inlicetis secregare respon-
deret, mentem Brunechildis auiae, secundae ut erat

---

[a] 4a ; cunctin 1   [b] 4a ; parsim 1
[c] sancti uiri *Jonas* ; civitatis suae *add.* 1   [d] *sc.* rumore

[1] This seems a more probable derivation than any alternative. For the
Saintois, cf. below, where *Sointense* becomes *Suggentensis* (chap. 37) and
Sogiontinsis (chap. 87).

[2] This chapter is taken verbatim, with very few additions, and some
omissions that obscure the sense of the original, from the *Vita Columbani* of

bore with nobility the simple-mindedness of Theudebert. She not only thought herself in no way inferior
to Brunechildis but frequently sent her contemptuous
messages. Brunechildis, for her part, reproached her
with having been her slave. Finally, when they had
thoroughly irritated each other exchanging messages
and talk of this sort, an interview was arranged on
the boundary between the district of Colroy and the
Saintois,[1] with the intention that the two queens should
patch up peace between Theuderic and Theudebert;
but on the advice of the Austrasians Bilichildis did not go.

36

By [2] the fourteenth year of Theuderic's reign, the 609
reputation [3] of the blessed Columbanus was increasing
everywhere in the cities and provinces of Gaul and
Germany. So generally reputed was he, and so venerated
by all, that King Theuderic used often to visit him at
Luxeuil humbly to beg the favour of his prayers, and as
often the man of God would rebuke him and ask why
he chose to surrender to mistresses rather than to enjoy
the blessings of lawful wedlock; for the royal stock
should be seen to issue from an honourable queen, not
from prostitutes. The king deferred to what the man of
God said and promised to abstain from illicit love; but
the Old Serpent slipped into the mind of that second

Jonas, completed in 640. References here are to the 1905 edition of Bruno
Krusch (*M.G.H. in usum scholarum*). It may at least be said for Theuderic
that Columbanus was politically as well as spiritually influential in
Burgundy; he had friends and supporters among the Burgundian
aristocracy.
    [3] *Vita Col.* I, chap. 18

Zezebelis, antiquus anguis adiit eamque contra uirum
Dei stimulatam superbiae aculeo excitat quia cerneret
uiro Dei Theudericum oboedire. Verebatur enim ne,
si abiectis concubines reginam aulae perfecisset,[a]
dignitates atque honoris sui modum amputasset. Euenit [1]
ergo ut quadam die beatus Columbanus ad Brune-
childem uenerit. Erat enim tunc apud Brocariacum
uilla.[2] Cumque illa eum in aula uenire cerniret, filios
Teuderici quos de adulterinis permixtionibus habebat
ad uirum Dei adducit. Quos cum uedisset, sciscitatur
quid sibi uellent. Cui Brunechildis ait : ' Regis sunt
filii : tu eos benedictione robora.' At ille : ' Nequaquam,' inquid, ' istos regalia sceptra suscepturus scias :
de lupinaribus emerserunt.'[3] Illa furens paruolus abire
iobet. Egrediens uir Dei regiam aulam, dum limitem
transiliret, fragor ex [b] terrorem incussit nec tamen
miserae feminae fororem conpescuit. Paratque deinde
insidias molire : uicinus monastirii per nuncius imperat
ut nulli eorum extra monasterii terminos iter pandatur,
neque receptacula monachis eius uel quelibet subsidia
tribuantur. Cernens beatus Columbanus regios animos
aduersum se permotus, ad eos properat ut [c] suis monitis
miserae [d] pertenaciae intentu frangat. Erat enim tunc
temporis apud Spinsiam uillam publecam.[4] Quo cum
iam sol occumbentem uenisset, regi nunciant uirum Dei
inibi esset nec regis domibus metare uellit. Tunc
Teudericus ait, melius esse uirum Dei oportunis subsidiis

[a] praefecisset *Jonas*
[b] fragor exorta totam domum quatiens omnibus terrorem *Jonas*
[c] 4a ; et 1
[d] miserat 1

[1] *Vita Col.* I, chap. 19
[2] Seine-et-Oise. Bourcheresse (Saône-et-Loire) is preferred by Jacobs
and an unidentified Brocaria near Étampes by Ewig.

Jezebel, his grandmother Brunechildis, and by the sting of pride provoked her against the holy man of God. Observing how Theuderic yielded to him, she feared that the substitution of a queen for mistresses at the head of the court would deprive her of part of her dignities and her honour. It happened [1] that one day the blessed Columbanus came to Brunechildis at the villa of Bruyères-le-Châtel.[2] She saw him coming through the courtyard and forthwith brought to the man of God the sons born in adultery to Theuderic. Seeing them, he enquired what they wanted of him, to which Brunechildis replied : 'These are the king's sons : pray strengthen them with your blessing.' ' Know,' rejoined Columbanus, ' that they shall never hold the royal sceptre, for they were born in adultery.'[3] Furious, she ordered the children to withdraw. As he left the royal courtyard and at the moment when his foot crossed the threshold, a roar of thunder shook him ; but it did not quench the fury of the wretched woman, who forthwith started to scheme the holy man's downfall. She sent instructions to those living round the monastery that no monk should be allowed to leave its confines or should be allowed a place of refuge or assistance. When he saw how the royal anger was kindled against him the blessed Columbanus repaired to the court to counsel the curbing of such immoderate wrath. The king was at the villa of Époisses.[4] It was sunset when the holy man arrived. The king was informed of his arrival and that he did not wish to enter the royal suite. Theuderic replied that it was better to do honour to the man of

---

[3] Their being born of concubines made no difference to the position of Merovingian princes or princesses.
[4] Côte-d'Or. See p. 104, n 1.

honorare quam Dominum ex seruorum eius offensam ad iragundiam prouocare. Iobet ergo regio cultu oportuna parare Deique famolo dirigi. Itaque uenerunt et iuxta imperium regis oblata offerunt. Que cum uidisset dapes et pocula cultu regio admenistrata, inquirit quid sibi de ista uellint. Aient ille : ' Tibi a rege fore directa.' Abuminatus ea ait : ' Scriptum est, Munera impiorum reprobat Altissemus [1] ; non enim dignum est ut famolorum Dei ora cibis eius polluantur qui non solum suis uerum etiam aliorum habitaculis famulis Dei aditum deniget.' His dicta, uascula omnia in frustra disrupta sunt uinaque ac sicera solo diffusa ceteraque separatim dispersam. Pauifacti menistri rei geste causam regi nunciant. Illi pauore perculsus, cum auia delucolo ad uirum Dei properant. Precantur de commisso ueniam ; se in postmodum emendare pollicentur. His pacatus promissis ad monasterium rediit.

Sed polliciti uadaemonii iura non diu seruata uiolantur ; exercentur miseriarum incrimenta, solitoque a rege adulteria patrantur. Quae audita, beatus Columbanus litteras ad eum uerberibus plenas direxit comminaturque excomunicationem si emendare dilatando non uellit. Ad haec rursum permuta Brunechildis, regis animum aduersum Columbanum excitat omnique conatu perturbare intendit, oraturque proceris, auligas, optamatis omnis ut regis animum contra uerum Dei perturbarint, episcopusque sollicitare adgressa, et de eius religione detrahendo et statum [a] regulae [2] quam suis

---

[a] *Jonas* ; statim 1, 4a

[1] Ecclesiasticus xxiv. 19 (Vulg. Ecclus. xxxiv. 23)

[2] ed. O. Seebass, *Zeitschrift für Kirchengeschichte*, xv (1895), pp. 366-86 and xvii (1897), pp. 215-34. The Rule and Penitential of Columbanus are discussed by J. F. Kenney, *The Sources for the early History of Ireland*, I, pp. 197-200, and most recently by G. S. M. Walker, *Sancti Columbani Opera* (Dublin 1957), who also edits and translates the texts.

God with timely gifts than to kindle the wrath of the Lord by offending one of His servants. So he ordered gifts to be prepared on a royal scale and sent to the man of God. His servants obediently went and offered these presents to Columbanus who, at the sight of the dishes and goblets presented to him with royal pomp, enquired what they meant. They replied, ' The king ordered them to be brought to you.' But he thrust them away with a curse, saying, ' It is written, The Almighty reproves the gifts of the impious.[1] It is unbecoming that the lips of God's servants should be polluted with that man's dainties, for he denies them not only their own homes but the homes of others.' At these words the vessels were broken in pieces, wine and cider spattered the floor and everything was thrown about in confusion. The terrified servants hastened to tell the king what had happened. When dawn broke the king, equally terrified, went with his grandmother to the man of God and begged his forgiveness, promising to live better in future. Placated by these promises, Columbanus returned to his monastery.

But their promises were not kept for long, for both subsided into their crimes and the king gave himself up to his habitual adultery. At this, the blessed Columbanus wrote him a letter full of reproach and threatened him with excommunication if he did not forthwith mend his ways. But Brunechildis, stirred up again, inflamed the king against Columbanus and did all she could to distress him. She besought the noblemen and courtiers and all the magnates to influence the king against the man of God, and dared to work upon the bishops to bring his profession into disrepute and to question the rule [2] he had imposed on his monks. Acceding to the

custodienda monachis indederat macularet. Obtem-
perantis igitur auli [a] regiae persuasionibus misere reginae,
regis animum contra uerum Dei perturbant, cogentes ut
accideret hac religione probaret. Abactus itaque rex ad
uirum Dei Lussouium uenit, conquestusque cum eo cur
ab conprouincialibus moribus discisceret et inter septa
secretiora omnibus christianis aditus non pateret.[1]
Beatus itaque Columbanus, ut erat audax atque animo
uegens, talibus obicienti regi respondit, se consuetudinem
non habere ut secularium hominum et relegioni alienis
famulorum Dei habitationes pandant introitum ; se et
oportuna aptaque loca ad hoc habere parata quo
omnium hospitum aduentus suscipiatur. Ad haec rex :
' Si,' inquid, ' largitatis nostre munera et solamenis
supplimentum capere cupis, omnibus in locis omnium
patebit introitus.' Vir Dei respondit : ' Si quod nunc
usque sub regulare disciplinae abenis constrictum fuit
uiolare conaris, nec tuis muneribus nec quibuscumque [b]
subsidiis me fore ad [c] te sustentaturum. Et si hanc ob
causam tu hoc in loco uenisti ut seruorum Dei caenubia
distruas et regularem disciplinam macules, cito [d] tuum
regnum funditus ruiturum et cum omni propaginae
regia dimersurum.' Quod postea rei probabit euentus.
Iam enim timerario conatu rex refecturium ingressus
fuerat. His ergo territus dictis, foris celer repetat.
Diris [e] post haec uir Dei increpationibus rex urguetur
contraque Teudericus ait : ' Martirii coronam a me tibi
inlaturam speras.' Non esse tantae demenciae ut hoc
tantum patraret scelus, sed pociores consilii se ageret

[a] auligae *Jonas*   [b] *Jonas* 4a ; quibusquae 1
[c] a *Jonas*   [d] 1, 4a ; scito 4b, c
[e] 1 ; duris *Jonas*, 4a

[1] On the normal Frankish practice of admitting all comers, except

wretched queen's prayers, the courtiers did stir up the king's anger against the holy man so that he should actually go in person to enquire into the state of the monastery. The king, carried away, went to seek him out at Luxeuil and there demanded why his practices differed from the practices of the Gallic sees and why, also, an interior precinct of his monastery was not open to all Christians.[1] The blessed Columbanus, unabashed and seething with rage, was emboldened to reply to the king that it was not allowed them to throw open the home of God's servants to laymen and to those hostile to his rule, but that nonetheless he had had suitable accommodation prepared for guests of whatever sort. The king rejoined : ' If you wish to enjoy the gifts of my bounty and to keep the benefit of my protection, you are to throw open the entire monastery to all comers.' ' And if,' retorted the holy man, ' you seek to violate what hitherto has been held firm by the rigour of our rule, I will have none of your gifts, nor your protection ; and be sure that if you have come here to force the retreat of God's servants and to shake the discipline of the rule, your kingdom shall speedily crumble and you with all your family shall be destroyed ' (this of course is what did happen). The king had already had the imprudence to set foot in the refectory, but these terrifying words caused him to withdraw promptly. The holy man then showered reproaches upon him but Theuderic replied, ' You are hoping that I shall give you the crown of martyrdom, but I am not such a fool as to commit so great a crime.' He urged him to be more sensible, to perform his public hospitality and to take notice that

occasionally women, to all monastic buildings, see E. Lesne, *Histoire de la Propriété Ecclés.* i, pp. 398-9.

utilia paraturum, ut qui ab omnium saecularium mores discescat, quo uenerit, ea uia repetare studeat. Auligum simul consona uoce uota prorumpunt, se habere non uelle his in locis qui omnibus non societur. Ad haec beatus Columbanus se dicit de cinubii septa non egressurum nisi uiolenter abstrahatur.

Discessit ergo rex relinquens uirum quendam procerem nomen Baudulfum. His enim cum remansisset, uirum Dei a monasterio pellet et poenes Vesoncionem oppidum ad exulandum perducit, quoadusque ex eo regali sentencia quod uoluisset decerneret. Post [1] haec uir Dei cernens quod nullis costudiis angeretur a nulloquo molestiam ferret—uidebant enim omnes in eum Dei uirtutem flagrare, ideoque omnes ab eius iniuriis secregabantur ne socii culparum forent—ascendit ergo dominica die in uerticem ardui cacuminis montis illius. [2] Ita enim situs urbis habetur, cum domorum [a] densitas in diffuso latere procliui montis sita sit, prorumpent ardua in sublimibus cacuminibus qui, undique abscissi, fluminis Dovae alueo uallante, nullatenus commeantibus uiam pandit. Ibique usque ad mediam diem expectat si aliqui iter ad monasterium reuertendi prohibeat. Et cum nullus contrarius existeret, ipse per mediam urbem cum suis ad monasterium regreditur. Quo audito Brunechildis ac Theudericus quod scilicet ab exilio reuertisset, atrociorebus irae aculeis stimulantur ; iubent [b] Bertharium [3] comitem attencius perquirendum uirorum cum presidio, simulque et Baudulfum quem superius direxerat destinarunt. Quo cum uenissent, beatum Columbanum in eclesia

[a] sc. dumorum. *I owe this conjecture to Mr A. P. Douglas.*
[b] iubentque militum cohortem ut rursum uirum Dei uim abstrahant et ad pristinum prorsus exilium reuocent *Jonas, who then relates a miracle redounding to the credit of Columbanus, which Fredegar omits.*

if he continued to defy the conventions of the country he should return whence he came. At the same time the courtiers all cried out that they had no desire to have there a man who would have nothing to do with them. But Columbanus asserted that he would not leave the monastic precincts unless forced to do so.

The king then departed, leaving behind one of the magnates, named Baudulf, who forthwith chased the holy man out of his monastery and led him to exile in the town of Besançon till such time as the king should declare his pleasure. Now [1] it was apparent to the man of God that he was neither being guarded nor subjected to molestation, for the divine virtue that all saw shining in him protected him from harm. Nobody would have dared to become an accomplice in the crime of which he was the victim. One Sunday he climbed to the top of a steep hill [2]—for the town is so sited that thickets cluster on the precipitous side of the mountain, the top of which is hard to come at since the drop is sheer and the river Doubs flows all round it—and there he waited till midday, to see if anyone were posted to prevent him returning to his monastery. No one appeared, and so he crossed the town with his companions and returned to the monastery. When they heard that he had left his place of exile, Brunechildis and Theuderic grew still more angry and post-haste sent a troop after him with Count Berthar [3] and Baudulf, their agent on the former occasion. On arrival, they found the blessed Columbanus in church, chanting psalms and prayers with all

---

[1] *Vita Col.* i, chap. 20
[2] cf. Caesar's description of the town, *Bell. Gall.* i, chap. 38
[3] see chap. 38, below

posetum sallentioque ac oratione deditum cum omni
congregatione fratrum repperiunt, sicque uirum Dei
adlocuntur : ' Vir Dei, precamur ut tam regiis quam
etiam nostris oboedias preceptis, egressusque eo itenere
quo primum his aduentasti in locis.' At ille : ' Non
enim,' inquid, ' reor placere Conditore semul natali solo
ob Christi timorem relecto dinuo repedare.' Cumque
nullatenus cerneret sibi uirum Dei obaudire, relictis
quibusdam, quibus ferocia animi forcior inerat,
Bertharius abscessit. Hii uero qui remanserant uirum
Dei hortantur ut illis misereatur, qui ad tale opus
patrandum infeliciter fuerant relicti, eorumque periculo
consoleret ; qui si eum uiolenter non abstraherent
mortis eos pericolum incurrere. At ille se ait iam saepius
testatum esse, nisi uim abstraheretur se non discessurum.
Illi gemino uallati periculo, undique urguenti formi-
dinae, palleum quo indutus erat adtingunt ; alii genibus
prouoluti cum lacrimis precantur ut pro tanti sceleris
culpam illis ignosceret, qui non suis desideriis sed regiis
obtemperarent preceptis.

Videns itaque uir Dei pericolum aliorum *a* fore si
suae seuiretate satisfaceret, cum omni eiulatu atque
maerore egreditur, depotatis custodibus, qui quousque
ditionis suae regno pelleretur, non eum relinquerent.
Inter quos primus Ragumundus erat, qui eum Nametis
usque perduxit. Sicque [1] a regno Theuderici expulsus,
iterum Hiberniam insulam repedare disposuit. Sed ut
nulli paenitus iter gradiendum fit pontificius [2] nisi permissum Altissimi, ipsi uero sanctus Italiam expetens,

---

a Jonas ; pericolorum 1 ; periculum fore 4a

[1] From this point Fredegar condenses into a few words Jonas'
account of Columbanus' journey across France, and then back again, first
to Lake Constance under the protection of Theudebert, and finally to
Italy. For

his brethren. They addressed him thus : ' Man of God, we beg you to obey our orders and the king's, and to return hence the way you came.' But he replied, ' I have no reason to think that it would please the Creator of the world if I returned to the place that I left simply through obedience to Christ.' Berthar saw that the holy man would not obey him and accordingly withdrew, and left him to men of tougher calibre. But those left to deal with him besought the man of God to have mercy on them, for it was their misfortune to give effect to cruel orders. He should consider the danger they were in, for they ran the risk of death if they failed to remove him by force. He had, he said, already sufficiently often repeated that violence alone could compel him to leave. The men, sensing danger from two directions and a prey to every fear, seized the vestments he wore, while others knelt before him begging him with tears to forgive their great crime : it was none of their doing but the king's orders.

The holy man now saw how great a danger to others could lie in his continuing to satisfy his own severe standards, and set out from his monastery, grief-stricken and in tears. Soldiers went with him, for their orders were to see him off the lands subject to the king. Ragamund, their commander, conducted him as far as Nantes. Hounded [1] from Theuderic's kingdom, the holy man planned to return to Ireland. But since no person sets out anywhere without the permission of the Most High,[2] the blessed Columbanus went in fact to Italy.

---

the worse fate of another bishop who rebuked Theuderic and Brunechildis see the *Vita Desiderii* of King Sisebut (*M.G.H. Script. Rer. Mero.* III, p. 636).

    [2] see E. Löfstedt, ' Some changes of sense in Late and Mediaeval Latin,' *Eranos*, 1946, p. 344, on *pontificium*

monasterium in loco nomen Bobio illuc construens, sancte conuersationis, plenus dierum migrat ad Christum.

37

610 Anno xv regni Theuderici, cum Alesaciones ubi fuerat enutritus preceptum patris sui Childeberti tenebat, a Theudeberto rito barbaro [1] peruadetur. Vnde placetus inter his duos regis ut Francorum iudicio [3] finiretur, Saloissa castro [2] instituunt. Ibique Theudericus cum escaritus utrumque decem milia accessit, Theudebertus uero cum magno exercito Austrasiorum inibi prilium uellens committendum adgreditur. Quod cum undique Theudericus ab exercitum Theudeberti circumdaretur, quoactus atque conpulsus Theudericus timore perterritus per pactionis uinculum Alsatius ad parte Theudeberti firmauit ; etiam et Suggentensis et Turensis et Campanensis,[4] quos saepius repetibat, idemque amisisse uisus est. Regressi uterque ad sidebus propriis.

His diebus et Alamanni in pago Auenticense Ultraiorano hostiliter ingressi sunt. Ipsoque pago predantes, Abbelenus et Herpinus comitis cum citeris de ipso pago comitebus cum exercito pergunt obuiam Alamannis. Vterque falange Wangas [5] iungunt ad prelium.

---

[1] cf. chap. 17, above

[2] Bas-Rhin

[3] Although R. Buchner, in his edition of Fritz Kern, *Gottesgnadentum und Widerstandsrecht*, p. 227, takes this to be a case of peaceful arbitration, the *iudicium* may just possibly be the judgement of battle and the *placitum* the agreement about the place of battle (see Fustel de Coulanges, *Recherches sur quelques problèmes d'histoire*, pp. 516 ff.) ; but cf. chaps. 40 and 53, below where this is much more doubtful.

[4] On the identification of these places see Martin, *Études Critiques*, pp. 186-95 : the Saintois is the region lying south of Toul (cf. chap. 35, above), the Thurgau is the Swiss Thurgau lying between the river Reuss

There he built a monastery at a place called Bobbio ; and then, in holiness of life and full of days, he completed ✓ his pilgrimage to Christ.

37

In the fifteenth year of Theuderic's reign, Alsace, where 610 he had been brought up and which he held by written authority from his father Childebert, was raided by Theudebert according to barbarian custom.[1]   The two kings therefore agreed to meet at the stronghold of Seltz,[2] so that their dispute might be resolved by Frankish judgement.[3]   Theuderic arrived with two detachments, each of ten thousand warriors, and Theudebert with a great force of Austrasians, intent on joining battle.   Surrounded on all sides and terror-stricken, Theuderic had no option but to cede Alsace by formal agreement to Theudebert.   At the same time he lost the Saintois, the Thurgau and the Campania,[4] which were the subject of frequent disputes.   Thereupon both kings went home.

At the same time the Alamans invaded and ravaged the district of Avenches, east of the Jura.   Abbelin and Herpin, in company with the other counts of the district, led an army to intercept them.   The two forces met and an engagement was fought at Wangen,[5] and the

---

and Lake Constance, and the Campania is the part of Champagne to the south of Troyes.   E. Ewig, *Die fränkischen Teilungen*, p. 690, still holds to Krusch's view that *Campanensis* is not the Campania of Troyes but the Kembsgau, or district of Chambiz, lying south of Strasbourg in the Alsatian Sundgau.

[5] See the important article of E. Tièche, 'Fredegars Notiz über die Schlacht bei Wangen,' *Museum Helveticum*, VI, pp. 1-18, on the syntax of this passage.   Wangen lies N.E. of Avenches.

Alamanni Transioranus superant, pluretate eorum gladio
trucedant et prosternunt, maximam partem territurio
Auenticense incendio concremant, plurum nomirum [a]
hominum exinde in captiuitate duxerunt. Reuersique
cum predam pergunt ad propriam. Theudericus has
iniurias deinceps integra adsiduetate consilium iniebat
quo pacto Theudebertum potuisset oppremere.

Eo anno Belechildis a Teudeberto interfecitur.
Theudebertus puella nomen Teudechilde accepit
uxorem.

611   Anno xvi Theuderici legationem ad Chlothario
diregit, indecans se contra Theudebertum, eo quod suos
frater non esset,[1] hostiliter uelle adgredere : Chlotharius
in solatium Theudeberti non esset. Docatum Denteleni,
quem contra Theudeberto cassauerat, si Theudericus
Theudebertum superabat, Chlotarius super memorato
Denteleno docato suae dicione receperit. Hanc
conuenenciam a Theudericum et Chlotharium legatus
intercurrentes firmatum Theudericus mouit exercitum.

38

612 Anno xvii regni sui Lingonas de uniuersas regni sui
prouincias mense Madio exercitus adunatur, dirigensque per Andelaum, Nasio [2] castra ceptum, Tollo
civitate perrexit et cepit. Ibique Theudebertus cum
Austrasiorum exercitum obuiam pergens, Tollensem
campaniam confligunt certamine. Theudericus superat
Teudebertum eiusque exercitum prostrauit; caesa sunt
exercitus eodem prilio nimia multitudo uirorum fortium.
Theudebertus terga uertens, per territurio Mittensem

---

[a] *Krusch's emendation* : nomirum *sc.* numerum, *cf.* p. 57, l. 15 ; plurum
nominum l   [1] cf. chap. 27, above

victorious Alamans slaughtered a large number of Transjurans, set fire to great areas of the territory of Avenches and took away a host of prisoners to servitude. Finally they returned home, laden with plunder. After this calamity Theuderic gave much thought to the best means of avenging himself on Theudebert.

It was at this time that Theudebert assassinated Bilichildis and took to wife a girl named Theudichildis.

In the sixteenth year of his reign, Theuderic sent a 611 deputation to Chlotar to say that he proposed to attack Theudebert—who was no brother of his [1]—and would Chlotar please not help Theudebert. He promised that if he were the victor he would restore to Chlotar the duchy of Dentelin (of which we spoke earlier), taken from him by Theudebert. The deputies worked out the terms of the agreement between Chlotar and Theuderic, and the latter proceeded to raise an army.

38

In the month of May in the seventeenth year of his reign, 612 Theuderic's army, summoned from every province of his kingdom, assembled at Langres. Marching through Andelot, it took the stronghold of Naix [2] and advanced upon the city of Toul, which also fell to it. Theudebert now appearing with an Austrasian army, battle was joined in the open country before Toul. Theuderic won and cut Theudebert's force to pieces ; many a brave warrior was slain in that battle. Theudebert himself took to flight, went through the territory of Metz and

---

[2] Naix-sur-Ornain (Meuse)

I

ueniens, transito Vosago Coloniam fugaciter peruenit.
Theudericus post tergum cum exercitum insequens,
beatos et apostolicos uir Lesio Mogancensis urbis
episcopus diligens utiletatem Theuderici et odens
stulticiam Theudeberti, ad Theuderico ueniens dixit :
' Quod coepisti perfice, satis te uteliter oportet huius
rei causam expetire.   Rustica fabula dicetur, lopus
ascendisset in montem et cum filiae suae iam uenare
coepissent eos ad se in monte uocat dicens : "Quam
longe ocolus uester in unamquemque parte uidere
preualet, non habetis amicus nisi paucus qui uestro
genere sunt." Perfecite quod coepistis.' [1]   Theudericus
cum exercitum Ardinnam transiens Tholbeaco peruenit.
Theudebertus cum Saxonis, Thoringus uel ceteras gentes
que de ultra Renum uel undique potuerat adunare,
contra Theudericum Tholbiaco perrexit.   Ibique dinuo
commissum est prilium.   Fertur a Francorum ceterasque
gentes ab antiquito sic forte nec aliquando fuisse prilium
conceptum.   Ibique tantae estrages ab uterque exercitus
facta est, ubi falange in congresso [a] certamenis contra se
priliabant, cadauera occisorum [b] undique non haberint
ubi inclinis iacerint, sed stabant mortui inter citerorum
cadauera stricti quasi uiuentes.   Sed Domino precedente iterum Teudericus Theudebertum superat, et a
Tolbiaco usque Colonia exercitus Theudeberti gladio
trucedatus per loca oram terre coperuit.   Ipsoque die
Colonia perrexit, omnes thynsaurus Theudeberti inibi
recepit.   Dirigensque Theudericus ultra Renum post
tergum Theudeberti Bertharium cobicularium, qui
diligenter Theudebertum insequens, cum iam cum
paucis fugiret, Theudebertum captum Bertharius

[a] ingresso 1, 4a.   *I adopt Hellmann's conjecture.*
[b] 4a ; occisorunt 1

over the Vosges and so reached Cologne. While Theuderic was in pursuit, the holy and blessed Bishop Leudegasius of Mainz, who loved Theuderic's valour as much as he despised Theudebert's folly, approached Theuderic and said : ' Finish what you have begun and exploit to the full the outcome of your action. There is a countryman's tale that tells how a wolf went up into the hills with her cubs, and when they had started to hunt she called them round her and said: " As far as your eyes can see, and in whatever direction, you have no friends, except a few of your own kind." So finish what you have begun.'[1] Theuderic and his warriors marched through the forest of the Ardennes and reached Zülpich, where Theudebert came to meet him with all the Saxons, Thuringians and other peoples from across the Rhine or elsewhere that he had been able to summon. There they fought. It is said that from time immemorial no such battle had ever been fought by the Franks and the other peoples ; the carnage on both sides was such that in the fighting line there was no room for the slain to fall down. They stood upright in their ranks, corpse supporting corpse, as if they still lived. By God's grace Theuderic again defeated Theudebert and cut down his men from Zülpich to Cologne. The whole countryside was strewn with their bodies. The same day he advanced to Cologne and secured Theudebert's entire treasure. He sent on Berthar, his chamberlain, across the Rhine in hot pursuit of Theudebert, who was in flight with a handful of followers. The captive Theudebert was

---

[1] Kurth, *Histoire poétique*, p. 415, argues that if the moral is that wolf does not eat wolf then in its original form the story must have been put into Lesio's mouth to stop the brothers fighting, not to urge on one against the other.

Coloniam conspectum Theuderici presentat exhibetum.
Vestis regalibus Theudebertus expoliatus [1] equosque
eius cum estratura regia, haec totumque Bertharium a
Theuderico concedetur ; Theudebertus uinctus Caby-
lonno distinatur. Filius eius nomen Merouius paruolus
iusso Theuderici adprehensus a quidam per pede ad
petram percutitur, cerebrum [a] eius capite aeruptum,
amisit spiritum. Chlotharius docatum Denteleno secundum conuenentiam Theuderici integro suae dicione
redegit ; ob quam rem Theudericus, cum iam totum
Auster dominarit, nimia indignatione commotus, contra
613 Chlotharium exercitum anno xviii regni sui de Auster
et Burgundias mouere precepit, legationem prius
dirigens, ut se Chlotharius de iam dicto docato Dente-
lenoe omnimodis remouerit ; alioquin nouerit se exercitum Theuderici undique regnum Chlotharium impleturum. Quo uerbo quem legati nunciant probauit
euentus.

39

613 Ipso quoque anno iam exercitus contra Chlotharium
adgredebat, Theudericus Mettis profluuium uentris
moritur. Exercitus protinus redit ad propriis sedebus.

40

Brunechildis cum filius Teuderici quattuor Sigybertum,
Childebertum, Corbum et Meroeum Mettis resedens,
Sigybertum in regnum patris instituere nitens,
Chlotharius [b] factione Arnulfo et Pippino [2] uel citeris

[a] 4a ; caelebrum 1
[b] *chap. 40*, 1

brought by Berthar and paraded before Theuderic at Cologne, where he was stripped of his royal clothing.[1] His horse and its royal trappings were all given by Theuderic to Berthar; and Theudebert was sent in chains to Chalon. His little son, Merovech, was seized on Theuderic's orders : a soldier took him by the heels and dashed out his brains on a stone ; and so he died. In accordance with his agreement with Theuderic, Chlotar now took the entire duchy of Dentelin ; but this in-furiated Theuderic, already master of all Austrasia. He turned his army against Chlotar and, in the eighteenth year of his reign, raised levies in Austrasia and Burgundy, 613 first sending a mission to Chlotar to get him to retire, lock, stock and barrel, from the duchy of Dentelin. If he did not, he threatened to overrun Chlotar's lands with his warriors ; and as events proved, his ambassadors' threats were carried out.

39

Theuderic was already, in this same year, on the march 613 against Chlotar when he died of dysentery at Metz. His men returned without delay to their own lands.

40

Brunechildis was at Metz with the four sons of Theuderic —Sigebert, Childebert, Corbus and Merovech. Her endeavour was to make Sigebert his father's successor. Chlotar was incited by the faction of Arnulf, Pippin [2]

---

[1] tonsured ?
[2] Bishop Arnulf of Metz and Pippin I (of Landen), founders of the Arnulfing or Carolingian family. See the genealogical table on p. 123.

procerebus Auster ingreditur. Cumque Antonnaco ascessisset, et Brunechildis cum filiis Theuderici Vurmacia resederet, legatos nomenibus Chadoindo et Herpone ad Chlotharium direxit, contestans ei ut se de regno Theuderici quem filiis reliquerat remouerit. Chlotharius respondebat et per suos legatus Brunechilde mandabat, iudicio Francorum [1] electorum quicquid precedente Domino a Francis inter eosdem iudicabatur, pollicetur esset implere.[a] Brunechildis Sigybertum seniorem filium Theuderici in Thoringia diriget apud [b] quem Warnarium maiorem domus et Alboenum cum citeris procerebus destinauit, gentes que ultra Renum adtraherint qualiter Chlothario potuissent resistere. Post tergum indiculum direxit ut Alboenus cum citeris Warnacharium interfecerit, eo quod se in regno Chlothariae uellet transferre. Quo indiculo relecto, Albuenus deruptum proiecit in terra. Inuentus est a puero Warnachariae, super tabulam caeram linitam dinuo ipsi soledatur. Quo indiculo relecto, Warnacharius cernens se uitae periculom habere, deinceps uehementer cogitare coepit quo pacto filii Theuderici opprimerentur et regnum Chlothariae aelegerit. Gentes que illic [c] adtractae fuerant, consilio secreto de solatio Brunechilde et filiorum Theuderici procul fecit abesse.[d] Exinde regressi,[2] cum Brunechilde et filios Teuderici Burgundias adpetunt, missos per uniuerso Auster discurrentes exercitum mouere nitebantur.

[a] *sc.* pollicetur se esse impleturum
[b] 4a ; a l
[c] illis l ; illic *all other MSS*
[d] adesse 1, 3, 4a, 5a, 5b

and other magnates to enter Austrasia. When he was near Andernach, Brunechildis, who was at Worms with Theuderic's sons, sent to him on their behalf an embassy comprising Chadoin and Herpo, with the demand that he should abandon the kingdom left by Theuderic to his sons. Chlotar then replied to Brunechildis through his envoys that he undertook to abide by whatever decision should, with God's help, be arrived at by a gathering of Franks [1] chosen for that purpose. Forthwith Brunechildis despatched Theuderic's eldest son, Sigebert, to Thuringia with Warnachar, mayor of the palace, Alboin and other great men, to win over the peoples across the Rhine to resist Chlotar ; but she sent after them a private letter to Alboin with instructions that he should kill Warnachar and the others, for they were planning to go over to Chlotar. Alboin tore up the letter after reading it and threw the bits on the ground ; but one of Warnachar's men found them and pieced them together on a wax tablet. Thus Warnachar read the letter, saw that his life was in danger and hastily considered ways of dispossessing Theuderic's sons and of making Chlotar king. He secretly released the peoples he had already bound to help Brunechildis and Theuderic's sons. On their return, the envoys [2] made for Burgundy with Brunechildis and Theuderic's sons and sent messengers through Austrasia to raise an army.

---

[1] cf. chap. 37, above
[2] The subject of this sentence might possibly be the *gentes* of the preceding sentence.

41

Burgundaefaronis [1] uero tam episcopi quam citeri leudis timentis Brunechildem et odium in eam habentes, Warnachario consilium inientes, tractabant ut neque unus ex filiis Theuderici euaderet sed eos totus oppressus Brunechilde delirent et regnum Chlothariae expetirent ; quod probauit euentus.

42

Cumque iusso Brunechilde et Sigyberto filio Theuderici exercitus de Burgundia et Auster contra Chlothario adgrederetur, ueniensque [a] Sigybertus in campania territuriae Catalauninsis super fluuium Axsoma, ibique Chlotharius obuiam cum exercito uenit, multus iam de Austrasius secum habens factione Warnachariae maiorem domus. Sic iam olim tractauerat consencientibus Aletheo patricio, Roccone, Sigoaldo et Eudilanae ducibus. Cumque in congresso certamine debuissent cum exercitum confligere, priusquam priliare cepissent signa dantis exercitus Sigyberti terga uertens, redit ad propriis sedibus. Chlotharius paulatim, ut conuinerat, post tergum cum exercitum sequens usque Ararem Sauconnam fluuium peruenit. Captis filiis Theuderici tres Sigiberto, Corbo et Meroeo quem ipse de fontes excipit, Childebertus fugaciter ascendens nec umquam postea fuit reuersus. Austrasiorum exercitus inlesus reuertit ad propriis sedibus. Factionem Warnachariae maioris domus cum reliquis maxime totis procerebus de regnum Burgundiae Brunechildis ab Erpone comestaboli de pago Vltraiorano ex uilla Orba una cum

[a] chap. 42, 1

[1] Perhaps, as Zöllner argues (' Die Herkunft der Agilulfinger,' p. 247), the indigenous Burgundian nobility, unbowed by the Frankish victory of

41

The notables of Burgundy,[1] however, bishops as well as secular lords, feared and hated Brunechildis ; and they took counsel with Warnachar to ensure that none of Theuderic's sons should escape : all should be killed with Brunechildis and their kingdom given to Chlotar. And this, in effect, is what happened.

42

A force of Burgundians and Austrasians set out on instructions from Brunechildis and Sigebert, son of Theuderic, to meet Chlotar. When Sigebert had advanced into Champagne to the river Aisne in the territory of Châlons-sur-Marne, Chlotar came to intercept him with a force that included many Austrasians who supported Warnachar, mayor of the palace ; for he had already come to an understanding with Warnachar, with the prior approval of the patrician Alethius and Dukes Rocco, Sigoald and Eudila. Just when the battle was about to begin, Sigebert's army took to its heels at an agreed signal and made off home. Chlotar, as arranged, followed slowly with his army and reached the Saône. He took prisoner three of the sons of Theuderic—Sigebert, Corbus and Merovech—to the last of whom he was godfather. Childebert escaped and never again returned. The Austrasian army returned home without loss. But the mayor, Warnachar, in conjunction with most of the Burgundian magnates, saw to it that Brunechildis was arrested at the villa

534 ; yet Fustel de Coulanges (*La Monarchie Franque*, p. 633) made a strong case for their being no more than royal officials in Burgundy.

Theudilanae germana Theuderici producitur et Chlothario Rionaua [1] uico super Vincenna fluuio presentatur. Sigybertus et Corbus filius Theuderici iusso Chlothariae interfecti sunt.[2] Meroeus secrecius iusso Chlothariae in Neptrico perducetur, eodem amplectens amore quod ipso de sancto excepisset lauacrum, Ingobode graffione commendatur, ubi plures post annos uixit. Chlotharius, cum Brunechildis suum presentatur conspectum et odium contra ipsam nimium haberit, repotans ei eo quod decem reges Francorum per ipsam interfecti fuissent—id est Sigybertus et Meroeus et genitor suos Chilpericus,[3] Theudebertus et filius suos Chlotharius, item Meroeus filius Chlothariae, Theudericus et eiusdem filiae tres, qui ad presens estincti fuerant—per triduo eam diuersis tormentis adfectam,[a] iobetque eam prius camillum [b] per omne exercito sedentem perducere, post haec comam capitis, unum pedem et brachium ad ueciosissemum aequum caudam legare : ibique calcibus et uelocitate cursus membratim disrumpetur.[4]

Warnacharius in regnum Burgundiae substituetur maior domi, sacramentum a Chlotharium acceptum ne umquam uitae suae temporebus degradaretur.[c] In Auster Rado idemque hoc gradum honoris adsumpsit. Firmatum est omnem regnum Francorum sicut a priorem Chlotharium fuerat dominatum, cunctis thinsauris dicione Chlothariae iunioris subiecitur, quod feliciter post [d] sedecim annis tenuit, pacem habens cum

---

[a] 1 ; adflictam 3, 5b
[b] caballum? camelum? *If the latter, ' mule ' might be meant. However,* Vita Eligii (M.G.H. Script. Rer. Mero., iv) *implies that ' mule ' and ' camel ' were not confused. The Byzantines sometimes paraded criminals on camels. For a comparable incident see* Historia Wambae, c. 30 (M.G.H. Script. Rer. Mero., v, p. 525).
[c] 4a ; detradaretur 1   [d] 1 ; per 4c[1]

of Orbe, in Transjuran territory, by the constable Herpo and taken to Chlotar in company with Theudila, a sister of Theuderic. Chlotar was at the village of Renève [1] on the river Vingeanne. He had Sigebert and Corbus, sons of Theuderic, killed [2] but for Merovech he felt a godfather's affection and ordered him to be sent in secrecy to Neustria and placed under Count Ingobad's protection. Merovech continued living there for some years. Brunechildis was brought before Chlotar, who was boiling with fury against her. He charged her with the deaths of ten Frankish kings—namely, Sigebert, Merovech, his father Chilperic,[3] Theudebert and his son Chlotar, Chlotar's son the other Merovech, Theuderic and Theuderic's three sons who had just perished. She was tormented for three days with a diversity of tortures, and then on his orders was led through the ranks on a camel. Finally she was tied by her hair, one arm and one leg to the tail of an unbroken horse, and she was cut to shreds by its hoofs at the pace it went.[4]

Warnachar became mayor of the palace in Burgundy after Chlotar had sworn that he should never be deposed during his lifetime, and Rado obtained the corresponding dignity in Austrasia. The entire Frankish kingdom was united as it had once been under the first Chlotar and it fell with all its treasure to the rule of the second Chlotar, who thereafter was king for sixteen happy

---

[1] Côte-d'Or
[2] cf. *Vita Col.* I, chap. 29
[3] In Book III, chap. 93, Fredegar gives the name of the assassin sent by Brunechildis as Falco. Goubert, *Byzance avant l'Islam*, II, pt. I, p. 38, calls this pure calumny because Fredegar alone makes the charge ; but the addition of the name hardly suggests an invention.
[4] cf. *Vita Desiderii*, chap. 21 ; and Fredegar, Book III, chap. 59, which reports an alleged prophecy of Brunechildis' death.

uniuersas gentes uicinas. Iste Chlotharius fuit patienciae deditus, litterum eruditus, timens Deum, ecclesiarum et sacerdotum magnus muneratur, pauperibus aelimosinam tribuens, benignum se omnibus et pietatem plenum ostendens, uenacionem ferarum nimium assiduae utens et posttremum mulierum et puellarum suggestionibus nimium annuens. Ob hoc quidem blasphematur a leudibus.

43

613 Cum anno xxx regni sui in Burgundia et Auster regnum arepuisset, Herpone duci genere Franco locum Eudilanae in pago Vltraiorano instituit. Qui dum pacem in ipso pago uehementer arripuisset sectari, malorum nugacitate reprimens, ab ipsis pagensibus [1] instigante parte aduersa, consilio Aletheo patricio et Leudemundo episcopo et Herpino comite per rebellionis audatiam Herpo dux interficetur. Chlotharius com in Alesacius villa Marolegia cuinomento cum Bertethrudae regina accesserat pacem insectans, multus iniqui agentes gladio trucidarit.

44

Leudemundus quidem episcopus Seduninsis ad Bertetrudem reginam ueniens, sigricius consilio Aletheo patricio uerba ignominiosa dixit, quod Chlotharius eodem anno omnimodis migraret de seculo, ut thinsauris quantum potebat secretisseme ad Sidonis suam ciuitatem transferrit, eo quod esset [2] locum tutissimum : Aletheos

---

[1] It is likely that Alethius and Leudemund were both Burgundians (see Zöllner, ' Die Herkunft der Agilulfinger,' p. 252).

[2] The sense may be that the queen rather than the treasure would be safe in Sion. (cf. Zöllner, ibid.)

years, during which he kept peace with all the neighbouring peoples. This Chlotar, who was strong-minded and well-read, was also a God-fearing man, for he was a munificent patron of churches and priests, an almsgiver to the poor, kindly disposed to all and full of piety. On the other hand, his devotion to the chase was excessive and he took too much notice of the views of women young and old, for which his followers censured him.

43

Thus in the thirtieth year of his reign Chlotar became 613
master of Burgundy and Austrasia. He made the Frank Herpo duke of the territory lying east of the Jura in place of Eudila ; and Herpo took vigorous measures to establish peace in his territory and to put down evildoers. But he was killed in a rising of the inhabitants,[1] egged on by his enemies with the insolent backing of Alethius the patrician, Bishop Leudemund and Count Herpin. Chlotar and his Queen Bertetrudis repaired to the villa of Marlenheim in Alsace ; and there he restored order and executed many of those found guilty.

44

Bishop Leudemund of Sion came secretly to Queen Bertetrudis and repeated to her, at the instigation of the patrician Alethius, the following falsehood : in this same year Chlotar would die without a doubt and she should privately send all the treasure she could to his city of Sion, where it [2] would be perfectly safe. He added that Alethius was thinking of giving up his wife

esset paratus suam relinquens uxorem Bettethrudem reginam acceperit ; eo quod esset regio genere de Burgundionibus,[1] ipse post Chlotharium possit regnum adsumere. Regina Bertetrudis cum haec audisset, uerens ne ueritatem subsisterit lacrimas prorumpens abiit in cobiculum. Leudemundus cernens se huiuscemodi uerbis habere periculum, fugaciter per nocte Sedunis perrexit. Exinde latante fuga Lussouio ad domno Austasio abbate peruenit. Post haec ab ipso abbati cum domno Chlothario his culpis excusatur, ad suam reuersus est ciuitatem. Chlotharius Masolaco uilla [2] cum procerebus resedens Aletheum ad se uenire precepit. Huius consilium iniquissimum conpertum est : gladium trucidare iussit.

616   Anno xxxiii regni Chlothariae Warnacharium maioris domus cum uniuersis pontificibus [a] Burgundiae seo et Burgundaefaronis Bonogillo [3] villa ad se uenire precepit. Ibique cunctis illorum iustis peticionibus annuens preceptionebus roborauit.[4]

45

Langobardorum gens quemadmodum tributa duodece milia soledorum dicione Francorum annis singulis dissoluebant referam, uel quo ordine duas ciuitates Agusta et Siusio cum territuriis ad parte Francorum cassauerant non abscondam. Defuncto Clep eorum principe duodecim ducis Langobardorum xii annis sine regibus transegerunt.[5] Ipsoque tempore, sicut super scriptum legitur,[6] per loca in regno Francorum pro-

---

[a] 4a ; ponticibus 1

[1] Fredegar may mean, as Buchner argues (*Die Provence in mero. Zeit*, p. 90), that the queen, not Alethius, was of royal Burgundian blood.

and of marrying the queen, provided that, being of royal Burgundian blood,[1] he could succeed Chlotar as king. Queen Bertetrudis was frightened at the prospect of what she had heard. She burst into tears and took to her room. Leudemund saw that the conversation had put him in danger ; so, fleeing during that night to Sion, he finally took refuge at Luxeuil with the Lord Abbot Eustasius. Later, the abbot obtained Chlotar's pardon for him and permission to return to his city. Meanwhile, Alethius was summoned before Chlotar and his great men at the villa of Mâlay-le-Roi.[2] His wicked plan was laid bare and he was sentenced to be executed.

In the thirty-third year of his reign, Chlotar 616 summoned to the villa of Bonneuil[3] his mayor Warnachar and all the bishops and notables of Burgundy. He there listened to all their just petitions and confirmed his concessions in writing.[4]

45

I am now going to tell how the Lombards came to pay the Franks a yearly tribute of twelve thousand gold solidi and I shall not conceal how they ceded to the Franks the two cities of Aosta and Susa, together with their territories. After the death of King Cleph the Lombards lived for twelve years without kings, under the rule of twelve dukes.[5] During this period they made (as already related [6]) a raid into Frankish territory, and

---

[2] near Sens (Yonne)
[3] near Paris
[4] see F. Beyerle, ' Volksrechtliche Studien,' *Zeitschrift der Savigny-Stiftung, Germ. Abt.* XLVIII (1928), p. 311
[5] Paul's account (*Hist. Lang.* II, chap. 32) differs.
[6] in Book III, chap. 68

ruperunt. Ea presumptione in conposicione Agusta et
Siusio ciuitates cum integro illorum territurio et populo
partibus Gunthramni tradiderunt.[1] Post haec legationem ad Mauricio imperatore dirigunt : hii duodice
ducis singulis legatariis destinant, pacem et patrocinium
imperiae petentes. Itemque et alius legatarius duodicem
ad Gunthramnum et Childebertum destinant, ut patrocinium Francorum et defensionem habentes, duodece
milia soledus annis singulis his duobus regibus in tributa
implerint, uallem cuinomento Ametegis partebus idemque Gunthramni cassantis ; his legatis, ubi plus
congruebat, patrocinium sibi firmarint. Post haec
integra deuocione patrocinium elegunt Francorum.
Nec mora post permissum Gunthramni et Childeberti
Autharium ducem super se Langobardi sublimant in
regnum. Alius Autharius idemque dux [2] cum integro
suo docato se dicione imperiae tradedit, ibique permansit.
Et Autharius rex tributa quod Langobardi ad parte
Francorum spondederant annis singulis reddedit. Post
eius discessum filius eius Ago [3] in regno sublimatur ;
similiter implisse denuscetur.

617   Anno XXXIIII regni Chlothariae legatus tres nobilis
ex gente Langobardorum Aghyulfus, Pompegius et
Gauto ab Agone regi [4] ad Clothario destinantur,
petentes ut illa duodece milia soledorum quas annis
singulis Francorum aerariis dissoluebant debuissent
cassare ; exhibentes ingeniose secrecius trea milia soledos
quos Warnacharius millae, Gundelandus millae et
Chucus [5] millae acciperunt. Chlothario uero XXXVI
milia soledorum insemul exhibebant : quod consilio

---

[1] Susa was in Byzantine hands ; Fredegar can only mean that the
Lombards acquiesced in its surrender to the Franks. On this, and Frankish
interests generally in the Alps and northern Italy, see G. Löhlein, ' Die
Alpen- und Italienpolitik der Merowinger im 6. Jahrhundert.'

as retribution for their audacity they ceded the cities of Aosta and Susa, with all their lands and inhabitants, to King Guntramn.[1] They then sent a deputation to the Emperor Maurice : each of the twelve dukes sent a deputy to beg peace and protection of the emperor. At the same time the twelve sent other missions to Guntramn and Childebert to buy Frankish help and protection at the price of an annual tribute to these two kings of twelve thousand solidi. The twelve dukes offered King Guntramn, by way of pledge, the valley of Lanzo, in order that the mission could secure protection on the best terms possible. They then placed themselves without reserve under Frankish overlordship. By permission of Guntramn and Childebert the Lombards soon chose Duke Authari for their king, and another duke of the same name [2] commended himself and his duchy to the emperor, to whom he remained loyal. Every year King Authari paid the promised Lombard tribute to the Franks ; and when, after his death, he was succeeded by his son Ago,[3] the payment continued to be made.

In the thirty-fourth year of Chlotar's reign, King Ago [4] sent to him a deputation of three noble Lombards named Agilulf, Pompeius and Gauto, with a request that the annual tribute of twelve thousand solidi paid into the Frankish treasuries should be cancelled ; and they took the wise precaution of making private gifts, of one thousand solidi each, to Warnachar, Gundeland and Chuc.[5] At the same time they offered Chlotar thirty-six thousand 617

---

[2] Perhaps the duke known to Paul as Droctulft (*Hist. Lang.* III, chap. 18)
[3] Agilulf was not the son of Authari.
[4] Agilulf died in 616.
[5] respectively mayors of the palace in Burgundy, Neustria and, probably, Austrasia

K

supra scriptis, qui occulti exseniati [a] fuerant, Chlotharius ipsa tributa ad parte Langobardorum cassauit et amiciciam perpetuam cum Langobardis sacramentis et pactis firmauit.

46

618 Anno xxxv regni Chlothariae Bertetrudis regina moritur, quam unico amore Chlotharius dilexerat [b] et omnes leudis bonitate eius cernentes uehementer amauerant.

47

622 Anno xxxviiii regni Chlothariae Dagobertum filium suum consortem regni facit eumque super Austrasius regem instituit, retinens sibi quod Ardinna et Vosacos uersus Neuster et Burgundia excludebant.

48

623 Anno xl regni Chlothariae homo nomen Samo natione Francos de pago Senonago [1] plures secum negutiantes adsciuit,[c] exercendum negucium in Sclauos coinomento Winedos perrexit. Sclaui iam contra Auaris coinomento Chunis [2] et regem eorum gagano ceperant reuellare.

---

[a] *sc.* xeniis donati *Krusch*
[b] 4a ; direxerat 1
[c] adciuit 1 ; adduxit 3, 4a, 5b

[1] In Hainaut ; or possibly the district of Sens (Krusch and Labuda). Ch. Verlinden, *Rev. belge de philol. et d'hist.* xii (1933), pp. 1090-5, sees Samo as an adventurer, not as a simple merchant, probably interested in the slave-trade. A case for his being a diplomatic agent is made by G. Labuda in an article written in Polish, of which a résumé is provided by V. Chaloupecký (' Considérations sur Samon, le premier roi des Slaves,' *Byzantinoslavica*, xi, 1950, pp. 223-39). Labuda stresses the remarkable value of the information given by Fredegar on central European affairs.

gold solidi. Accordingly the king took the advice of the above-mentioned men who had been secretly bought, excused the Lombards their tribute and confirmed on oath a pact of eternal friendship with them.

46

Queen Bertetrudis died in the thirty-fifth year of Chlotar's reign. The king was particularly devoted to her and the whole court recognised her goodness and loved her dearly for it. 618

47

In the thirty-ninth year of his reign, Chlotar associated his son Dagobert with him in his rule and placed him as king over the Austrasians. But he reserved for himself the Austrasian lands stretching towards Neustria and Burgundy on the near side of the Ardennes and the Vosges. 622

48

In the fortieth year of Chlotar's reign, a certain Frank named Samo, from the district of Soignies,[1] joined with other merchants in order to go and do business with those Slavs who are known as Wends. The Slavs had already started to rise against the Avars (called Huns)[2] and against their ruler, the Khagan. The Wends had long 623

---

[1] owe this reference to Professor Bognetti. Dr. E. B. Fryde informs me that Labuda's argument that Samo led the Slavs of Moravia or Czechs is based on archaeological evidence that could be interpreted another way.

[2] These Avars were not descendants of Attila's Huns. 'Khagan' was their ruler's title, not his name as Fredegar supposes.

Winidi befulci Chunis fuerant iam ab antiquito, ut cum Chuni in exercitum contra gentem qualibet adgradiebant Chuni pro castra adunatum illorum stabant exercitum, Winidi vero pugnabant. Si ad uincendum preualebant, tunc Chuni predas capiendum adgrediebant, sin autem Winidi superabantur Chunorum auxilio fulti uirebus resumebant. Ideo befulci uocabantur a Chunis eo quod dublicem in congressione certamine uestila *a* priliae facientes, ante Chunis precederint.[1] Chuni hiemandum *b* annis singulis in Esclauos ueniebant, uxores Sclauorum et filias eorum strato sumebant; tributa super alias oppressiones Sclaui Chunis soluebant. Filii Chunorum quos in uxores Winodorum et filias generauerant tandem non subferentes maliciam ferre et oppressione, Chunorum dominatione negantes, ut supra memini,*c* ceperant reuellare. Cum in exercito Winidi contra Chunus fuissent adgressi, Samo negucians, quo memoraui superius, cum ipsos in exercito perrexit. Ibique tanta ei fuit utiletas de Chunis facta ut mirum fuisset et nimia multitudo ex eis gladio Winidorum trucidata fuisset. Winidi cernentes utilitatem Samones eum super se eligunt regem, ubi xxx et v annos regnauit feliciter. Plures prilia contra Chunis suo regimini Winidi iniaerunt: suo consilio et utilitate Winidi semper Chunus superant. Samo xii uxores ex genere Winidorum habebat, de quibus xxii filius et quindecem filias habuit.

a 1 ; ?uexilla *Krusch* ; *other MSS omit*
b 5b ; aemandum 1   *c* 4a ; memine 1

[1] There are several possible explanations of this difficult passage, none entirely satisfactory. The best, that of Theodor Mayer, ' Fredegars Bericht über die Slawen,' is that the Slavs were known, in their own language, as *Byvolci*, the people who looked after the buffaloes (*byvolů*) of the Avars. The nearest homophone in Latin known to Fredegar or his informant was *befulti* (=*befulci*), and of this rare word he gives a reasonable

since been subjected to the Huns, who used them as Befulci. Whenever the Huns took the field against another people, they stayed encamped in battle array while the Wends did the fighting. If the Wends won, the Huns advanced to pillage, but if they lost the Huns backed them up and they resumed the fight. The Wends were called Befulci by the Huns because they advanced twice to the attack in their war bands, and so covered the Huns.[1] Every year the Huns wintered with the Slavs, sleeping with their wives and daughters, and in addition the Slavs paid tribute and endured many other burdens. The sons born to the Huns by the Slavs' wives and daughters eventually found this shameful oppression intolerable ; and so, as I said, they refused to obey their lords and started to rise in rebellion. When they took the field against the Huns, Samo, the merchant of whom I have spoken, went with them and his bravery won their admiration : an astonishing number of Huns were put to the sword by the Wends. Recognising his parts, the Wends made Samo their king ; and he ruled them well for thirty-five years. Several times they fought under his leadership against the Huns and his prudence and courage always brought the Wends victory. Samo had twelve Wendish wives, who bore him twenty-two sons and fifteen daughters.

---

explanation in the context. What the Slavs actually did was to drive the Avars' buffalo-waggons on campaigns ; what Fredegar makes them do is to fight first, and then, set on their feet again if necessary by the Avars, to continue the battle. Two other instances where Fredegar misunderstands a Slav word are (1) in this chapter, *gagano*, and (2) in chapter 72, *Walluc*. Other less satisfactory solutions are to derive *befulci* from *bubulcus* (mod. Ital. *bifolco*), an oxherd, or to suppose a scribal corruption of *bifurci* and imagine a two-pronged attack (something of this lies behind Labuda's solution, that *befulci* is a hybrid, *bis* + *folc*, meaning 'a double regiment') ; neither agrees with the careful explanation given by Fredegar.

49

623 Ipsoque anno XL Chlothariae, Adloaldus rex Langobardorum filius Agone regi cum patri suo successisset
in regno,[1] legato Mauricio imperatoris [2] nomen Eusebio [3]
ingeniose ad se uenientem benigne suscepit. Inunctus
in balneo nescio quibus ungentes, ab ipsi Eusebio
persuadetur et post inuncionem nec quicquam aliud nisi
quod ab Eusebio hortabatur facere non potebat.
Persuasos ab ipso, primatis et nobiliores cunctis in regno
Langobardorum interficere ordinarit ; eisdem [a] estinctis,
se cum omni gente Langobardorum imperio traderit.
Quod cum iam uel duodecem ex eis, nullis culpis
extantibus, gladio trucedasset, reliqui cernentes eorum
esse uitae periculum Charoaldum [b] ducem Taurinen-
sem, qui germanam Adloaldo regi habebat uxorem
nomen Gundebergam, omnes seniores et nobilissimi
Langobardorum gentes uno conspirante consilio in
regnum elegunt sublimandum.

50

Adloaldus rex uenino auctus interiit. Charoaldus statim
regnum adripuit.[4] Taso,[c] unus ex ducebus Langobardorum, cum agerit Tuscana prouincia superbia
elatus, aduersus Charoaldo regi coeperat rebellare.

51

Gundeberga regina, cum esset pulchra aspecto, benigna
in cunctis et piaetate plenissema christiana, aelimosinis

[a] *Krusch* ; eiusdem 1   [b] *chap. 50,* 1   [c] 4a ; Taro 1
[1] in 616
[2] The Emperor Heraclius, not Maurice, was his contemporary.

49

In this same fortieth year of Chlotar's reign, the Lombard 623
ruler Adaloald who had succeeded to the kingdom of
his father Agilulf,[1] received with kindness a representative of the Emperor Maurice,[2] named Eusebius,[3] who
cleverly approached him and persuaded him to be
massaged in his bath with some sort of ointment which
had the effect of subjecting him to Eusebius' will and
to none other. He was prevailed upon by him to order
the killing of all the great men and lords of the Lombard
kingdom and, with them out of the way, to place himself
and all the Lombard people under the Emperor. But
when he had put to death twelve innocent magnates,
the rest saw the danger that faced them. So all the
Lombard lords unanimously chose as king the duke
of Turin, Charoald, who had married Gundeberga,
King Adaloald's sister.

50

King Adaloald was poisoned and died. Charoald at
once assumed the crown,[4] but a Lombard duke named
Taso—governor of Tuscany—in his pride started a
rebellion against King Charoald.

51

The lovely Queen Gundeberga was in all things good-
natured and full of Christian piety. She was generous

---

[3] This story is not reported by Paul, who states that Adaloald lost his
reason and was deposed (*Hist. Lang.* IV, chap. 41).
[4] in 626

larga, praecellenti bonitatem eius, diligebatur a cunctis.
Homo quidam nomen Adalulfus ex genere Langobardorum, cum in aula palatiae adsiduae obsequium regis
conuersaretur, quadam uicae ad reginam ueniens cum
in eius staret conspectum Gundeberga regina eum sicut
et citeris diligens dixit honeste staturae Adalulfo fuisse
formatum. Ille haec audiens ad Gundebergam secrecius
ait dicens : ' Furmam status meae laudare dignasti,
stratus tui iobe subiungere.' Illa fortiter denegans
eumque dispiciens in faciem expuit. Adalulfus cernens
se uitae periculum habere, ad Charoaldo regem protinus
cocurrit, petens ut sigrecius quod ad suggerendum
habebat exponeret. Locum acceptum dixit ad regem :
' Domina mea, regina tua Gundebarga, apud Tasonem *a*
ducem secrecius tribus diebus locuta est, ut te uenino
interficerit, ipsum coniugatum sublimarit in regnum.'
Charoaldus rex, his mendatiis auditis credens, Gundo-
bergam in Laumello *b* castro in unam turrem exilio
trudit. Chlotharius legatus diriens ad Charoaldum
regem, inquirens qua de re Gundebergam reginam
parentum Francorum [1] humiliasset, ut exilio retrudisset,
Charoaldus his uerbis mendaciis quasi uiretatem sub-
sisterint respondebat. Tunc unus ex legataries nomen
Ansoaldus non quasi iniunctum *c* habuisset sed ex se ad
Charoaldo dixit : ' Liberare potebas de blasphemeo
causam hanc. Iube illum hominem, qui huiuscemodi
uerba tibi nunciauit, armare et procedat alius de parte
reginae Gundebergae, quique armatus ad singulare
certamine. Iudicium Dei his duobus confligentibus
cognuscatur, utrum huius culpae repotationes Gundeberga sit innoxia an fortasse culpabelis.' Cumque haec
Charoaldo regi et omnibus primatis palatiae suae
placuisset, iobet Adalulfum armatum conflictum adire

in almsgiving and universally loved for her bounty. A certain Lombard named Adalulf, who was constantly at court in the king's service, one day found himself in her presence. The queen was as well disposed to him as she was to all others and accordingly remarked what a fine upstanding man he was. Hearing this, he said quietly to the queen, 'You deign to like my looks; pray, then, bid me sleep with you.' But she violently refused and spat in his face to show her contempt for him. Adalulf saw that he had endangered his life and thereupon made haste to King Charoald, for whom he said he had secret information. An audience being granted, he said to the king : ' My lady Queen Gundeberga has for three days been scheming with Duke Taso. She wants to poison you and then marry him and place him on the throne.' King Charoald took these lies seriously. He sent the queen into exile to the fortress of Lomello, where she was shut up in a tower. Chlotar sent a deputation to Charoald to enquire why he had humiliated his kins-woman[1] Queen Gundeberga, and sent her into exile. Charoald replied by reporting the above-mentioned lies as if they had been the truth, whereat Ansoald, one of the deputation, remarked to Charoald as if on his own account, without any authority : ' You could get out of this difficulty without loss of face by ordering your informer to arm himself and do single combat with a representative of the queen. By such combat the judge-ment of God would determine Gundeberga's innocence or—who can tell ?—guilt.' King Charoald and all his magnates liked this advice. Adalulf was ordered to arm

---

[a] 4a ; Asonem 1   [b] 4b[2] ; Caumello 1   [c] 4a ; inunctum 1
[1] cf. chap. 34, above, and, for her further treatment, chap. 71 below

certamine, ut de partae Gundebergae, procurrentibus ^a consubrinis Gundebergam et Aripertum,[1] homo nomen Pitto [2] contra Adalulfu armatus adgreditur. Cumque confligissent certamine, Adalulfus a Pittone interficetur. Gundeberga statim de exilio post anno tercio regressa, sublimatur in regno.

52

624 Anno XLI Chlothariae regis cum Dagobertus iam utiliter regnarit in Auster, quidam ex procerebus de gente nobile Ayglolfingam nomen Chrodoaldus [3] in offensam Dagoberti cadens, instigantibus [4] beatissimo uero ^b Arnulfo pontifice et Pippino maiores domus seu et citeris prioribus sublimatis in Auster; eo quod esset ipse Chrodoaldus rebus pluremis ditatos, ceterorum facultatibus cupiditatis ^c peruasor, superbiae deditus, elatione plenus, nec quicquam boni in ipso repperiebatur. Cumque Dagobertus ipsum iam uellet pro suis facinoribus interficere, Chrodoaldus ad Chlotharium terga uertit ut suam cum filio uitam obtenere dignarit. Chlotharius cum Dagobertum uidisset, inter citeris conlocutionibus Chrodoaldi uitam praecatur; Dagobertus promittens, si id quod male gesserat emendabat, Chrodoaldus uitae periculum non haberit. Sed nulla extante mora, cum Chrodoaldus cum Dagoberto Treuerus accessisset iusso Dagoberti interfectus est; quem Bertharius homo Scarponinsis [5] aeuaginato gladio ad ostium cubiculi capo truncauit.

^a sc. procurantibus *Krusch*   ^b sc. uiro
^c sc. add instincto *Krusch*

[1] This is the Charibert of chap. 34, above.
[2] Paul, *Hist. Lang.* IV, chap. 47 reports that her champion was Carellus, her slave.

himself for the fight ; while Gundeberga and her cousin
Aripert [1] arranged that a certain Pitto [2] should be
Adalulf's opponent in arms. They fought, and Pitto
killed Adalulf. So Gundeberga was forthwith re-
established as queen, after three years in exile.

52

In the forty-first year of Chlotar's reign, when Dagobert 624
was happily ruling over Austrasia, an Agilolfing lord
named Chrodoald [3] fell into disfavour with Dagobert
through the instrumentality [4] of the blessed Bishop
Arnulf, Pippin, mayor of the palace, and other
Austrasian magnates. This Chrodoald, a rich man
on his own account, was for ever greedily seizing the
property of others. He was as proud and as insolent as
could be and lacked any redeeming quality. Because
these crimes made Dagobert wish to kill him, Chrodoald
fled to Chlotar to ask him graciously to intervene with
his son Dagobert to spare his life. When Chlotar was
seeing Dagobert he asked, among other matters, for a
pardon for Chrodoald; and Dagobert promised that if he
mended his ways he would be in no danger. But shortly
afterwards Chrodoald was killed on Dagobert's orders
when he had gone with the latter to Trier. A certain
Berthar, of Charpeigne,[5] drew his sword and cut off his
head at the door of his bed-chamber.

---

[3] cf. chap. 87, below
[4] Redress against this kind of attack on a man's character before the
king (other examples are in chaps. 54 and 61, below) is provided for in the
Germanic laws (cf. *Lex Salica*, 18, *Lex Ribvaria*, 42).
[5] or Scarponne (Meurthe), on the Moselle

53

625 Anno xlii regni Chlothariae Dagobertus cultu regio et
iusso patris honeste cum leudibus Clippiaco [a1] nec
procul Parisius uenit, ibique germanam Sichieldae [2]
regina, nomen Gomatrudae, in coniugium accepit.
Transactis nupciis, diae tercio inter Chlotharium et
filium suum Dagobertum grauis horta fuit intencio,
petensque Dagobertus cuncta que ad regnum Austrasiorum pertinebant suae dicione uelle recipere ; quod
Chlotharius uehementer denegabat, eidem ex hoc nihil
uelle concedere. Elictis ab his duobus regibus duodicem
Francis [3] ut eorum disceptatione haec finirit intentio ;
inter quos et domnus Arnulfus pontifex Mettensis cum
reliquis episcopis elegitur et benignissime, ut sua erat
sanctitas, inter patrem et filium pro pacis loquebatur
concordia. Tandem a pontificebus uel sapientissimis
uiris procerebus pater paceficatur cum filio. Reddensque
ei soledatum quod aspexerat ad regnum Austrasiorum,
hoc tantum exinde, quod citra Legerem uel Provinciae
partibus situm erat suae dicione retenuit.[4]

54

626 Anno xliii regni Chlothariae Warnacharius maior
domi moritur. Filius eius Godinus animum leuetates
inbutus, nouercam suam Bertane eo anno accepit
uxorem. Vnde Chlotharius rex aduersus eum nimia
furore permutus [5] iobet Arneberto duci, qui Godini
germanam uxorem habebat, eum cum exercito inter-
ficeret. Godinus cernens suae uitae periculum habere,
terga uertens cum uxore ad Dagoberto regi perrexit in

---

[a] *Krusch* ; nec : : : clippi[aco] procul 1

[1] now Saint-Ouen-sur-Seine (Paris) ; but cf. chap. 58, below

53

In the forty-second year of Chlotar's reign, Dagobert 625
came royally attired at his father's order with a fine
following to Clichy,[1] near Paris ; and there he received
in marriage Gomatrudis, sister of Queen Sichildis.[2] But
three days after the wedding there broke out a serious
quarrel between Chlotar and his son Dagobert ; for the
latter demanded that all the lands belonging to the
kingdom of Austrasia should be subordinated to him,
and Chlotar stoutly refused to comply and would concede
nothing. So the two kings chose twelve Frankish lords
to decide the issue.[3] One of the bishops among those
chosen was Arnulf of Metz who, such was his integrity,
was always a peacemaker between father and son. The
bishops and the wiser of the lords eventually reconciled
Dagobert with his father and Chlotar ceded to him all
that belonged to Austrasia, only keeping for himself the
territory lying beyond the Loire and in Provence.[4]

54

Warnachar, mayor of the palace, died in the forty-third 626
year of Chlotar's reign and in that same year his son,
the light-hearted Godinus, married his step-mother
Bertha. Chlotar was furious at this [5] and ordered Duke
Arnebert (who had married a sister of Godinus) to raise
a force and kill him. Finding his life in danger, Godinus
and his wife fled to King Dagobert in Austrasia ; but
such was his fear of the king that he took refuge in the

[2] wife of Chlotar
[3] cf. chap. 37, above
[4] i.e. the Austrasian territory in that region
[5] This fury is echoed in *Lex Ribvaria*, 72 (2).

Auster et in eclesia sancti Apri[1] regio timore perterritus fecit confugium.[a] Dagobertus per legatus pro eius uita saepius Chlothario regi depraecabat. Tandem a Chlothario promittitur Godino[b] uita concessa, tamen ut Bertanem, quam contra canonum instituta uxorem acciperat, relinquerit. Quod cum ipsa reliquisset et reuersus est in regnum Burgundiae, Berta continuo ad Chlotharium perrexit, dicens si Godinus conspecto Chlothariae presentatur, ipsum regem uellet interficere. Godinus iusso Chlothariae per precipua loca sanctorum, domni Medardi Soissionas et domni Dionisis Parisius, ea preuentione sacramenta daturus adducitur ut semper Chlothariae deberit esse fidelis, ut congruae locus esset repertus, quo pacto separatus a suis interficeretur. Chramnulfus unus ex procerebus et Valdebertus domesticus dicentes ad Godino ut Aurilianis in ecclesia sancti Aniani et Thoronos ad limina sancti Martini ipsoque sacramento adhuc impleturus adiret. Quod cum in suburbano Carnotis, Chramnulfo indecante et transmittente, ora prandiae in quedam uillola uenisset, ibique Ramnulfus et Waldebertus super ipsum cum exercito inruunt eumque interficiunt et eos qui cum ipso adhunc resteterant, quosdam interficiunt aliusque expoliatus in fugam uertentes relinquunt.

Eo anno Palladius eiusque filius Sidocus episcopi Aelosani,[2] incusante Aighynane duci quod rebellione Wasconorum fuissent consciae, exilio retruduntur. Boso, filius Audoleno de pago Stampinse iusso Chlothario ab Arneberto duci interficetur, repotans ei estobrum[c] cum regina Sighilde. Eo anno Chlotharius cum procerebus

[a] 4b² ; coniugium 1
[b] 5b ; Godoino 4b² ; Godoni 1
[c] sc. stuprum
[1] in the suburbium of Toul

church of Saint-Epvre.[1]   Dagobert repeatedly sent deputations to Chlotar to obtain a pardon for Godinus ; and finally Chlotar said he would spare his life on condition that Godinus gave up Bertha, whom he had married contrary to canon law.   So Godinus did give up Bertha and returned to the kingdom of Burgundy.   But Bertha went straight to Chlotar and averred that if Godinus appeared before the king it would be with the intention of killing him.   In consequence, Chlotar had Godinus conducted to the principal holy places, the churches of Saint Médard at Soissons and Saint Denis at Paris on the pretext of making him swear lifelong fidelity but in fact only with the object of finding a suitable place to kill him, when separated from his companions.   A magnate called Chramnulf and Waldebert, the domesticus, told Godinus that he must now visit the churches of Saint Aignan at Orleans and of Saint Martin at Tours to repeat his oath.   When he had reached the outskirts of Chartres and was about to break his fast at a farm to which Chramnulf had brought him, Waldebert and Chramnulf and their men went for him and killed him.   They also killed some of those who were still with him but let others escape after they had been plundered.

In this year Palladius and his son Sidoc, bishops of Eauze,[2] were charged by Duke Aighyna with having been implicated in the Gascon rebellion.   They were sent into exile.   Boso of Étampes, son of Audolenus, was killed by Duke Arnebert on instructions from Chlotar, who accused him of misconduct with Queen Sichildis.

---

[2] Fredegar alone implies that they were co-bishops (Duchesne, *Fastes Épiscopaux*, II, p. 95).

et leudibus Burgundiae Trecassis coniungitur, cum eorum esset sollicitus si uellint, decesso iam Warnachario, alium eius honores gradum sublimare ; sed omnes unianimiter deligantes *a* si, nequicquam si uelle maiorem domus elegere, regis graciam obnoxie *b* petentes cum rege transagere.

55

627 Anno XLIIII regni Chlothariae, cum pontificis et uniuersi proceres regni sui tam de Neuster quam de Burgundia Clippiaco ad Chlotharium pro utilitate regia et salute patriae coniuncxissent, ibique homo nomen Ermarius, qui gubernatur palatiae Gairiberto filio Chlothario erat, a pueris Aeghynanae genere Saxonorum optimate interficetur. Paene fuerat exinde nimia multorum estragiis nisi pacientia Chlothariae interueniente semul et haec currente, fuisset repraesum.*c* Aeghyna iobente Chlothario in Monte Mercore resedit, pluram secum habens multitudinem pugnatorum. Produlfus auunculus Airiberti exercitum undique colliens, super ipsum cum Chairiberto uolebat inruere. Chlotharius ad Burgundefaronis specialius iobet ut, cuius pars suum uolebat deuertere *d* iudicium, eorum instantia et utilitate oppremiretur : ea pauore uterque iussione regio pacantur.

---

a *Krusch* ; delgantes 1 ; denegantes nequaquam se (si) *all other MSS*
b obnexe, *corr.* obnoxie 1 ; obnixe 4b²
c *sc.* repressum
d 4b² ; deuerte 1; *cf.* conflige *chap. 64*

Chlotar this year assembled the Burgundian nobles and courtiers at Troyes and inquired if they wished to appoint a successor to the position of Warnachar, who had died. But they unanimously decided that they would never have another mayor of the palace and earnestly begged the king of his goodness to deal direct with them.

55

In the forty-fourth year of Chlotar's reign, the bishops 627 and all the great men of his kingdom, Neustrians as well as Burgundians, assembled at Clichy on the king's business and to consider their country's problems. It was there that a certain Ermenarius, comptroller to Charibert, Chlotar's son, was killed by the followers of Aighyna, the Saxon nobleman. Great bloodshed would have ensued had not Chlotar wisely intervened and done everything to prevent it. On his orders Aighyna retired to Montmartre with many of his warriors. Brodulf, Charibert's uncle, gathered together a force from all parts with the object of falling, together with Charibert himself, upon Aighyna ; but Chlotar gave strict instructions to his Burgundians that they were promptly to crush whichever party to the quarrel flouted his decision ; and the fear this royal order inspired kept both parties quiet.

L

56

628   Anno XLV [1] regni sui Chlotharius moritur et suburbano
Parisius in ecclesia sancti Vincenti sepellitur. Dagobertus cernens genitorem suum fuisse defunctum,
uniuersis leudibus quos regebat in Auster iobet in
exercito promouere. Missos in Burgundia et Neuster
direxit ut suum deberint regimen eligere. Cumque
Remus uenisset, Soissionas peraccedens, omnes pontefecis et leudis de regnum Burgundiae inibi se tradedisse
nuscuntur, sed et Neustrasiae pontefecis et proceres
plurima pars regnum Dagoberti uisi sunt expetisse.
Airibertus frater suos nitibatur, si potuisset, regnum
adsumere,[a] sed eius uoluntas pro simplicitate parum
sortiter effectum. Brodulfus uellens nepotem estabilire
in regnum, aduersus Dagoberto muscipulare coeperat ;
sed huius rei uicissitudinem probauit aeuentus.

57

Cumque regnum Chlothariae tam Neptreco quam
Burgundias ad Dagobertum fuisset preoccupatum captis
thinsauris et suae dicione redactis, tandem miserecordia
mutus consilio sapientibus usus, citra [b] Legere et
limitem Spaniae quod ponitur partibus Wasconiae seu
et montis Parenei pagus et ciuitates, quod fratri suo
Gairiberto ad transagendum ad instar priuato habeto
cum uiuendum potuisset sufficere nuscetur concessisse :
pagum Tholosanum, Cathorcinum, Agenninsem, Petro-
corecum et Santonecum uel quod ab his uersus montis
Pereneos exludetur. Hoc tantum Chairiberto regendum

---

[a] 4b[2] ; adsumeret 1
[b] *sc.* inter *Krusch or* intra *Halphen*

[1] As Krusch shows, Chlotar died late in 629, the 46th year of his reign,
though only MS 1 gives it ; but Fredegar is correct, within his own

56

Chlotar died in the forty-fifth year [1] of his reign. He 628
was buried in the church of Saint Vincent on the outskirts of Paris. Learning of his father's death, Dagobert
ordered all his Austrasian followers to assemble in arms,
and sent deputations into Burgundy and Neustria to
ensure his choice as king. When he had passed through
Rheims and was on the way to Soissons, news reached
him that all the bishops and magnates of the kingdom
of Burgundy had submitted to him. Most of the
Neustrian bishops and magnates were said also to be
willing to obey him. His brother Charibert made an
attempt to seize the kingdom but his cause made little
headway since he was simple-minded ; and Brodulf also
started to plot against Dagobert in an attempt to secure
the kingdom for his nephew ; but in vain, as events
were to show.

57

So Dagobert took possession of all Chlotar's kingdom,
Neustria as well as Burgundy, and of all the treasure.
But then he felt sorry and, on good advice, made over
to his brother Charibert the territories and cities between
the Loire and the Spanish frontier in the general area of
Gascony and the Pyrenees. This would provide him
with sufficient upkeep for his household. The territories
were Toulouse, Cahors, Agen, Périgueux, Saintes and
whatever lay between there and the Pyrenees. Dagobert
placed all this under his rule and confirmed the donation

---

chronological system, to give it as the 45th year (see Courtois, ' L'avènement
de Clovis,' p. 159 and Ch. Higounet, ' Notes sur la succession de Clotaire II,'
Annales du Midi, XLVII, 1935).

concessit, quod et per pactiones uinculum estrinxit, ut amplius Airibertus nullo tempore aduersus Dagobertum de regno patris repetire presumerit. Airibertus sedem Tholosa aeliens,[a] regnat in partem prouinciae Aquetaniae. Post anno tercio quod regnare coepisset, tota Wasconia cum exercito superans suae dicione redegit ; alequantulum largiorem fecit regni sui spacium.

58

628 Dagobertus cum iam anno septimo regnans maxemam partem patris regni, ut super memini,[1] adsumsit Burgundias ingreditur. Tanta timore ponteficibus et procerebus in regnum Burgundiae consistentibus seo et citeris leudibus aduentus Dagoberti concusserat ut a cunctis esset mirandum ; pauperibus iustitiam habentibus gaudium uehementer inrogauerat. Cumque Lingonas ciuitatem uenisset, tanta inter uniuersis leudibus suis tam sublimis quam pauperibus iudicabat [b] iusticiam ut creditur omnino fuisset Deo placebile ; ubi nullus intercedebat premius [c] nec personarum accepcio nisi sola dominabatur iusticia, quem diligebat Altissimus. Deinde adgressus Diuione immoque Latona[2] resedens aliquantis diebus, tanta intentionem ad uniuersi regni sui populo iusticia iudicandi posuerat. Huius benignitatis desiderio plenus nec somnum capiebat oculis nec cibum saciabatur, intentissime cogitans ut omnes cum iustitia recepta de conspectu suo remearint. Eodem die quo de Latona ad Cabillonno deliberare properabat priusquam lucisceret, balneo ingrediens, Brodulfo auunculo fratri suo Chairiberto interficere iussit ; qui ab Amalgario et Arneberto ducibus et

in writing, so that henceforward Charibert should never lay further claim to any part of his father's kingdom. Charibert chose Toulouse for his seat and reigned over part of the province of Aquitaine. In the third year of his reign his army subjugated the whole of Gascony, and thus somewhat extended his kingdom.

58

When he had been reigning seven years and held, as I have said,[1] the greater part of his father's kingdom, Dagobert visited Burgundy. The profound alarm that his coming caused among the Burgundian bishops, magnates and others of consequence was a source of general wonder ; but his justice brought great joy to the poor. On arrival at the city of Langres he gave judgement for all, rich and poor alike, with such equity as must have appeared most pleasing to God. Neither bribe nor respect of persons had any effect on him : justice, dear to the Almighty, ruled alone. Then he went to Dijon and spent some days at Saint-Jean-de-Losne,[2] and did what he could to bring justice to his people throughout his realm. Such was his great good-will and eagerness that he neither ate nor slept, lest anyone should leave his presence without having obtained justice. On the very day that he planned to leave Saint-Jean-de-Losne for Chalon and while taking his bath before daybreak, he gave orders to kill Brodulf, his brother Charibert's uncle ; and these were carried out by the Dukes Amalgar and Arnebert and the

628

---

[a] 1 ; eligens 4b²   [b] 4b² ; indecabat 1   [c] sc. praemium
[1] chap. 47, above   [2] Côte-d'Or

Willibado patricio interfectus est. Cumque[a] Cabillonno, ubi iusticiae amorem qua coeperat perficienda Dagobertus intentionem dirigit, post per Agustedunum Auteciodero pergens, per ciuitatem Senonas Parisius uenit ; ibique Gomatrudem reginam Romiliaco uilla ubi ipsa matrimunium acceperat[1] relinquens, Nantechildem unam ex puellis de menisterio matrimonium accipiens reginam sublimauit. Vsque eodem tempore ab inicio quo regnare ciperat consilio primetus beatissime Arnulfi Mettensis urbis pontefice et Pippino maiorem domus usus, tante prosperetatis regale regimen in Auster regebat ut a cunctis gentibus inmenso ordine laudem haberit. Timorem uero sic forte sua concusserat utelitas ut iam deuotione adreperint suae se tradere dicionem ; ut etiam gente que circa limitem Auarorum et Sclauorum consistent ei prumptae expetirint ut ille post tergum eorum iret feliciter, et Auaros et Sclauos citerasque gentium nationes usque manum publicam suae dicione subiciendum fiducialiter spondebant.[b] Post discessum[2] beati Arnulfi adhuc consilius Peppino maiorem domus et Chunibertum ponteficem urbis Coloniae utens et ab ipsis fortiter admonetus, tantae prosperitatis et iustitiae amore conplexus uniuersas sibi subditas gentes, usque dum ad Parisius ut supra memini peruenit, regebatur ut nullus de Francorum regibus precedentibus suae laudis fuisset precellentior.

---

[a] *sc.* tumque *Krusch*   [b] spondebat 5a

[1] Paris ; but cf. chap. 53, above. Or Romilly ? (R. Latouche, *Textes d'histoire médiévale*, 1951, p. 90). The *Gesta Dagoberti*, which though not contemporary, contains genuine tradition, adds that Gomatrudis was abandoned on the advice of the Franks because she was sterile (ed. Krusch, *M.G.H. Script. Rer. Mero.* II, p. 408).

[2] not death

patrician Willebad. From Chalon, where he continued his work for justice, he next travelled to Auxerre by way of Autun, and then went on through Sens to Paris ; and leaving Queen Gomatrudis at the villa of Reuilly (where he had married her[1]), he took to wife a maiden of the bed-chamber named Nantechildis and made her queen. From the beginning of his reign up to that time he had taken advice from the blessed Arnulf, bishop of Metz, and from Pippin, mayor of the palace, and thus ruled Austrasia so prosperously that he earned unlimited praise of all peoples ; and his resolution spread such alarm that everywhere they hastened humbly to submit to him. Even the people who lived on the Slav-Avar frontier earnestly desired him to come to them. They confidently promised that he should dominate the Avars and the Slavs and all the other peoples, up to the frontiers of the Roman Empire. After the withdrawal [2] of his counsellor the blessed Arnulf he was advised by Pippin, mayor of the palace, and Chunibert, bishop of Cologne ; and he ruled his subjects so happily and with such regard for justice that none of his predecessors as king of the Franks earned more praise than he. So it was, as I have said, up to the time of his arrival at Paris.

59

629 Anno VIII regni sui cum Auster regio cultu circuerit,[a] quadam puella nomen Ragnetrudae aestrati suae adsciuit, de qua eo anno habuit filium nomen Sigybertum.

60

Reuertens in Neptreco, sedem patris suae Chlothariae diligens, adsiduae resedire disponens, cum omnem iustitiam quem prius dilixerat fuisset oblitus, cupiditates instincto super rebus ecclesiarum et leudibus sagace desiderio uellit omnibus undique expoliis nouos implere thinsauros, luxoriam super modum deditus tres habebat maxime ad instar reginas et pluremas concupinas. Reginae uero haec fuerent : Nantechildis, Vulfegundis et Berchildis. Nomina concubinarum, eo quod plures fuissent, increuit huius chronice inseri. Quod cum uersum fuisset cor eius sicut super meminemus et ad Deum eius cogitatio recessisset, tamen postea, atque utinam illi ad [b] mercedem ueram lucre fuisset, nam aelymosinam pauperibus super modum largiter aerogabat, si huius rei sagacitas cupiditates instincto non prepedisset, regnum creditur meruisset aeternum.

61

Cum leudes suae eiusque nequicie gemerint, haec cernens Peppinus, cum esset cautior cunctis et consiliosus ualde, plenissemus fide, ab omnibus delictus pro iustitiae amorem, quam Dagoberti consiliose instruxerat

---

[a] *sc.* circumiret
[b] ae, *corr.* ad 1 ; e mercede vera 4b[2]

59

In the eighth year of his reign, while he was making a 629 royal progress through Austrasia, Dagobert admitted to his bed a girl named Ragnetrudis ; and by her he had, in the course of the year, a son named Sigebert.

60

Then he returned to Neustria and, finding that he liked his father Chlotar's residence, decided to make it his home. But he forgot the justice that he had once loved. He longed for ecclesiastical property and for the goods of his subjects and greedily sought by every means to amass fresh treasure. He surrendered himself to limit- less debauchery, having three queens and mistresses beyond number. The queens were Nantechildis, Wulfegundis and Berchildis : the names of his mistresses it would be wearisome to insert in this chronicle ; there were too many of them. And so his heart was corrupted, as we noted earlier, and his thoughts turned away from God ; but—and would that this might have profited him to the obtaining of his true reward !—he had once been prodigal in his almsgiving ; and had this earlier wise almsgiving not foundered through the promptings of cupidity, he would indeed in the end have merited the eternal kingdom.

61

His followers complained of Dagobert's misconduct ; and this reached the ears of Pippin, of all men the most careful, a true counsellor, a man of unshakable fidelity and beloved of all for that passion for justice that he had

dum suo usus *a* fuerat consilio, sibi tamen nec quicquam oblitus iustitiam neque recedens a uiam bonitates, cum ad Dagoberto accederit, prudenter agebat in cunctis et cautum se in omnibus ostendebat. Zelus Austrasiorum aduersus eodem uehementer surgebat,*b* ut etiam ipsum conarint cum Dagobertum facere odiosum ut pocius interficeretur [1] ; sed iustitiae amor et Dei timor, quam diligenter amplexerat, ipsum liberauit a malis. Ipse uero eo anno cum Sigybertum filium Dagoberti ad Chairibertum regem accessit.

62

Chairibertus Aurilianis ueniens Sigybertum de sancto lauacro excipit.[2] Aega uero a citeris Neptrasiis consilio Dagoberti erat adsiduos. Eo anno legati Dagoberti, quos ad Aeraclio imperatore [3] direxerat, nomenibus Seruatus et Paternus, ad eundem reuertuntur nunciantes pacem perpetuam cum Aeraclio firmasse. Acta uero miraculi quae ab Aeraclio factae sunt non praetermittam.

63

Aeraclius cum esset patricius uniuersas Africae [4] prouincias, et Fogas, qui tiranneco ordine Mauricio imperatore interficerat, imperium adreptus nequissime

a huius 1, husus *Krusch* ; usus *all other MSS*
b sug(g)erebat 3, 4b², 5b

[1] I take this to mean that the Austrasians were incensed at Pippin's apparent failure to control the king. It cannot mean, as Dupraz argues, that Pippin's zeal *for* the Austrasians roused other interests at court against him (*Le Royaume des Francs*, p. 378), nor, as Baudot believes (*Le Moyen Age*, xxix, 1928, p. 145) that Austrasian anger with Dagobert caused the Austrasians to embroil Pippin with him the better to kill him.

prudently instilled into Dagobert in the days when the king used to listen to him. He did not become forgetful of what was just nor did he leave the paths of righteousness but in Dagobert's presence behaved in every way reasonably and always showed how prudent he was. The wrath of the Austrasians was thoroughly roused against him, to the extent of trying to blacken his character in Dagobert's eyes and so obtain his death.[1] But his love of justice and fear of that God whom he eagerly embraced saved him from evil. In this same year he journeyed with Sigebert (Dagobert's son) to King Charibert.

62

Charibert came to Orleans and stood godfather to Sigebert.[2] Before all other Neustrians Aega was Dagobert's most trusted adviser. In this year Servatus and Paternus, the ambassadors whom Dagobert had sent to the Emperor Heraclius,[3] returned home with the news that they had made with him a treaty of perpetual peace. I cannot silently pass over the extraordinary things that happened under Heraclius.

63

When Heraclius was patrician of all the provinces of Africa,[4] the tyrant Phocas (the killer of the Emperor Maurice) seized the empire and reigned most cruelly.

---

[2] According to Baudemundus, Sigebert was baptized by St Amand (*Vita*, ed. Krusch, *M.G.H. Script. Rer. Mero.* v, p. 442).
[3] Eastern Emperor, 610-41
[4] Heraclius' father was exarch of Carthage.

regerit et modum amentiae thinsauros in mare proiecerit,
dicensque Neptuno munera daret ; senatores cernentes
quod uellet imperium per stulticiam destruere, factionem
Aeracliae Fogatim adprehensum senatus, manibus et
pedibus truncatis, lapidem ad collum legatum in mare
proiciunt. Aeraclius consensu senatu imperio sublimatur.

64

Cum infestatione Persarum imperium temporebus
Maurici et Fogatis imperatorum multae prouinciae
fuissent uastate, more *a* solito dinuo contra Aeraclio [1]
imperator Persarum cum exercitum surgens, Calcedona
ciuitate nec procul a Constantinopoli Persi uastantes
prouinciae rei publicae peruenissent eumque rumpentes
incendio concremauerunt. Post haec Constantinopole
sedem imperiae propinquantis destruere conabantur.
Egrediens cum exercito Aeraclius obuiam, legatis discurrentibus Aeraclius imperatorem Persarum nomine
Cosdroe petit, ut hii duo imperatores singulare certamine coniungerent, suspensa procul uterque exercitus
multitudinem ; et cuius uicturia prestabatur ab Altissimo, imperium huius qui uincebatur et populum
inlesum receperit. Emperatur Persarum huius con-
uenentiae se egressurum ad prilio singulare certamen
spondedit. Aeraclius imperatur arma sumens, telam
priliae et falange a suis postergum preparatam relinquens,
singolare certamen ut nouos Dauit procedit ad bellum.
Emperator Persarum Cosdroes patricium quidam ex suis
quem fortissemum in prelio cernere potuerat huius

---

a chap. 64, 1

[1] Fredegar's account of Heraclius' Persian wars is often at variance
with Byzantine accounts.

Like a lunatic he threw the imperial treasure into the
sea with the remark that he was making a present to
Neptune. The senators saw that in his folly he wished
to ruin the empire and accordingly they formed a party
in support of Heraclius, seized Phocas, cut off his hands
and feet, tied a stone round his neck and threw him into
the sea. Heraclius was then made emperor by choice of
the senate.

64

Under the Emperors Maurice and Phocas a great many
provinces had been devastated by Persian attacks.
Following his usual practice, the Persian emperor sent
an army against Heraclius,[1] which ravaged through the
provinces of the empire till it reached Chalcedon, not
far from Constantinople. This town they took by assault
and set on fire. Then they made for Constantinople,
the imperial capital, with the intention of destroying it.
But Heraclius came out to meet them with an army. He
sent a mission to Chosroes, the Persian emperor, to
require him to do single combat with him, their two
armies to remain passive spectators. He to whom the
Almighty should give victory should receive the entire
empire and the subjects of the vanquished. The Persian
emperor agreed to this and promised to come and do
single combat. Heraclius armed himself, left behind him
his army drawn up in fighting array, and advanced to
the fray like a second David. But the Persian emperor
Chosroes honoured their pact by sending one of his
patricians, whose great valour he knew, to fight in his

conuenenciae ad instar pro se contra Aeraglio priliandum direxit. Cumque uterque cum aequetis hy duo congressione priliae in inuicem propinquarint, Aeraglius ait ad patricium, quem emperatore Persarum Cosdroae stemabat,[a] dixit : ' Sic conuenerat, ut singulare certamen priliandum debuissimus confligere [b] : quare postergum tuom alii secuntur ? ' Patricius ille girans capud conspecere qui postergum eius uenerit, Aeraglius aecum [c] calcaneum uehementer urguens, extrahens uxum [1] capud patriciae Persarum truncauit. Cosdroes emperatur cum Persis deuictus et confusus, terga uertens a suis propries tiranneco ordene Cosdroes interfecetur. Persi terga uertentes ad sedebus remeant propries. Aeraglius aeuecto nauale cum exercito Persas ingredetur totamque Persedam suae dicione redigit, captis exinde multis thinsauris et septem aeltiarnitis.[2] Tribus annis cerceter Perseda uastata eius dicione subgecetur. Post haec dinuo Persae [d] emperatorem super se creant.[3]

65

Aeraglius emperatur erat speciosus conspecto, pulchra faciae, status formam digne minsure, fortissemus citiris, pugnatur aegregius, nam et sepe leones in arenas et in aerimis plures singulares [e] interfecit. Cum esset litteris

[a] 1 ; aestimabat 4b[2]
[b] conflige 1, cf. deverte chap. 55 ; confligere all other MSS
[c] 1 ; equum 4b[2]
[d] Persas, corr. Persae 1
[e] Professor Mynors' conjecture ; singulos 1 ; singulis 4b[2]

[1] Uxus (also used in Book II, chap. 58) is a very rare word. If Hellmann's suggestion (' Das Fredegarproblem,' p. 44) that it may be derived from Persian ākus, a chisel, is accepted, then the chances are increased that Fredegar is here recounting a tale of eastern origin. Professor W. B. Henning, however, informs me that he cannot accept the derivation and

place against Heraclius. Advancing on horseback upon each other, Heraclius said to the patrician, whom he took for the Emperor Chosroes : ' Since we have agreed to single combat, why are those other warriors following behind you ? ' The patrician turned his head to see who was following him, whereupon in a flash Heraclius spurred his horse forward, drew his short sword [1] and cut off his opponent's head. So the Emperor Chosroes was defeated with his Persians, and all in confusion he turned to flight. But he was wickedly done to death by his own followers. The Persians continued to flee until they reached their own land. Then Heraclius put to sea with his army, invaded Persia, and subjected all that empire to his sway. He took much treasure including seven full sets of war-harness.[2] For nigh on three years was devastated Persia subject to him ; after which time the Persians once more chose an emperor for themselves.[3]

65

The Emperor Heraclius was striking in appearance for he was handsome, tall, braver than others and a great fighter. He would often kill lions in the arena and many a wild boar in unfrequented places. Being well-read

---

suggests as an alternative explanation that Fredegar's account may here go back through intermediaries to the source of the Greek historian Theophanes, who reports that Chosroes was killed (not of course in the situation envisaged by Fredegar) by arrows, τόξοις ; thus *uxus* or perhaps *uxum* (for once the τ was lost, the actual remnant, *όξοις, could easily evoke a spurius singular *όξος) may reflect a corrupt and subsequently misunderstood [τ]όξον or rather [τ]όξα.

[2] Harness (sc. compound of *harnesium*) for men, horses or chariots. Or should we read *aetilarnitos*, sc. *nobiles harnitos*, as Krusch suggests ?

[3] Chosroes was succeeded by his son, Siroes.

nimius aeruditus, astralogus effecetur ; per quod cernens a circumcisis gentibus diuino noto emperium esse uastandum, legationem ad Dagobertum regem Francorum dirigens, petens ut omnes Iudeos regni sui ad fidem catolecam baptizandum preciperit. Quod protenus Dagobertus empleuit.[1] Aeraglius per omnes prouincias emperiae talem idemque [a] facere decreuit. Ignorabat unde haec calametas contra emperium surgerit.

66

Agarrini, qui et Saracini sicut Orosiae liber testatur,[2] gens circumcisa ad latere montes Caucasi super mare Caspium [b] terram Ercoliae [3] coinomento iam olem consedentes, in nimia multetudine creuissent, tandem arma sumentis prouincias Aeragliae emperatores uastandum inruunt, contra quos Aeraglius milites ad resistendum direxit. Cumque priliare cepissint Saracini milites superant eosque gladio graueter trucedant. Fertur in eo prilio cento quinquagenta milia militum a Saracinis fuisse interfecta ; espolia eorum Saracini per legatus Aeraglio recipiendum offerunt. Aeraglius cupiens super Saracinus uindictam nihil ab his spolies recepere uoluit. Congregatis undique de uniuersas prouincias emperiae nimia multetudinem militum, transmittens Aeraglius legationem ad portas Caspias,[c] quas Alexander Magnos Macedus [4] super mare Cespium aereas fiere et serrare iusserat propter inundacione gentium seuissemorum que ultra montem Caucasi

---

[a] sc. item   [b] 4c[1] ; Cypium 1   [c] 4c[1] ; Cypias 1

[1] This lacks confirmation. Heraclius certainly persecuted Jews.
[2] It does not. Krusch suggests reading *Hieronymi* for *Orosiae* ; cf. Book II, chap. 2.

he practised astrology, by which art he discovered, God helping him, that his empire would be laid waste by circumcised races. So he sent to the Frankish King Dagobert to request him to have all the Jews of his kingdom baptized—which Dagobert promptly carried out.[1] Heraclius ordered that the same should be done throughout all the imperial provinces ; for he had no idea whence this scourge would come upon his empire.

66

The race of Hagar, who are also called Saracens as the book of Orosius attests [2]—a circumcised people who of old had lived beneath the Caucasus on the shores of the Caspian in a country known as Ercolia [3]—this race had grown so numerous that at last they took up arms and threw themselves upon the provinces of the Emperor Heraclius, who despatched an army to hold them. In the ensuing battle the Saracens were the victors and cut the vanquished to pieces. The story goes that the Saracens killed in this engagement 150,000 men ; then they sent a deputation to Heraclius with an offer to send him the spoils of battle ; but he would accept nothing because of his desire for vengeance on the Saracens. He raised a great force throughout the imperial provinces and sent representatives to the Caspian Gates, which the Macedonian Alexander the Great [4] had built of brass above the Caspian Sea and had had shut to check invasion by the untamed barbarians living beyond the

---

[3] Colchis ? (Krusch)
[4] Jordanes confirms this, *Getica*, chap. 7 § 50 (ed. Mommsen, *M.G.H. Auct. Ant.* v, p. 67).

M

culmenis habetabant, easdem portas Aeraglius aperire
precepit. Indique cento quinquagenta milia pugnatorum auroque locatus auxiliae suae contra Saracinus
priliandum aemittetur.[a] Saracini duos habentes princepis, ducenta fere [b] milia erant. Cumque castra nec
procul inter [c] se exercitus uterque posuissit, ita ut in
crastena bellum inirent confligentes, eadem nocte gladio
Dei Aeragliae exercitus percotitur : in castris quinqua-
ginta et duo milia ex militibus Aeragliae in stratum
mortui sunt.[1] Cumque in crasteno ad prilium debebant
adgredere, cernentes eorum exercitum milites partem
maxema deuino iudicio interfectam, aduersus Saracinus
nec ausi sunt inire prilium. Regressus omnes exercitus
Aeragliae ad propries sedebus, Saracini more quo
ceperant prouincias Aeragliae emperatores adsiduae
uastandum pergebant. Cum iam Hierusolemam propin-
quassint, Eraglius uedens quod eorum uiolenciae non
potuissit resistere, nimia amaretudines merorem adreptus infelex Euticiana aerese iam sectans,[2] Christi
cultum relinquens, habens uxorem filiam sorores suae,[3]
a febre uexatus crudeleter uitam finiuit.[4] Cui successit
emperiae gradum Constantinus filius eius, cuius tempore
pars publeca a Saracines nimium uastatur.

67

630 Anno nono regni Dagoberti Charibertus rex moretur,
relinquens filium paruolum nomini Chilpericum,
qui nec post moram defunctus est. Fertur faccione

---

[a] *Krusch* ; demittetur *Monod* ; : : mittetur 1 ; mittitur 4b[2]
[b] 4b[2] ; fer 1
[c] *sc.* a
[1] Battle of the Yarmūk (636)

Caucasus. Heraclius ordered these gates to be opened, and through them poured 150,000 mercenary warriors to fight the Saracens. The latter, under two commanders, were approximately 200,000 strong. The two forces had camped quite near one another and were ready for an engagement on the following morning. But during that very night the army of Heraclius was smitten by the sword of the Lord : 52,000 of his men died where they slept.[1] When, on the following day, at the moment of joining battle, his men saw that so large a part of their force had fallen by divine judgement, they no longer dared advance on the Saracens but all retired whence they came. The Saracens proceeded—as was their habit—to lay waste the provinces of the empire that had fallen to them. They were already approaching Jerusalem. Heraclius felt himself impotent to resist their assault and in his desolation was a prey to inconsolable grief. The unhappy king abandoned the Christian faith for the heresy of Eutyches [2] and married his sister's daughter.[3] He finished his days in agony, tormented with fever.[4] He was succeeded by his son Constantine, in whose reign the Roman Empire was cruelly ravaged by the Saracens.

67

Charibert died in the ninth year of Dagobert's reign. 630 He left an infant son called Chilperic who only survived him a short time. It is said that Dagobert's followers

---

[2] more exactly, Monothelitism, derived from the heresy of Eutyches
[3] Martina, daughter of his sister Mary
[4] 11 February 641

Dagoberti fuisset interfectus. Omnem regnum Chariberti unam cum Wasconiam Dagobertus protenus suae dicione redigit ; tinsaurus quoque Chariberti Baronto duci adducendum et sibi presentandom direxit. Vnde Barontus graue dispendio fecisse dinusceter, una cum tinsauraries faciens nimium exinde fraudolenter subtracsit.

68

630 Eo anno Sclaui coinomento Winidi in regno Samone neguciantes Francorum cum plure multetudine interfecissent et rebus expoliassint, haec fuit inicium scandali inter Dagobertum et Samonem regem Sclauinorum. Dirigensque Dagobertus Sycharium legatarium ad Samonem, paetens ut neguciantes quos sui interfecerant aut res inlecete usorpauerant cum iusticia faceret emendare. Samo nolens Sicharium uedere nec ad se eum uenire permitteret, Sicharius uestem indutus ad instar Sclauinorum cum suis ad conspectum peruenit Samonem. Vniuersa quod iniunctum habuerat eidem nunciauit. Sed, ut habit gentiletas et superbia prauorum, nihil a Samone que sui admiserant est emendatum, nisi tantum placeta uellens instetuere, de hys et alies intencionibus que inter partes orte fuerant, iustitia redderetur in inuicem. Sicharius, sicut stultus legatus, uerba inproperiae quas iniunctas non habuerat et menas aduersus Samonem loquitur, eo quod Samo et populus regni sui Dagobertum diberint seruicium. Samo respondens iam saucius *a* dixit : ' Et terra quam habemus Dagoberto est et nos sui sumus, si tamen nobiscum disposuaerit amicicias conseruare.' Sicharius

*4b² caucius 1

brought about his assassination.   Dagobert at once took control of the entire kingdom of Charibert, Gascony included ;   and he ordered Duke Barontus to take Charibert's treasure and bring it to him.   But a good part is known to have been lost through the fraudulent dealings of Barontus and the treasurers, since they agreed to embezzle a large share.

68

In this year the Slavs (or Wends, as they are called) 630 killed and robbed a great number of Frankish merchants in Samo's kingdom ;   and so began the quarrel between Dagobert and Samo, king of the Slavs.   Dagobert despatched Sicharius on an embassy to Samo to request him to make proper amends for the killing and robbing of the merchants by his people.   Samo had no wish to see Sicharius and would not admit him to his presence. But Sicharius dressed up as a Slav and so got with his followers into Samo's presence and fully delivered to him the message that he had been instructed to deliver. But, as is the way with pagans and men of wicked pride, Samo put right none of the wrong that had been done. He simply stated his intention to hold an investigation so that justice could be done in this dispute as well as in others that had arisen between them in the mean-time.   At this point the ambassador Sicharius, like a fool, addressed threatening words to Samo, for which he had no authority.   He declared that Samo and his people owed fealty to Dagobert.   Taking offence, Samo replied, ' The land we occupy is Dagobert's and we are his men on condition that he chooses to maintain friendly relations with us.'   Sicharius retorted :   ' It is

dicens : ' Non est possebelem ut christiani et Dei serui cum canebus amicicias conlocare possint.' Samo ae contrario dixit : ' Si uos estis Dei serui et nos Dei canes, dum uos adsiduae contra ipsum agetis, nos permissum accepimus uos morsebus lacerare.' [a] Aegectus est Sicharius de conspectum Samones.[1] Cum haec Dago- berto nunciassit, Dagobertus superueter iubet de uni- uersum regnum Austrasiorum contra Samonem et Winidis mouere exercitum : ubi trebus turmis falange super Wenedus exercitus ingreditur, etiam et Lango- bardi solucione Dagoberti idemque osteleter in Sclauos perrixerunt. Sclaui his et alies locis e [b] contrario preparantes, Alamannorum exercitus cum Crodoberto duci in parte qua ingressus est uicturiam optenuit ; Langobardi idemque uicturiam optenuerunt et plure- mum nummerum captiuorum de Sclauos Alamanni et Langobardi secum duxerunt. Aostrasiae uero cum ad castro Wogastisburc [2] ubi plurima manus forcium Venedorum inmurauerant circumdantes, triduo pri- liantes pluris ibidem de exercito Dagoberti gladio truci- dantur et exinde fogacetur, omnes tinturius et res quas habuerant relinquentes, ad propries sedebus reuertuntur. Multis post haec uecebus Winidi in Toringia et relequos uastandum pagus in Francorum regnum inruunt ; etiam et Deruanus dux gente Surbiorum, que ex genere Sclauinorum erant et ad regnum Francorum iam olem aspecserant, se ad regnum Samonem cum suis tradedit. Estaque uicturia qua Winidi contra Francos meruerunt, non tantum Sclauinorum fortitudo optenuit quantum

---

[a] 4b² ; laterare 1   [b] 4b² ; et 1

[1] cf. A. Jaksch, ' Fredegar und die Conversio Carantanorum (Ingo),' *M.I.Ö.G.* xli (1926), p. 44

impossible for Christians and servants of the Lord to live on terms of friendship with dogs.' ' Then if,' said Samo, ' you are God's servants, we are his hounds, and since you persist in offending Him we are within our rights to tear you to pieces ! ' And Sicharius was forthwith thrown out of Samo's presence.[1] When he came to report to Dagobert the outcome of his mission, the king confidently ordered the raising of a force throughout his kingdom of Austrasia to proceed against Samo and the Wends. Three corps set out against the Wends ; and the Lombards also helped Dagobert by making a hostile attack on Slav territory. But everywhere the Slavs made preparations to resist. An Alamannic force under Duke Crodobert won a victory over them at the place where they had entered Slav territory ; and the Lombards were also victorious and, like the Alamans, took a great number of Slavs prisoner. Dagobert's Austrasians, on the other hand, invested the stronghold of the Wogastisburg [2] where many of the most resolute Wends had taken refuge, and were crushed in a three-day battle. And so they made for home, leaving all their tents and equipment behind them in their flight. After this the Wends made many a plundering sortie into Thuringia and the neighbouring districts of the kingdom of the Franks. Furthermore Dervan, the duke of the Sorbes, a people of Slav origin long subject to the Franks, placed himself and his people under the rule of Samo. It was not so much the Slavic courage of the Wends that won

---

[2] The site is identified by Labuda with Wgost-Uhošťany in Bohemia, which lies near an ancient road that follows the river Egra.

dementacio Austrasiorum, dum se cernebant cum
Dagoberto odium incurrisse et adsiduae expoliarintur.

69

Eo anno Charoaldus rex Langobardorum legatus ad
Isacium patricium sigricius mittens, rogans ut Tasonem
docem prouinciae Toscane [1] quo potebat [a] ingenio
interfecerit. Huius beneficiae uecessitudinem tributa
quas Langobardi de manu publeca recibebant, trea
centenaria auri annis singolis, unde unum centenarium
auri Charoaldus rex partibus emperiae de praesente
cassarit. Hysacius patricius haec audiens tractabat
quebus ingenies haec potuissit emplere, Tasonem
ingeniose mandans, dum in offinsa Charoaldi regis erat,
cum ipsum amicicias oblegarit : ipse uero contra
Charoaldo rigi ei auxiliaretur. Tale preuentus est
fraude, Rauennam pergit. Hysacius ei obuiam mandans,
pre timore emperatoris Tasonem cum suis infra [b] murus
Rauenne urbis armatum non audebat recipere. Cumque
Taso credens, armam suorum foris urbem relinquens, in
Rauennam fuissit ingressus, statem que fuerant preparati
super Tasonem inruunt et ipsam et suos totus qui cum
eo uenerant interficiunt. Charoaldus rex unum centenarium auri, sicut promiserat, partebus Isaciae et
emperiae cassauit. Dua tantum centenaria deinceps ad
partem Langobardorum a patricio Romanorum annis
singolis emplentur ; unus centenarius cento libras auri
capit. Post haec continuo Charoaldus rex moretur.[2]

[a] 4b² ; putebat 1   [b] sc. intra

[1] Duke of Friuli according to Paul, who tells a similar story (*Hist. Lang.*
IV, chap. 38)
[2] 636

them this victory over the Austrasians as the demorali-
zation of the latter, who saw themselves hated and
regularly despoiled by Dagobert.

69

In this year the Lombard King Charoald sent secretly
to the patrician Isaac to ask him by what means he
could destroy Taso, duke of the province of Tuscany [1] ;
and in return for this service King Charoald promised
to pay the Empire a hundred pounds of gold out of an
annual tribute of three hundred pounds that he received
from it. Upon this proposal the patrician Isaac
considered how he could accomplish the deed. He
artfully put it to Taso that, since he had incurred the
hatred of Charoald, he should make friends with him
(Isaac) and thus obtain help from him against the king.
This ruse deceived Taso, who came to Ravenna. Isaac
sent a message to say that out of respect for the Emperor
he dared not receive him armed with a following
within the walls of Ravenna. Trustfully, Taso made
his retinue leave their arms outside the city and thus
entered Ravenna whereupon men specially posted for
the purpose threw themselves upon him and killed him
and the retinue. King Charoald kept his word, for he
sent a hundred pounds of gold to Isaac and the Empire ;
and annually the Roman patrician paid only two
centenaria of gold to the Lombards—a centenarium
being worth a hundred pounds. King Charoald died
just afterwards.[2]

70

Gundeberga regina, eo quod omnes Langobardi eidem fidem cum sacramentis firmauerant, Chrothacharium [1] quidam unum ex ducibus de terreturio Brissia ad se uenire precepit, eum conpellins uxorem quam habebat relinquerit et eam matremuniam acciperit ; per ipsam omnes Langobardi eum sublimauant in regno. Quod Chrotharius lebenter consenciens, sacramentis per loca sanctorum firmans, ne umquam Gundeberga postponerit nec de honorem gradis aliquid menuarit ipsamque uneco amore diligens, in omnebus honorem pristarit condigne. Gundoberga adtragente omnes Langobardorum primati Crotharium sublimant in regno. Chrotharius cum regnare cepissit, multus nubilium Langobardorum quos sibi sinserat contomacis, interfecit. Chrotharius fortissemam disciplinam et timorem in omnem regnum Langobardorum pacem sectans fecit. Chrotharius oblita sacramenta qua Gundeberge dederat eamque in unum cubicoli Ticinum in aula palaciae retrudit eamque ad privato habeto uiuere fecit. Quinque annus sub ea retrusione tenetur. Chrotharius per concubinas baccatur adsiduae. Gundoberga uero, eo quod esset christiana, in hanc tribulationem benedicebat Deum omnipotentem, ieiunies et oracionebus adseduae peruacabat.

71

Quando Deo conplacuit, Aubedo [a] ligatarius [b] dirictus a Chlodoueo [2] regi causam legationes usque ad Chrotharium regem Langobardorum, Papia coinomento Ticino [3] ciuitatem Aetaliae peruenisset, cernens regina

[a] *chap. 71,* 1   [b] 4b[2] ; legarius 1

70

Queen Gundeberga, to whom all the Lombards had sworn
fealty, sent for a certain Rothari,[1] a duke of the territory
of Brescia, and compelled him to abandon his wife in
order to marry her. She promised that with her support
he would be chosen king by all the Lombards. Rothari
gladly consented and swore in places holy to the saints
that he would never abandon Gundeberga nor impair
the honour of her royal rank, but would cherish her only
and in all things pay her due respect. The Lombard
lords were beguiled by Gundeberga and they did raise
Rothari to the throne. At the start of his reign he caused
a great many nobles, whom he knew to be his enemies,
to be executed. But he was a lover of peace and
established the strictest order (based on fear) throughout
the Lombard kingdom. He forgot his promises to
Gundeberga, for he confined her in a single room in the
palace at Pavia and made her lead a life of obscurity.
She was kept in this seclusion for five years. Rothari
gave himself up to his mistresses. But as she was a
Christian, Gundeberga blessed Almighty God in her
affliction and usefully employed her time in fasting and
prayer.

71

In God's good time, Aubedo, sent by King Clovis [2] on an
embassy to the Lombard King Rothari, reached the
Italian city of Pavia, or Ticinum.[3] Knowing that the

---

[1] This story does not appear in Paul's account of Rothari's succession
(*Hist. Lang.* IV, chap. 42).
[2] Clovis II, son and successor of Dagobert
[3] cf. chap. 51, above, for another version of the same story

quam sepius in legationem ueniens uiderat et ab ipsa benigne semper susceptus fuerat fuisse retrusam, quasi iniunctum habens exinde inter citera Chrothario regi sugessit quod illam parentem Francorum quam reginam habuerat, per quem etiam regnum adsumserat non dibuissit umiliare ; multum exinde regis Francorum et Franci essint ingrati. Quam Chrotharius de presenti, reuerenciam Francorum habens, iubit egredi foris ; et post quinque circeter annis per totam ciuitatem et foris Gundoberga regili ordine per loca sanctorum ad oracionem adgreditur. De uillas et opebus fisci quod habuerat Chrotharius ei restaurare praecepit, quod usque diem obetus sui et gradum dignetatis et opes plurebus ditata rigio culto post feliceter tenuit. Aubedo uero a Gundeberga regina forteter muneratur. Chrotharius cum exercito Genaua maretema, Albingano, Varicotti, Saona, Vbitergio et Lune ciuitates litore mares de imperio auferens uastat, rumpit, incendio concremans ; populum derepit, spoliat et captiuitate condemnat. Murus ciuitatebus supscriptis usque ad fundamento distruens, uicus has ciuitates nomenare praecepit.

72

Eo anno [1] in Abarorum cuinomento Chunorum regnum in Pannia surrexit uiaemens [a] intentio, eo quod de regnum certarint cui deberetur ad sucedendum : unus ex Abares et alius ex Bulgaris collicta multitudinem uterque in inuicem inpugnarint. Tandem Abaris

---

[a] 1 ; uehemens 4b[2]

[1] Fredegar is the only authority for this story.

queen, whom he had often seen during his missions and who had always received him well, was incarcerated, he put it in the course of conversation to King Rothari, as if on instructions, that it would be better not to ill-use a queen who was related to the Franks and who had been instrumental in obtaining the throne for him ; if he did, it would be much resented by the Frankish kings and their peoples. Rothari was afraid of the Franks and forthwith ordered the release of the queen. Thus after nearly five years Gundeberga proceeded through the city and its neighbourhood in royal state to pray at the holy places of the saints. Rothari ordered all the properties and fiscal domains that had been hers to be restored to her, and to her dying day she retained her position and her fortune and lived in contentment, in the midst of royal splendour. Aubedo was, of course, richly rewarded by the queen. Rothari went with his army and took from the Empire the maritime cities of Genoa, Albenga, Varigotti, Savona, Oderzo and Luni. He ravaged and destroyed them and left them in flames ; and the inhabitants, stripped of their belongings, were seized and condemned to servitude. He ordered that these cities should be known only as villages in future ; and he razed their walls to the ground.

72

In this year [1] there broke out a violent quarrel in the Pannonian kingdom of the Avars or Huns. The matter in dispute was the succession to the throne : should it be an Avar or a Bulgar ? The forces of the two parties

Burgarus superant. Burgaris superatis, noue milia uerorum cum uxoris et liberis de Pannonias expulsi, ad Dagoberto expetint, petentes ut eos in terra Francorum manendum receperit. Dagobertus iobit eos iaemandum Badowarius recipere, dummodo pertractabat cum Francis quid exinde fierit. Cumque dispersi per domus Baioariorum ad hyemandum fuissent, consilium Francorum Dagobertus Baioariis iobet ut Bulgarus illus cum uxoris et liberis unusquisque in domum suam una nocte Baiuariae interficerint. Quod protinus a Baiouaries est impletum ; nec quisquam ex illis remansit Bulgaris nisi tantum Alciocus [1] cum septinientis uiris et uxoris cum liberis, qui in marca Vinedorum saluatus est. Post haec cum Wallucem ducem [2] Winedorum annis plurimis uixit cum suis.

73

Eo anno quod partebus Spaniae uel eorum regibus contigerit non pretermittam. Defuncto Sisebodo rige climentissemo, cui Sintela ante annum circiter successerat in regnum,[3] cum essit Sintela nimium in suis inicus et cum omnibus regni suae primatibus odium incurrerit, cum consilium cytiris Sisenandus quidam ex proceribus ad Dagobertum expetit, ut ei cum exercito auxiliaretur qualiter Sintilianem degradaret ad regnum. Huius beneficiae repensionem missurium aureum nobelissimum ex tinsauris Gothorum quem Tursemodus rex ab Agecio patricio acceperat [4] Dagobertum dare promisit pensantem auri pondus quinnentus. Quo audito

---

[1] Probably the Alzeco of Paul, *Hist. Lang.* v, chap. 29
[2] ' Walluc ' was a title, not, as Fredegar thought, the duke's name.
[3] Sisebut was succeeded by Reccared II in 621, and Reccared, after a few months, by Suintila.

gathered together and there was a fight. In the end the Avars beat the Bulgars who, 9000 strong, were chased out of Pannonia with their wives and children. They sought asylum of Dagobert, begging him to take them in and give them a home in Frankish territory. Dagobert gave instructions that they might winter among the Bavarians, and in the meantime he would deliberate with the Franks about their future. When they were dispersed among the Bavarian homesteads for the winter, Dagobert took the advice of his Franks and ordered the Bavarians to kill the Bulgars with their wives and families during the night in their homes. The order was at once carried out. Only Alzeco,[1] with 700 men and their wives and families, survived : they found safety in the Wendish March. Alzeco and his following lived for many years with the Walluc or Wendish duke.[2]

73

I must not overlook what happened this year to Spain and her kings. Their most clement King Sisebut died and was succeeded by Suintila.[3] Suintila was very harsh to his followers and was hated by all the magnates of his kingdom. After he had reigned about a year one of them, Sisenand, on the advice of the rest, went to Dagobert in order to obtain an army that could over-throw Suintila. In return for this service he promised to give Dagobert a superb golden dish weighing 500 pounds from the treasure of the Goths. It had been given to King Thorismund by the patrician Aetius.[4]

---

[4] After Thorismund and his father Theodoric had assisted Aetius to defeat the Huns at the battle of the Catalaunian Fields (451). cf. Book II, chap. 53.

Dagobertus, ut erat cupedus, exercitum in ausilium Sisenandi de totum regnum Burgundiae bannire precepit. Cumque in Espania deuolgatum fuisset exercitum Francorum ausiliandum Sisenando adgredere, omnis Gotorum exercitus se dicione Sisenando subaegit. Abundancius et Venerandus cum exercito Tolosano tanto usque Cesaragustam ciuitatem cum Sisenando acesserunt ; ibique omnes Goti de regnum Spaniae Sisenandum sublimant in regnum.[1] Abundancius et Venerandus cum exercito Tolosano munerebus onorati reuertunt ad propries sedibus. Dagobertus legacionem ad Sisenando rigi Amalgario duce et Venerando dirigit, ut missurium illum quem promiserat eidem dirigerit. Cumque ad Sisenando regi missurius ille legatarius fuissit tradetus, a Gotis per uim tolletur, nec eum exinde excobere permiserunt.[2] Postea discurrentes legatus ducenta milia soledus missuriae huius praecium Dagobertus a Sisenandum accipiens ipsumque pensauit.

74

631 Anno decemo regni Dagoberti, cum ei nunciatum fuissit exercitum Winitorum Toringia fuisse ingressum, cum exercito de regnum Austrasiorum de Mettis urbem promouens, transita Ardinna, Magancia [3] cum exercito adgreditur, disponens Renum transire, scaram de electis uiris fortis de Neuster et Burgundia cum ducebus et grafionebus secum habens. Saxones missus ad Dagobertum dirigunt, petentes ut eis tributa quas fisci dicionebus dissoluebant indulgerit ; ipse uero eorum

---

[1] 631
[2] However, Brunechildis is said to have given the church of Saint Germain d'Auxerre a *missorium* of silver, *qui Thorosmodi nomen scriptum habet ;*

Hearing this, the greedy Dagobert caused an army to be raised in Burgundy for the assistance of Sisenand. As soon as it was known in Spain that the Franks were on the march in support of Sisenand, the entire Gothic army submitted to him. Abundantius and Venerandus united their forces at Toulouse but had only got to Saragossa when they fell in with Sisenand ; and there all the Goths of the Spanish kingdom proclaimed Sisenand king.[1] Laden with gifts, Abundantius and Venerandus went home with the army of Toulouse. Dagobert despatched an embassy to King Sisenand, consisting of Duke Amalgar and Venerandus, to claim the promised dish. It was handed to the ambassadors by King Sisenand but the Goths took it back by force and would not allow it to be taken away.[2] After much negotiating, Dagobert received from Sisenand 200,000 solidi in compensation for the loss of the dish.

74

In the tenth year of his reign Dagobert learned that the Wendish army had entered Thuringia. He raised a force in Austrasia, placed himself at its head in the town of Metz, crossed the Ardennes and approached Mainz [3] with the object of crossing the Rhine. With him was a corps of picked warriors from Neustria and Burgundy under their dukes and counts. The Saxons sent messengers to Dagobert to ask him to excuse them the tribute that they paid to his fisc ; and they promised

631

---

pensat libras 37 ; habet in se historiam Eneae cum litteris Grecis (Gesta Pont. Autissiod. chap. 20, ed. Duru, Bibliothèque historique de l'Yonne, 1, p. 337).

[3] The Ardennes were thus reckoned by Fredegar to extend over the right bank of the Moselle to include the Idarwald and the Hunsrück.

N

studio et utiletate Winidis resistendum spondent et
Francorum limete de illis partebus custodire promittent.
Quod Dagobertus consilio Neustrasiorum adeptus prestetit ; Saxones, qui uius peticionebus suggerendum
uenerant sacramentis, ut eorum mus erat, super arma
placata*a* pro uniuersis Saxonebus firmant.*b* Sed parum
haec promissio sortitur aefectum ; tamen tributo
Saxones quem reddere consuaeuerant per preceptionem
Dagoberti habent indultum. Quinnentas uaccas in-
ferendalis annis singolis a Chlothario seniore censiti
reddebant,[1] quod a Dagoberto cassatum est.

75

632 Anno undecimo regni Dagoberti, cum Winidi iusso
Samone forteter seuerint et sepius transcesso eorum
limite regnum Francorum uastandum Toringia et
relequos pagus ingrederint, Dagobertus Mettis orbem
ueniens, cum consilio ponteuecum seo et procerum,
omnesque primatis regni sui consencientebus, Sigybertum [2] filium suum in Auster regem sublimauit
sedemque ei Mettis ciuitatem habere permisit. Chunibertum Coloniae urbis ponteuecem et Adalgyselum
ducem palacium et regnum gobernandum instetuit.
Tinsaurum quod suffecerit filium tradens, condigne ut
decuit eum uius culmine sublimauit ; seo *c* quodcumque
eidem largitus fuerat sigillatem praeceptionebus robo-
randum decreuit. Deinceps Austrasiae eorum studio
limetem et regnum Francorum contra Winedus utiliter
definsasse nuscuntur.

a *sc.* plagata
b 4b² ; firmat 1

zealously and bravely to stand up to the Wends and to guard that sector of the Frankish frontier. Dagobert, on Neustrian advice, agreed to these Saxon proposals ; and the Saxon envoys took an oath upon weapons, clashing them together as their custom is, for the whole Saxon people. But the promise was of little effect. Nonetheless, Dagobert excused the Saxons the tribute they owed him : since the time of the first Chlotar they had given 500 cows yearly.[1] This ceased with Dagobert.

75

In the eleventh year of Dagobert's reign the Wends, on 632 Samo's orders, were raiding widely and often crossing the frontier to lay waste the Frankish kingdom, spreading out over Thuringia and other territory. Dagobert came to the city of Metz and there, on the advice of his bishops and lords and with the consent of all the great men of his kingdom, placed his son Sigebert [2] on the throne of Austrasia and allowed him to make Metz his headquarters. Bishop Chunibert of Cologne and Duke Adalgisel were chosen to control the palace and the kingdom. Having given his son a sufficient treasure, he provided him with all that his rank required and confirmed the gifts he had made by separate charters. Thereafter, it is reported that the Austrasians bravely defended their frontier and the Frankish kingdom against the Wends.

---

[c] *Krusch* ; eo 1, 4b[2]

[1] cf. Greg. *Hist.* iv, chap. 14 ; and also cont. chap. 31 below.

[2] Sigebert III. See further, Krusch, *Studien zur fränkischen Diplomatik* (1937), p. 54.

76

633 Cumque anno duodecemo regni Dagoberti eidem filius nomen Chlodoueos de Nanthilde regina natus fuissit, consilio Neustrasiorum eorumque admonicione per pactiones uincolum cum Sigybertum filium suum firmasse dinuscetur, et Austrasiorum omnes primati, ponteuecis citirique leudis Sigyberti manus eorum ponentes insuper, sacramentis firmauerunt ut Neptreco et Burgundia soledato ordene ad regnum Chlodouiae post Dagoberti discessum aspecerit ; Aoster uero idemque ordine soledato, eo quod et de populo et de spacium terre esset quoaequans, ad regnum Sigyberti idemque in integretate deberit aspecere ; et quicquid ad regnum Aostrasiorum iam olem pertenerat, hoc Sigybertus rex suae dicione rigendum reciperet [a] et perpetuo dominandum haberit, excepto docato Dentileni,[1] quod ab Austrasius iniquiter abstultus [b] fuerat, iterum ad Neustrasius subiungeretur et Chlodoueo regimene subgiceretur. Sed has pacciones Austrasiae, terrorem Dagoberti quoacti uelint nonlint firmasse uisi sunt. Quod postea temporebus Sigyberti et Chlodouiae regibus conseruatum fuisse constat.

77

Radulfus dux [2] filius Chamaro, quem Dagobertus Toringia docem instetuit, pluris uecibus cum exercito Winedorum demicans, eosque uictus uertit in fogam. Vius superbiae aelatus et contra Adalgyselum ducem diuersis occansionebus inimicicias tendens, paulatem contra Sigybertum iam tunc ciperat reuellare.[3] Sed, ut

[a] 4b[2] ; recipere 1   [b] 4b[2] ; abtultus 1

76

We learn that in the twelfth year of his reign, having had 633
a son named Clovis by Queen Nantechildis, Dagobert
made an agreement with his son Sigebert on the advice
and at the wish of the Neustrians. All the Austrasian
magnates, the bishops and all the warriors of Sigebert,
swore with hands raised that after Dagobert's death
Neustria and Burgundy united should belong to Clovis
while Austrasia, which had the same population and
extent of territory, should be entirely Sigebert's. Sigebert
should have and retain for ever all that had belonged to
the Austrasian kingdom with the exception of the duchy
of Dentelin,[1] formerly unjustly seized by the Austrasians ;
Dentelin should again belong to the Neustrians and be
ruled by Clovis. The Austrasians were apparently
compelled willy-nilly by their fear of Dagobert to ratify
this agreement, which in the event was faithfully
observed in the time of King Sigebert and King Clovis.

77

Duke Radulf,[2] son of Chamar, who was made duke of
Thuringia by Dagobert, fought repeated engagements
with the Wends ; and he beat them and put them to
flight. These victories turned his head : time and again
he behaved aggressively towards Duke Adalgisel, and
this led on to preparations for a revolt against Sigebert.[3]

---

[1] cf. chap. 20, above. For this arrangement see Chamard, *Rev. Quest.
Hist.* xxxv, 1884, p. 12.
[2] This Radulf, father of Hetan and grandfather of Gozbert, may be
identified with the Duke Hruodi of the *Passio Kiliani* (ed. Levison, *M.G.H.
Script. Rer. Mero.* v, p. 723).
[3] cf. chap. 87, below

dictum est, sic agebat : ' Qui diligit rixas, meditatur discordias.'

78

635 Anno quarto decimo rigni Dagoberti, cum Wascones forteter revellarent et multas predas in regno Francorum quod Charibertus tenuerat facerint, Dagobertus de uniuersum regnum Burgundiae exercitum promouere iobet, statuens eis capud exercitus nomeni Chadoindum referendarium,[1] qui temporebus Theuderici quondam regis multis prilies probatur strenuos. Quod cum decem [2] docis cum exercetebus, id est Arinbertus, Amalgarius, Leudebertus, Wandalmarus, Waldericus, Ermeno, Barontus, Chairaardus ex genere Francorum, Chramnelenus ex genere Romano, Willibadus patricius genere Burgundionum, Aigyna genere Saxsonum, exceptis comitebus plurimis qui docem super se non habebant, in Wasconia cum exercito perrixsissent et totam Wasconiae patriam ab exercito Burgundiae fuissit repleta, Wascones deinter moncium rupes aegressi, ad bellum properant. Cumque priliare cepissint, ut eorum mus est terga uertentes, dum cernerent se esse superandus, in faucis uallium montebus Perenees latebram dantes, se locis tutissemis per rupis eiusdem moncium conlocantes latetarint, exercitus postergum eorum cum ducibus insequens, pluremo nummero captiuorum Wascones superatus, seo et ex his multetudinem interfectis, omnes domus eorum incinsis, paeculies et rebus expoliant. Tandem Wascones oppressi seo perdomiti, ueniam et pacem subscriptis ducibus petentes, promittent

[1] The only case of a referendary acting as commander-in-chief in the field. The referendary's normal, clerical duties are best described in the *Vita Ansberti*, chap. 4 (ed. Levison, *M.G.H. Script. Rer. Mero.* v).

He behaved thus because, as they say, he who likes fighting picks quarrels.

78

In the fourteenth year of his reign, since the Gascons 635 were in revolt and were making severe raids into the Frankish kingdom that had been Charibert's, Dagobert raised his forces throughout Burgundy and put in command of them the referendary Chadoind.[1] In Theuderic's reign Chadoind had shown much bravery in many combats. He made for Gascony with his army in company with ten [2] dukes and their forces—namely, the Franks Arnebert, Amalgar, Leudebert, Wandalmar, Walderic, Hermenric, Barontus and Chaira, the Roman Chramnelen, the Burgundian patrician Willebad, the Saxon Aighyna and in addition many counts who had no duke over them. The whole of Gascony was over-run by the Burgundian host ; and the Gascons, ready for war, emerged from their mountain fastnesses. But when battle had been joined and they saw that they were going to be beaten, the Gascons turned to flight, as their way was, and sought refuge in the Pyrenean gorges, where they hid in the heights among inaccessible rocks. The army with the dukes followed them, took many prisoners, killed many, burned all their homes and took their goods and chattels. So in the end the Gascons were overcome and subjugated, and they begged for quarter from the above-mentioned dukes, promising to present

---

[2] Eleven are named, though we may, following Martin (*Études Critiques*, p. 351), exclude Willebad on the grounds that a patrician was distinct from and superior to a duke. However, *decem* could be a scribal error for *undecem*.

se gluriae et conspectum Dagoberti regi presentaturus [a] et, suae dicione traditi, cumta ab eodem iniuncta empleturus. Feliciter haec exercitus absque ulla lesionem ad patriam fuerant repedati, si Arnebertum docem maxime cum seniores et nobiliores exercitus sui per neglienciam a Wasconebus in ualle Subola [1] non fuissit interfectus. Exercitus uero Francorum qui de Burgundia in Wasconia accesserat patrata uicturia redit ad propries sedebus. Dagobertus ad Clippiaco resedens mittit nuncius in Brittania que Brittanes male admiserant ueluciter emendarint et dicione suae se traderint; alioquin exercitus Burgundiae, qui in Vasconiam fuerat, de presenti in Brittanias debuissint inruere. Quod audiens Iudacaile rex Brittanorum, corso ueluci Clippiaco cum multis munerebus ad Dagobertum perrexit, ibique ueniam petens cumta que sui regnum Brittaniae pertenentes leudibus Francorum inlecete perpetrauerant, emendandum spondedit et semper se et regnum quem regibat Brittaniae subiectum dicione Dagoberti et Francorum regibus esse promisit. Sed tamen cum Dagobertum ad minsam nec ad prandium discumbere noluit, eo quod esset Iudechaile relegiosus et temens Deum ualde. Cumque Dagobertus resedissit ad prandium, Iudacaile aegrediens de palacium ad mansionem Dadone [2] referendario, quem cognouerat sanctam relegionem sectantem, accessit ad prandium. Indique in crasteno Iudacaile rex Brittanorum Dagobertum uale dicens, in Brittaniam repedauit; condigne tamen a Dagoberto munerebus honoratur. [3]

636　　Anno quinto decimo regno Dagoberti Wascones omnes seniores terre illius cum Aiginane duci ad

---

[a] *sc.* praesentaturos

themselves before the glorious face of King Dagobert, to submit to his power and to do whatever he should order. The army would have come back without loss had not Duke Arnebert been slain by the Gascons through his own negligence, together with the lords and nobles of his army, in the valley of the Soule.[1] But the Frankish army that had passed through Burgundy to Gascony came home victorious ; and Dagobert, then at Clichy, sent a mission into Brittany to require the Bretons to make prompt amends for what they had done amiss and to submit to his rule. Otherwise, he said, the Burgundian army that had been in Gascony would at once advance on Brittany. When he heard this, the Breton king Judicael went at once to Clichy with a quantity of gifts to ask pardon of King Dagobert. He promised to make good whatever his subjects had unjustly taken from Frankish subjects and undertook that he and his kingdom of Brittany should always remain under the lordship of Dagobert and the Frankish kings. However, he declined to eat or sit down to table with Dagobert, for he was religious and full of the fear of God. When Dagobert did sit down to table, Judicael left the palace and went to dine at the residence of the referendary Dado,[2] whom he knew to lead a religious life. On the following day King Judicael took leave of Dagobert and returned, laden with gifts, to Brittany.[3]

In the fifteenth year of Dagobert's reign, all the 636 Gascon lords and their duke Aighyna came to seek

---

[1] Basses-Pyrénées
[2] Also known as Audoenus (St Ouen, bishop of Rouen) ; *Vita Audoini* ed. Levison, *M.G.H. Script. Rer. Mero.* v.
[3] Judicael was the last independent ruler of Brittany. He finally retired to the cloister.

Dagobertum Clipiaco uenerunt ; ibique in eclesia domni Dioninsis rigio temore perterriti confugium fecerunt. Clemenciam Dagoberti uitam habent indultam. Ibique sacramentis Wascones firmantes semul et promittentes se omni tempore Dagoberto eiusque filies regnumque Francorum esse fedilis : quod more soleto, sicut sepe fecirant post hac probauit *a* aeuentus. Permissum Dagoberti Wascones regressi sunt in terra Wasconiae.

79

637   Anno sexto decemo regni sui Dagobertus profluuium uentris Spinogelo uilla super Secona fluuio nec procul a Parisius aegrotare cepit. Exinde ad baseleca sancti Dionensis *b* a suis defertur. Post paucos dies cum suae uitae sentirit pericolum, Aeganem sub celeretate ad se uenire praecipit, reginam Nantildem et filium suum Chlodoueum eidem in mano conmendans, se iam discessurum senciens, consilium Aegane peragratum habens, quod cum eius instancia regnus strenuae gubernari possit. Hys gestis post paucus dies Dagobertus amisit spiritum [1] sepultusque est in ecclesia sancti Dionensis,*c* quam ipse prius condigne ex auro et gemmis et multis preciosissemis espetebus ornauerat et condigne in circoito fabrecare preceperat,[2] patrocinium ipsius precioso expetens. Tante opes ab eodem et uillas et possessiones multas per plurema loca ibique sunt conlate ut miraretur

---

a 4b² ; proliauit 1
b 1 ; Dionisi(i) *all other MSS*
c 1 ; Dionisii 4b²

[1] Courtois, ' L'avènement de Clovis,' p. 159, shows that Dagobert died on 19 January 638, having fallen ill in the last days of 637. Then followed an interregnum of nearly two years, before the accession of Clovis II in

Dagobert at Clichy ; but fear of the king overcame them and they took refuge in the church of Saint-Denis. Dagobert, however, was merciful and spared their lives ; and they swore always to be faithful to the king, to his sons, and to the kingdom of the Franks. But this oath they kept in their usual manner, as events were to prove. The Gascons then went home, with Dagobert's leave.

79

In the sixteenth year of his reign Dagobert had an attack 637 of dysentery at his villa of Épinay-sur-Seine, near Paris. They carried him from the villa to the church of Saint-Denis. Some days later, realizing that his life was in danger, he sent in haste for Aega and commended to him his Queen Nantechildis and Clovis, his son. He felt himself at death's door and, judging Aega a wise counsellor, considered that through him the kingdom would be well governed. Not many days after doing this, Dagobert gave up the ghost.[1] He was buried in the church of Saint-Denis which he had magnificently embellished with gold, gems and precious things and had decorated from end to end in a remarkable way,[2] in the hope of ensuring the precious patronage of the saint. He gave the church such riches and so many domains and possessions in different places that many were struck

---

October 640. The best explanation of the interregnum is that a Frankish prince was expected to reach a minimum age of seven years before being proclaimed king.

[2] Dagobert's munificence to the abbey is discussed in the second of L. Levillain's important articles entitled ' Études sur l'abbaye de Saint-Denis à l'époque mérovingienne,' *Bibl. de l'École des Chartes,* LXXXVI (1925), p. 22.

a plurimis. Sallencium ibidem ad instar monastiriae sanctorum Agauninsium instetuere iusserat[1] ; sed facilletas abbatis Aigulfi eadem[a] instetucionem nuscetur refragasse. Post Dagoberti discessum filius suos Chlodoueos sub tenera aetate regnum patris adsciuit ; omnes leudis de Neuster et Burgundia eumque Masolaco uilla[2] sublimant in regno.

80

640-2   Aega uero cum rigina Nantilde quem Dagobertus reliquerat, anno[b] primo regni Chlodouiae, secundo et inmenente tercio eiusdem regni anno condigne palacium gobernat et regnum. Aega uero inter citiris primatebus Neustreci prudencius agens et plenitudenem pacienciae inbutus cumtis erat precellentior. Eratque genere nobele, opes habundans, iusticiam sectans, aeruditus in uerbis, paratus in rispunsis ; tantummodo a plurimis blasphemabatur, eo quod esset auariciae deditus. Facultatis pluremorum, que iusso Dagoberti in regnum Burgundiae et Neptreco inlecete fuerant usurpate et fisci dicionebus contra modum iusticiae redacte, consilio Aegane omnibus restaurantur.

81

Eo anno[3] Constantinus emperatur moretur. Constans filius eius sub tenera aetate consilio senato emperio sublimatur. Idem eius tempore grauissime a Sarracinis uastatur imperiom. Hierusolema a Saracinis capta[4]

---

[a] sc. eam   [b] chap. 80, 1

[1] cf. Greg. Hist. III, chap. 5 ; and chap. 1, above
[2] near Sens (Yonne)   [3] 641   [4] 637

with astonishment. He instituted a perpetual chant in the church on the model of the monastery of Saint Maurice,[1] but this practice is known to have been allowed to fall into desuetude through the feebleness of Abbot Aegulf. After the death of Dagobert the kingdom fell to his son Clovis, still a minor. All the warriors of Neustria and Burgundy raised him to the kingship at the villa of Mâlay-le-Roi.[2]

80

Aega ruled justly over the palace and the kingdom 640-2 together with Nantechildis, Dagobert's widow, during the first, the second and the beginning of the third year of the reign of Clovis. He stood out among the other Neustrian magnates and excelled them all through his ability to act with decision and his instinct to consider before he acted. He was of noble birth and very wealthy. Moreover, he was careful to be just, was an able talker and was always ready with an answer ; but generally he was blamed for a tendency to avarice. It was on his advice that whatever on Dagobert's orders had been unjustly taken for the royal fisc in the kingdoms of Burgundy and Neustria was restored to its rightful ownership.

81

This year [3] the Emperor Constantine died and was succeeded as Emperor, on the motion of the senate, by his son Constans, who was still a minor. In Constans' reign the empire suffered very great devastation at the hands of the Saracens. Having taken Jerusalem [4] and

ceterasque ciuitates aeuersae. Aegyptus superiur et inferior a Saracines peruadetur, Alexandria capetur et praedatur.[1] Afreca tota uastatur et a Saracines possedetur paulolum ibique Gregorius patricius a Saracinis interfectus.[2] Constantinopolis tantum cum Traciana prouincia et paucis insolis, etiam et Romana prouincia emperiae dicione remanserat, nam maxeme totum emperium a Saracines graueter fuit adtritum ; etiam et in postremum emperatur Constans constrictus adque conpulsus, effectus est Saracinorum tributarius, ut uel Constantinopoles cum paucis prouincies et insolis suae dicione reseruaretur.[3] Trebus annis circeter et fertur adhuc amplius per unumquemque diem mille soledus auri aeraries Saracinorum Constans emplebat. Tandem resumtis uiribus Constans emperium aliquantisper recoperans tributa Saracines emplendum refutat.[4] Quemadmodum haec factum fuissit aeuentum anno in quo expletum est in ordene debeto referam et scribere non selebo,[a] donec de his et alies optata si permiserit Deus perficiam, uius libelli cumta mihi ex ueretate cogneta inseram.

82

Eo anno [5] Sintela rex Espaniae, qui Sisenando in regno successerat, defunctus est. Vius filius nomini Tulga sub tenera aetate Spanies peticionem patris sublimatur in regno. Gotorum gens inpaciens est quando super se fortem iogum non habuerit. Vius Tulganes aduliscenciam omnes Spania more soleto uiciatur, diuersa conmittentes insolencia. Tandem unus ex primatis nomini Chyntasindus collictis plurimis senatorebus

[a] sc. silebo
[1] 643   [2] 647   [3] 654   [4] 658   [5] 640

razed other cities, they attacked upper and lower Egypt, took and plundered Alexandria,[1] devastated and quickly occupied the whole of Roman Africa, and killed there the patrician Gregory.[2] Only Constantinople, the province of Thrace, a few islands and the duchy of Rome remained in imperial control, for the greater part of the Empire had been overrun by Saracens. So reduced, Constans became in the last resort their tributary, merely controlling Constantinople and a handful of provinces and islands.[3] It is said that for three years and more Constans paid one thousand gold solidi a day to the Saracens ; but then he somewhat recovered his strength, little by little won back his empire and refused to pay tribute.[4] How this came about I shall set down under the right year in its proper sequence ; and I shall not remain silent if, God willing, I finish this and other matters as I desire ; and so I shall include everything in this book that I know to be true.

82

This year [5] died Suintila, king of Spain and successor to Sisenand, and he was succeeded by his own nominee, his son Tulga, who was still a minor. The Gothic people become restive when not ruled with a heavy hand, and during this Tulga's boyhood all Spain, true to form, abandoned itself to every sort of arbitrary insubordination, until at length, at a gathering of many of the Gothic senators and the rest of the people, one of the magnates, named Chindaswinth, was chosen king of

Gotorum citerumque populum regnum Spaniae sublimatur. Tulganem degradatum et ad onus clerecati tunsorare fecit.[1] Cumque omnem regnum Spaniae suae dicione firmassit, cognetus morbum Gotorum quem de regebus degradandum habebant, unde sepius cum ipsis in consilio fuerat [2] quoscumque ex eis uius uiciae prumtum contra regibus qui a regno expulsi fuerant cognouerat fuesse noxius, totus sigillatem iubit interfici aliusque exilio condemnare eorumque uxoris et filias suis fedelebus cum facultatebus tradit. Fertur de primatis Gotorum hoc uicio repremendo ducentis fuisse interfectis ; de mediogrebus quingentis interfecere iussit. Quoadusque hoc morbum Gotorum Chyntasindus cognouissit perdometum non cessauit quos in suspicionem habebat gladio trucidare. Goti uero a [a] Chyntasindo perdomiti nihil aduersus eodem ausi sunt, ut de regebus consuaeuerant inire consilium. Chyntasindus cum esset plenus diaerum filium suum nomine Richysindum in omnem regnum Spaniae regem stabiliuit.[3] Chyntasindus paenetentiam agens, aelymosinam multa de rebus propries faciens, plenus senectutae, fertur nonagenarius moretur.[4]

83

642 Anno tercio regni Chlodouiae Aega Clipiaco uilla uixatus a febre moretur. Ante paucis diaebus Ermenfredus, qui filiam Aegane uxorem acceperat, Chainulfo comiti in Albiodero uico [5] in mallo interfecit. Ob hanc

[a] 4b², 5b ; a uero (sc. uiro) 1, 3

[1] 641

[2] cf. Greg. *Hist.* iii, chap. 30. Visigothic practice in such matters, which was in some ways at variance with Frankish practice, is best discussed by F. Kern, *Gottesgnadentum und Widerstandsrecht* (ed. Buchner, 1954), esp. p. 352.

Spain. When he had dethroned Tulga he had him tonsured [1] ; and then, having made sure of his power throughout the Spanish kingdom and knowing the Gothic weakness for dethroning their kings (for he had often been involved with them in such conspiracies),[2] he ordered the killing, one by one, of all those whom he knew to have been compromised in rebellion against kings who had been dethroned. Others he condemned to exile, and gave their wives, daughters and inherited possessions to his followers. The story goes that to repress this criminal tendency he caused to be executed two hundred of the Gothic chieftains and five hundred of lower standing ; and until he was certain that he had tamed this disease, he never ceased to execute those whom he suspected. Thus mastered by Chindaswinth, the Goths never dared to raise against him the sort of conspiracy that they had raised against his predecessors. When he was full of days, the king established his son Reccaswinth upon the Spanish throne,[3] and then gave himself up to works of penance and to generous alms-giving from his private resources. He was a great age—ninety, they say—when he died.[4]

83

In the third year of the reign of Clovis, Aega succumbed to fever and died at Clichy. Some days previously Ermenfred, who had married Aega's daughter, had killed Count Chainulf in the court held at Augers,[5] in consequence of which his possessions were savagely 642

---

[3] 649   [4] 652
[5] Seine-et-Marne

rem grauissema stragis de suis rebus iussionem et permissum Nantilde a parentebus Ainulfi et populum pluremum fiaetur. Ermenfredus in Auster Remus ad baselecam sancte Remediae fecit confugium ibique diebus plurimis hanc infestacionem deuitando et rigio temore residit.

84

Post discessum Aegane Erchynoaldus maior domus, qui consanguaeneus fuerat de genetrici Dagoberto, maior domi palacium Chlodouiae effecetur. Eratque homo paciens, bonetate plenus, cum esset paciens et cautus, humiletatem et benignam uoluntatem circa sacerdotibus omnebusque pacienter et benigne respondens nullamque tumens superbiam neque cupeditatem saeuiaebat [1] ; tanta in suo tempore pacem sectans fuit ut Deum esset placebelem. Erat sapiens, sed in primum maxeme cum simplecetate, rebus minsuratem ditatus, ab omnibus erat dilectus. Igitur post discessum Dagoberti regi quo ordine eiusdem tinsauri inter filius deuisi fuerant nun obmittam sed delucedato ordene uius uolumine inseri procurabo.

85

Cum Pippinus maior domi post Dagoberti obetum et citiri ducis Austrasiorum qui usque in transito Dagoberti suae fuerant dicione retenti Sigybertum unanemem conspiracionem expetissint Pippinus cum Chuniberto, sicut et prius amiciciae cultum in inuicem conlocati fuerant, et nuper sicut et prius amiciciam uehementer se firmeter perpetuo conseruandum oblegant, omnesque

attacked by Chainulf's family and many others, with the approval and permission of Queen Nantechildis. Ermenfred sought refuge in the Austrasian church of Saint Rémi at Rheims, and stayed there many days to escape from attack as well as from the royal wrath.

84

Erchinoald, a relation of Dagobert's mother, was made mayor of the palace to Clovis after the death of Aega. He was a gentle, good-natured man, in brief both patient and canny, very humble and kindly towards the bishops, ready with a civil answer to all questioners and quite without pride or greed.[1] So long as he lived he sought peace, as is well-pleasing to God. He was certainly clever, but open and straightforward about it ; he lined his own pockets to be sure, but quite moderately ; and everyone was very fond of him. Anyway, I must not forget to say how, on Dagobert's death, his treasure was divided among his sons, and I will take care to record it accurately in this book.

85

After Dagobert's death, Pippin the mayor of the palace and the other Austrasian dukes who had hitherto been Dagobert's subjects unanimously sought Sigebert for their king. Pippin and Chunibert, once good friends, had just come together again and agreed always to help and support one another. Jointly and with suitable

---

[1] A different picture is given by St Ouen in his *Vita Eligii*, II, chap. 27 (ed. Krusch, *M.G.H. Script. Rer. Mero.* IV, p. 714).

leudis Austrasiorum secum uterque prudenter et cum dulcedene adtragentes, eos benigne gobernantes eorum amiciciam constringent semperque seruandum. Aegetur, discurrentebus legatis partem Sigiberti debetam de tinsauris Dagoberti Nantilde regine et Chlodoueo rigi a Sigyberto requiretur, quod reddendum placitus instetuaetur. Chunibertus pontefex urbis Coloniae et Pippinus maior domi cum aliquibus primatebus Austri a Sigyberto dericti uilla Conpendio usque perueniunt, ibique tinsaurum Dagoberti iubente Nantilde et Chlodoueo instancia Aegane maiorem domus presentatur et aequa lanciae deuidetur ; terciam tamen partem de quod Dagobertus adquisiuerat Nantildis regina percepit. Chunibertus et Pippinus hoc tinsaurum quod pars fuit Sigyberti Mettis facint perducere ; Sigyberto praesentatur et discribetur. Post fertur anni circolo Pippinus moretur, nec parua dolore eiusdem transitus cumtis generauit in Auster, eo quod ab ipsis pro iusticiae cultum et bonetatem eiusdem delictus fuissit.

86

Grimoaldus filius eius cum essit strinuos, ad instar patris diligeretur a *ª* plurimis, Otto quidam filius Vrones domestici,[1] qui baiolos Sigyberto ab adoliscenciam fuerat, contra Grimoaldo superbiam tomens et zelum ducens eumque dispecere conaretur : Grimoaldus cum Chuniberto pontefice se in amiciciam constringens, ceperat cogitare quo ordine Otto de palacio aegiceretur et gradum patris Grimoaldus adsumeret.

ª *chap. 86,* 1

blandishments they drew the Austrasian notables into their orbit, ruled them generously, won their support and knew how to keep it. Sigebert now sent messengers to ask Queen Nantechildis and King Clovis for his share of Dagobert's treasure, and a court was summoned to settle how it should be returned. Bishop Chunibert of Cologne and Pippin, mayor of the palace, and certain other Austrasian magnates were sent by Sigebert to Compiègne where, on instructions from Nantechildis and Clovis and with the consent of the mayor Aega, Dagobert's treasure was brought and divided into equal parts. Queen Nantechildis had one-third of all that Dagobert had amassed ; Chunibert and Pippin had Sigebert's share taken to Metz, where it was presented to Sigebert and inventoried. Pippin died about a year later. His death was a matter of deep grief to all Austrasians, who loved him for his concern for justice and his goodness.

86

His son Grimoald, a man of enterprise, was loved, like his father, by most people. A certain Otto, however, son of the domesticus [1] Uro and tutor to Sigebert since his childhood, was swollen with pride and carried away by envy against Grimoald, and tried to displace him. For his part, Grimoald swore friendship with Bishop Chunibert and considered how he could get Otto put out of office and succeed to his father's position.

---

[1] Court official. For Dagobert's efforts to hold a balance between the Austrasian factions led by the family of Otto and by the Arnulfings, see Ewig, *Die fränkischen Teilreiche*, p. 113.

87

639 Cumque anno octauo Sigybertus regnarit, Radulfus dux
Toringiae uehementer contra Sigybertum reuellandum
disposuissit,[1] iusso Sigyberti omnes leudis Austrasiorum
in exercitum gradiendum banniti sunt. Sigybertus
Renum cum exercito transiens gentes undique de uniuersis regni sui pagus ultra Renum cum ipsum adunati sunt. Primo in loco Faram filio Chrodoaldo[2]
nomini, qui cum Radulfo unitum habebat consilium,
exercitus Sigyberti trucedans rupit ipsoque interfecit.
Omnem populum uius Fare qui gladium aeuasit
captiuetate depotant. Omnes primati et exercitus
dextras in inuicem dantes ut nullus Radulfo uitam
concederet ; sed haec promissio non sortitur effectum.
Sigybertus deinde Buchoniam[3] cum exercito transiens,
Toringiam properans, Radulfus haec cernens, castrum
lignis monitum in quodam montem super Vnestrude
fluuio in Toringia construens, exercitum undique
quantum plus potuit collegens, cum uxorem et liberis in
hunc castrum ad se definsandum stabilibit. Ibique
Sigybertus cum exercitum regni sui ueniens castrum
undique circumdat exercitus, Radulfus uero intrinsecus
ad prilio forteter praeparatus sedebat. Sed hoc prilio
sine consilio initum est. Haec adoliscencia Sigyberti
regis patrauit,[4] cum aliae eodem diae uellint procedere
ad bellum et aliae in crasteno, nec unitum habentes
consilio. Grimoaldus et Adalgyselus ducis haec
cernentes, Sigyberti pericolum zelantes eum undique
sine intermissione custudiunt. Bobo[5] dux Aruernus
cum parte exercitus Adalgyseli et Aenouales comex
Sogiontinsis[6] cum paginsebus suis et citeri exercitus

---

[1] cf. chap. 77, above   [2] cf. chap. 52, above
[3] probably the general area of the Rhön and Vogelsberg

87

In the eighth year of Sigebert's reign, Radulf duke of 639
Thuringia impetuously rose in revolt.[1] Sigebert summoned all the leading men of Austrasia to suppress him,
crossed the Rhine with an army and was joined by all
the peoples of his kingdom who lived in the districts
across the river. Sigebert's army first fell upon a son of
Chrodoald named Fara,[2] an accomplice of Radulf, and
killed him ; and all Fara's people who escaped death were
taken off to servitude. The commanders and the rank
and file swore to one another that they would none of them
spare Radulf's life. The oath was not kept. Sigebert and
his army passed through the forest of Buchonia [3] and
hastened on without pausing into Thuringia. Observing
this, Radulf put up a wooden stockade round his position
on a rise above the banks of the Unstrut, in Thuringia,
and when he had assembled every possible man from all
parts, fortified himself with his wife and children within
this field-work to withstand a siege. Sigebert arrived
with his army and invested the camp while Radulf sitting
tight within prepared for a vigorous defence. But battle
was joined imprudently, owing to the youthfulness of
King Sigebert.[4] Some were for fighting that same day,
others preferred to await the morrow ; and they were
unable to give unanimous counsel. Seeing this, the
Dukes Grimoald and Adalgisel took great pains to guard
Sigebert, appreciating the danger that he ran. Bobo,[5]
duke of Auvergne, with some of Adalgisel's men, and
Innowales, count of the Saintois,[6] with his compatriots

---

[4] He was about eleven.

[5] cf. W. Levison, ' Das Testament des Diakons Adalgisel-Grimo vom
Jahre 634,' *Aus Rheinischer und Fränkischer Frühzeit*, pp. 131-2. The Auvergne
was Austrasian property.

[6] cf. chaps. 35 and 37, above

manus plura contra Radulfum ad portam castri protenus pugnandum perrexerunt. Radulfus cum aliquibus ducebus exercitus Sigyberti fiduciam haberit quod super ipsum nun uoluissent uiribus inruere, de castrum per porta prorumpens super exercitum Sigyberti cum suis inruens, tanta stragis a Radulfo cum suis de exercito Sigyberti fiaetur ut mirum fuissit. Macansinsis hoc prilio non fuerunt fedelis. Fertur ibique plurima milia homenum fuisse gladio trucidati. Radulfus patrata uicturia in castrum ingredetur. Sigybertus cum suis fedelebus graue amaretudines merorem adreptus super aequum sedens lacremas oculis prorumpens plangebat quos perdederat. Nam et Bobo dux et Innowales comex, citiri nouilium fortissemi pugnatoris seo et plura manus exercitus Sigiberti regi qui cum ipsis in congressione certamenes sunt adgressi conspiciente Sigyberto hoc prilio fuerunt trucidati. Nam et Fredulfus domestecus, qui amicus Radulfo fuisse dicibatur, hoc prilio occu- puit. Sigybertus eadem nocte nec procul ab ipso castro in tenturies cum suos mansit exercito. In crasteno uedentes quod Radulfo nihil preualuissint, missus dis- currentebus ut paceueci [a] Renum aeterum transmearint, cum Radulfo conuenenciam Sigybertus et eiusdem exer- citus ad propries sedebus remeantur. Radulfus superbia aelatus admodum regem se in Toringia esse cinsebat, [1] amicicias cum Winidis firmans, ceterasque gentes quas uicinas habebat cultum amiciciae oblegabat, in uerbis tamen Sigiberto regimini non denegans, nam in factis forteter eiusdem resistebat dominacionem.

[a] 1 ; pacifice 4b[2]

[1] On the implications of this claim see W. Schlesinger, ' Über germanisches Königtum ' (Das Königtum, p. 129).

and a large part of the remaining forces, advanced at once to the entrance of the camp to attack Radulf. But Radulf was in touch with certain dukes in Sigebert's army and knew that they would not attack him with their men. So out he came through the camp entrance and threw himself and his warriors on Sigebert's and made a carnage to be marvelled at. The men of Mainz turned traitor in this battle. Several thousands of warriors fell there, they say. Radulf went back into the camp after his victory while Sigebert, like his followers, was seized with wildest grief and sat there on his horse weeping unrestrainedly for those he had lost ; for Duke Bobo, Count Innowales, the bravest warriors of his nobles and the greater part of the army that had followed them to battle had been slain before Sigebert's eyes. Furthermore, the domesticus Fredulf, allegedly a friend of Radulf, also fell in battle. Sigebert and his army spent that night in their tents not far from the enemy encampment, and on the day following, seeing that he could do nothing against Radulf, he sent a delegation to request that he might recross the Rhine unmolested and be permitted, he and his men, to go home. Radulf was in transports of pride. He rated himself King of Thuringia [1] and concluded treaties of alliance with the Wends and made overtures to other neighbouring peoples. He did not in so many words deny Sigebert's overlordship but in practice did all he could to resist his power.

88

641 Anno decimo regno Sigyberti Otto, qui aduersus Grimoaldo inimicicias per superbia tomebat, faccionem Grimoaldo a Leuthario duci Alamannorum interfecetur. Gradus honoris maiorem domi in palacio Sigyberto et omnem regnum Austrasiorum in mano Grimoaldo confirmatum est uehementer.[1]

89

643 Anno quarto regni Chlodouiae cumque Nantildis regina cum filio suo Chlodouio regi post discessum Aeganem Aurilianes in Burgundiae *a* regnum uenissit, ibique omnes seniores, ponteueces, ducebus et primatis de regnum Burgundiae ad se uinire precepit. Ibique cumtus Nantildis sigillatem adtragens Flaogatum genere Franco maiorem domus in regnum Burgundiae aelectionem ponteuecum et cumtis docebus a Nantilde regina hoc gradum honores stabilitur neptemque suam nomini Ragnoberta Flaochadum disponsauit. Espunsalias *b* has nessio qua factione fiunter ; nam alium consilium secrete Flaochatus et Nantildis regina macenauant, quem credetur non fuisse Deo placebelem ideoque non mancepauit effectum. Cumque Erchynoaldus et Flaochadus maiores domi inter se quasi unum inissint consilium, consencientes ab inuicem, hunc gradus honorum, alterutrum solatium prebentes disponent habere felicetur. Flaochadus cumtis ducibus de regnum Burgundiae seo et pontefecis per epistolas etiam et

---

a Burdiae, *corr.* Burgundiae 1   *b* 1 ; sponsalias 4b[2]

[1] Fredegar does not tell of the subsequent usurpation of Grimoald when, for two years (660-2) the Austrasian throne was occupied, not by Sigebert's son Dagobert II (an exile in Ireland till his return in 676), but by Grimoald's son, Childebert III. See *Liber Historiae Francorum*, chap. 43.

88

In the tenth year of Sigebert's reign fell Otto, afire with 641 hatred of Grimoald, at whose instigation he was slain by Leuthar, duke of the Alamans. The dignity of mayor of Sigebert's palace and control of all the kingdom of Austrasia was thus decisively assured to Grimoald.[1]

89

In the fourth year of the reign of Clovis, after the death 643 of Aega, Queen Nantechildis came with her son, King Clovis, to Orleans in the kingdom of Burgundy; and there she summoned to her all the lords and bishops and dukes and chief men of Burgundy. She won them over, one after another, and then, by choice of all the bishops and dukes, raised the Frank Flaochad to the dignity of mayor of the palace in the kingdom of Burgundy. She gave to him in marriage her niece Ragnoberta : I do not know who arranged this match. Flaochad and Queen Nantechildis were plotting a different project which seems not to have been according to the will of God who did not allow it to come to pass. The two mayors of the palace, Erchinoald and Flaochad, had, so to speak, a single aim and were of one mind ; and so they supported one another and prepared to exercise their high office in friendliness. Flaochad promised by letter to all the dukes and bishops of the Burgundian kingdom, and

---

L. Dupraz *Le Royaume des Francs*, chap. 4, makes an unconvincing attempt to explain away this usurpation, the reality of which was demonstrated once for all by L. Levillain, ' Encore la succession d'Austrasie au vii⁰ siècle,' pp. 296-306. In his *Life* of Wilfrid (ed. B. Colgrave, Cambridge 1927, chap. 28), Eddius Stephanus tells how the English bishop helped in the restoration of Dagobert to the Austrasian throne, thereby bringing down on himself the enmity of Ebroin and the Neustrians.

sacramentis firmauit, unicuique gradum honoris et dignetatem seo amiciciam perpetuo conseruarit.[1] Hanc dignetatem sublimatus Flaochadus regnum Burgundiae peruagatur consilium adseduae iniens, priorem inimiciciam qua cordis arcana dio celauerat memorans, Villebadum patricium interfecere disponebat.[2]

90

Willebadus cum esset opebus habundans et pluremorum facultates ingenies diuersis abstollens, ditatus inclete fuissit et inter patriciatum gradum et nimiae facultates aelacionem superbiae esset deditus, aduersus Flaochadum tumebat eumque dispicere quonaretur. Flaochadus collictis secum pontefecis et ducibus de regnum Burgundiae Cabilonno pro utiletate patriae tractandum minse Madio placitum instituit. Ibique et Willebadus multitudinem secum habens aduenit. Flaochadus ibidem Willebado interfecere nitebatur. Haec cernens Willebadus palacium noluit introire. Flaochadus foris contra Willebadum preliandum adgreditur. Amalbertus uero, germanus Flaochado ad pagandum [a] intercurrens ubi iam in congressione certamene conflige [b] debuerant, Willebadus Amalberto secum retenens de hoc aeuasit pericolum. Intercurrentes et citiris persunis separantur inlese. Flaochadus deinceps uehementem inibat consilium de interetum Villebadi.

Eo anno Nantildis regina moretur.[3] Ipsoque anno minse Septembre Flaochadus cum Chlodoueo regi et

---

[a] sc. pacandum   [b] 1 ; confligi 4b[2]

[1] cf. chap. 54, above

[2] Behind this feud may lie the wrath of certain Burgundians, probably from the Lyons-Valence district, led by Willebad, at having a Frank imposed on them as mayor (cf. Ewig, *Die fränkischen Teilungen*, p. 708 and *Die*

confirmed it by oath, that he would protect them all in their ranks and dignity and at the same time would assure them of his unswerving friendship.[1] In virtue of this promotion, Flaochad took careful counsel and went on progress through the kingdom of Burgundy ; and once more he discovered an old hatred that had long lain hidden in his heart : he planned to kill the patrician Willebad.[2]

90

Willebad had become very rich by seizing the properties of a great many people by one means or another. Seemingly overcome with pride because of his position of patrician and his huge possessions, he was puffed up against Flaochad and tried to belittle him. The latter summoned the bishops and dukes of the Burgundian kingdom to Chalon, and fixed the day for the Mayfield to consider matters of national interest. Willebad arrived with a great following. Flaochad here planned an attempt on his life, but Willebad got to hear of this and refused to enter the palace. Out came Flaochad to fight him but Amalbert, Flaochad's brother, interposed to pacify them at the very moment when they were on the point of fighting. Willebad forcibly secured Amalbert and escaped immediate danger. Others now intervened and they separated without harming one another. But thereafter Flaochad set about planning Willebad's death as a matter of urgency.

In this year died Queen Nantechildis.[3] And in the month of September of the same year Flaochad left

___

fränkischen Teilreiche, pp. 107 and 119). A different view is taken by Martin, *Études critiques*, p. 233, who detects no resistance movement but only a personal feud.
[3] 641/2

Erchynoaldo idemque maiorem domus et aliquibus primatebus Neustrasies de Parisiaco promouens per Senonas et Auticiodero Agustedunum accesserunt, ibique Chlodoueus Willibadum patricium ad se uenire precepit. Willibadus cernens inimicum consilium Flaochado et germano suo Amalberto, Amalgario et Chramneleno ducebus de suo intereto fuisse initum, colligens secum pluremam multitudinem de patriciatus sui termenum, etiam et ponteuecis seo nobelis et fortis quos congrecare potuerat, Agustedunum gradiendum iter adrepuit. Cui obuiam a Chlodoueo regi, Erchynoaldo maiorem domus et Flaochado Ermenricus domesticus dirigetur, eo quod Willebadus trepedabat utrum peracederit an suum deuitandum periculo repedarit, ut ab Ermenrici promissionebus preuentus, usque adgrederit Agustedunum ; quem ille credens condigne munerebus honorauit. Postergum eius Agustedunum accessit ibique tenturia cum suis nec procul ab urbe posuit. Eodemque diae quo ibidem peraccesserat Ailulfo Valenciae [1] urbis episcopo et Gysone comite ad preuedendum que agebantur Agustedunum dirixerat, qui a Flaochado in urbe retenti sunt.

In crasteno Flaochadus, Amalgarius et Chramnelenus, qui consilium de interetum Villebadi unianemeter conspirauerant, de urbem Agustedunum maturius promouentis citirique docis de regnum Burgundiae cum exerceto eis subiunguntur. Erchynoaldus cum Neustrasius quos secum habebat idemque arma sumens ad hoc bellum adgreditur. Willebadus ae contra tela priliae construens quoscumque potuit adunare, falangis uterque in congressione certamenes iungent ad prilium. In ea

---

[1] Possibly to be identified with that Agilolf who was one of the four advisers of Dagobert in his revision of the *Lex Baiuuariorum* : it was a strong

Paris with King Clovis, his mayor Erchinoald and certain of the Neustrian magnates, and went together to Autun by way of Sens and Auxerre. King Clovis there ordered the patrician Willebad to appear before him ; but Willebad saw that Flaochad, his brother Amalbert and the Dukes Amalgar and Chramnelen had plotted as enemies to kill him. Therefore he assembled a large force from the limits of his patriciate, as well as all the bishops, nobles and warriors whom he could collect, and took the road to Autun. King Clovis, mayor Erchinoald and Flaochad sent the domesticus Ermenric to meet him and to lead him on by promises to Autun, since Willebad was alarmed and uncertain whether to proceed further into the city, or whether he would escape danger on his return. Willebad trusted this domesticus. He showered presents upon him, proceeded behind him towards Autun and camped with his followers not far from the city. On the day of his arrival he sent Bishop Ailulf of Valence [1] and Count Gyso into Autun to discover what was going on there. They were detained in the city by Flaochad.

The next day Flaochad, Amalgar and Chramnelen, who were in agreement about the plan to kill Willebad, came early out of the city and were joined by the remaining Burgundian dukes, followed by their men. Erchinoald also seized his weapons and came out, with such Neustrians as he had with him, to do battle. Willebad for his part equally made preparations for battle and assembled round him as many warriors as answered his call. And so the two companies met. As the fight turned out, Willebad was attacked by Flaochad

---

Burgundian team (cf. Zöllner, ' Die Herkunft der Agilulfinger,' p. 256).

pugna Flaochadus, Amalgarius et Chramnelenus idemque Wandelbertus ducis cum suis in congressione certamenis contra Willebado pugnandum confligunt ; nam citiri ducis uel Neustrasiae, qui undique eodem debuerant circumdare, se retenentes aspiciaebant spectantes aeuentum, super Willebadum noluerunt inruere. Ibique Willebadus interfecetur, plurimi cum ipso de suis gladio trucedantur. Eo certamine citiris primus Bertharius comis palatii Francus de pago Vltraiorano contra Willebado confligit. Aduersus quem frendens Manaulfus Burgundio exiens deinter citiris cum suis aduersus Bertharium priliandum ; Bertharius eo quod prius illi amicus fuissit dicens : ' Veni sub clepeum meum, de hoc periculo te liberabo.' Cumque ad eum liberandum clepeum aeleuassit, Manaulfus cum conto Bertharium in pectore percuciens, citiri qui cum eum uenerant ipsumque circumdantes eo quod Bertharius nimium reliquis precessisset, uolneratur graueter. Tunc Chaubedo [1] filius Berthario, cernens patrem in pericolum mortis, curso uelucissemo patri auxiliandum perrexit, Manaulfo conto percusso in pectore terra prostrauit, citiris qui patri percusserant totusque interfecit. Sic Bertharium suum genetorum, ut fedelis filius prestante Domino liberabit a morte. Hy uero docis qui cum eorum exercito super Villebado inruere noluerant, tinturia Willebadi episcoporum et citerorum qui cum eum uenerant depredandum. Pluretas inibi auri et argenti capetur reliquisque rebus et aequitis ab hys qui priliare noluerunt percepti sunt. [2]

His ita gestis Flaochadus in crasteno de Agostedunum promouens Cabilonno perrexit. Ingressus in

---

[1] The same Chaubedo witnesses a charter dated 22 June 654, in

and the Dukes Amalgar, Chramnelen and Wandelbert with their men, while the remaining dukes and the Neustrians who should have surrounded them remained spectators, awaiting the outcome with no wish to throw themselves on Willebad. There Willebad was killed, and many of his followers were cut down with him. A count of the palace, Berthar, a Transjuran Frank, was first of them all to attack Willebad ; and the Burgundian Manaulf, gnashing his teeth with fury, left the ranks and came forward with his men to fight Berthar. Berthar had once been a friend of his, and said : ' Come under my shield, I will get you out of this danger,' and he lifted his shield to cover Manaulf. But the latter aimed a blow at his chest with his lance and his men surrounded him (for Berthar had come on too far by himself) and severely wounded him. But when Chaubedo,[1] Berthar's son, saw his father in danger of his life, he rode full pelt to his assistance, threw Manaulf to the ground with his spear through him, and set about killing all those who had wounded his father. And so by God's help, like the true son he was, he saved Berthar his father from instant death. Those dukes who had preferred not to throw their men upon Willebad now pillaged the tents of his bishops and the rest of his following, and much gold and silver fell to them. The non-fighters then made off with the horses and whatever else was left behind.[2]

On the morning after these happenings, Flaochad left Autun and advanced to Chalon, which he entered.

J. Havet, *Œuvres*, I (1896), p. 240, though I fail to see why Havet considered him probably identical with the Aubedo of chap. 71.

[2] P. Le Gentilhomme, *Mélanges de Numismatique Mérovingienne* (1940), p. 105, plausibly associates Willebad's scattered treasure with the coins discovered at Buis (Saône-et-Loire).

P

urbe, in crastenum urbi, nessio quo caso, maxeme tota incendio concrematur. Flaochadus iudicio Dei percussus, uixatus a febre conlocatur in scaua,[a] aeuicto nauale per Ararem fluuio quoinomento Saoconna Latona properans, in aetenere undecemo diae post Willibadi interetum amisit spiritum sepultusque est in ecclesia sancti Benigni suburbano Diuioninse. Credetur a plurimis,[1] hy duo Flaochadus et Willebadus, eo quod multa in inuicem per loca sanctorum de amicicias oblegandum sacramenta dedirant et uterque in populis sibi subgectis copeditates instincto iniqui oppresserunt semul et a rebus nudauerunt, quod iudicius Dei de eorum oppressione plurema multetudine liberassit et eorum perfedia et mendacia eos uterque interire fecissit.

---

[a] *See Bede's note on this word*, Retractatio in Actus Apostolorum, *ed. M. L. W. Laistner* (Mediaeval Academy of America, 1939), p. 145. *A. R. Lewis translates ' coaster'* (The Northern Seas, p. 106).

[1] For contemporary views cf. *Vita Eligii*, ed. Krusch, *M.G.H. Script. Rer. Mero.* IV, p. 715 and *Vita Sigiramni*, ibid. p. 613

On the following day this city was burnt to the ground by some mischance of which I am ignorant ; and Flaochad was struck down by divine judgement and attacked by fever. He was placed in a skiff on the river Arar (the Saône, they call it) and they made haste to Saint-Jean-de-Losne ; but he died on the way. It was eleven days after Willebad's death. He was buried in the church of Saint Bénigne, outside Dijon. Many believed [1] that since Flaochad and Willebad had time and again sworn mutual friendship in places holy to the saints and in addition had both greedily oppressed and robbed their people, it was God's judgement that delivered the land from their overweening tyranny and laid them low for their faithlessness and lying.

CONTINVATIONES

I

Igitur [a][1] Chlodoueus filius Dagoberti, de genere alieni-genarum [b][2] reginam accipiens nomine Baldethilde [c] prudentem atque eligantem, genuitque ex ea filios tres Chlothario, Childerico et Theuderico.[d] Habebatque maiorem domi palatii uirum strenuum atque sapientem nomine Erchinoaldo. Chlodoueus itaque in regno pacem habuit absque bella. In extremis uero uitae annis amens effectus uitam caruit regnauitque annis xviii.[3] Franci [e] quoque Chlotharium filium eius maiorem in regno statuunt cum prefata regina matre.

2

Eodem quoque tempore mortuus est Erchinoaldus maior domus palatii. Franci in incerto uacellantes [g] accepto consilio, Ebroino huius honoris cura ac dignitate statuunt. His [h] diebus Chlotharius rex a ualida febre correptus obiit in iuuentute regnauitque annis iiii.[4]

---

[a] *chap. 91*, 5. *I adopt Krusch's capitulation, though not his paragraphing.*
[b] 4b² ; alienarum 4a   [c] 4b² ; Belechilde 4a
[d] 4b² ; Childerico et Theuderico et Chlothario 4a   [e] *chap. 92*, 5
[f] 4b² ; anno 4a   [g] 4b² ; uallantes 4a   [h] *chap. 93*, 5

[1] The first ten chapters of the continuation are excerpted from the *Liber Historiae Francorum*, chaps. 43-53 (ed. Krusch, *M.G.H. Script. Rer. Mero.* ii). On this see G. Kurth, 'Étude critique sur le Liber Historiae Francorum,' *Études Franques*, i, 1919. The continuator adds some additional matter of his own.
[2] *Saxonorum*, *Lib. Hist. Franc.* chap. 43. She had been an Anglo-Saxon slave (cf. *Vita S. Balthildis*, chap. 2, ed. Krusch, ibid. p. 483).
[3] 657. Chlotar III succeeded him, perhaps after a short interregnum,

CONTINUATIONS

I

Now [1] Clovis, son of Dagobert, chose for his queen a foreigner [2] named Baldechildis, a sensible and attractive woman. By her he had three sons—namely Chlotar, Childeric and Theuderic. And the mayor of his palace, by name Erchinoald, was forceful and intelligent. So peace reigned in the kingdom of Clovis, and there were no wars. In his latter years, it is true, his mind became affected, and he died after reigning for eighteen years.[3] The Franks thereupon made his eldest boy, Chlotar, king, with the queen-mother by his side.

2

Erchinoald, mayor of the palace, died at the same time. Uncertain what to do, the Franks debated the matter and then bestowed on Ebroin the care and dignity of that office. About this time King Chlotar was seized with a fever and died, still in his youth, after reigning four years.[4] His brother Theuderic succeeded him, and

---

in October or November of the same year (cf. Courtois, ' L'avènement de Clovis,' p. 160). Clovis II's madness is plain lust for evil in *Lib. Hist. Franc.* chap. 44, the author of which champions the abbey of Saint-Denis against the king who robbed it of one of the saint's relics.

[4] Chlotar III died in the 16th year of his reign (673). The mistake may have arisen from the use made by the Neustrian author of *Lib. Hist. Franc.* of an Austrasian catalogue of kings, where the four years referred to Chlotar's reign over all three Frankish kingdoms (cf. Dupraz, *Le Royaume des Francs*, pp. 248 ff., though Levillain and others will not allow that Chlotar ever did rule over Austrasia).

Theudericus uero frater eius in regno successit ; Childericus enim frater in Auster a Francis in regno [a] eleuatus est aput Vulfoaldum ducem.

Eo [b] tempore Franci aduersus Ebroinum insidias praeparant, contra Theudericum consurgunt eumque a regno deiciunt. Crines capitis eius abscidentes tutunderunt Ebroinumque et ipsum tutundent et in Burgundia Luxouio monasterio inuitum dirigunt. Propter Childericum in Auster legacionem mittunt. Vna cum Vulfoaldo duce ueniens et eum super cunctum [c] regnum suscipiunt.

Erat [d] enim ipse Childericus rex leuis atque citatus nimis, gentem inuicem Francorum in sedicionem mittens in scandalum ac derisum, donec odium non modicum inter ipsos creuit usque ad scandalum et ruinam. Quo ingrauiscente, uno Franco nobile nomine Bodilone ad stipidem tensum [e] cedere contra legem praecepit.[1] Videntes hec Franci in ira magna commoti, Ingobertus uidelicet et Amalbertus uel reliqui maiores natu Francorum sedicionem contra ipsum Childericum concitauerunt. Memoratus Bodilo super eum cum reliquis quam plures surrexit insidiaturos in regem ; in Lauchoni silua [f2] una cum regina eius praegnante nomine Belichilde quod dici dolus est interfecit. Vulfoaldus quoque per fugam lapsus euasit, in Auster reuersus est. Franci uero Leudesio filio Erchinoaldi nobile in maiorem domatum statuunt per consilium beati Leudegarii et consorciorum eius. Ebroinus [g] hec

---

[a] 4b² ; in regno *om.* 4a   [b] *chap. 94,* 5   [c] 4b² ; cuntum 4a
[d] *chap. 95,* 5   [e] 4b² ; censo 4a
[f] 4b² ; in Lauconis siluam 4a   [g] *chap. 96,* 5

[1] cf. *Lex Salica,* 51
[2] Or Bondy, between Saint-Denis and Chelles ; but Levillain, following

his other brother, Childeric, was made king by the Franks of Austrasia, with the backing of Duke Wulfoald.

At that time the Franks plotted against Ebroin, and rose against Theuderic and deposed him. They shaved off the hair of both and tonsured them ; and Ebroin, thus tonsured, they despatched unwilling to the monastery of Luxeuil in Burgundy. Then they sent to Austrasia for Childeric ; and when he arrived with Duke Wulfoald, they made him king over the entire kingdom.

But this King Childeric was altogether too light and frivolous. The scandal and contempt that he aroused stirred up sedition among the Frankish people, until bitter hatred sprang up and he became a rock of offence to his own ruin. To make matters worse, he ordered, illegally, that a noble Frank named Bodilo, should be bound to a stake and thrashed [1] ; and this infuriated the Franks who saw it. Ingobert, Amalbert and other Frankish notables stirred up insurrection against Childeric ; and that same Bodilo together with the other conspirators fell upon the king, and slew him and, I am sorry to say, his pregnant queen, Belechildis, in the Forest of Livry.[2] Wulfoald escaped by flight and returned to Austrasia. The Franks now took the advice of the blessed Leudegar and his party : they bestowed the mayoralty of the palace upon the noble Leudesius, son of Erchinoald. When Ebroin heard of these troubles and of

---

H. Stein (' Encore la succession d'Austrasie,' p. 305) prefers the Bois de Lognes (Seine-et-Marne), S.E. of Lagny-sur-Marne. Another possibility that cannot be ruled out, as it is by Stein, is Leucone in Picardy. The fragmentary *Life* of St Lambert implies that the corpses were retrieved for burial by St Ouen (ed. Levison, *M.G.H. Script. Rer. Mero.* v, p. 612).

audiens has dissensiones, consilio accepto Francos inuicem discordantes conuocatis in ausilium sociis personis quam plurimis, cum multo comitatu exercituum [a] a Luxouio caenubio egressus in Francia regreditur. Vsque [b] Isra fluuium ueniens peraccessit, custodibus dormientibus interfecit ad Sanctam Maxenciam [1] adque Isra fluuium transiens quos ibi inuenit de insidiatoribus suis occidit. Leudesius maiorem domus una cum thesauros regis [2] per fugam dilapsus euasit. A Baciuo uilla [3] euadens aufugit ibique, adueniente Ebroino, thesauros [c] quos ibi repperit adpraehendit. Inde egressus Crisceco uilla ueniens in Pontio,[4] Leudesio sub dolo fidem promitti se simulans fefellit, facto placito ut coniuracione facta cum pacae discederint. Sed Ebroinus fallaciter agens ut solebat, conpatri suo insidias praeparans ipsum Leudesium interficit ; regem Theudericum in regno restituto, ipse suum principatum sagaciter restaurauit. Sanctum Leudegarium [5] episcopum crudelissimis tormentis caesum gladio peremi iussit ; Gaerenum germanum eius diuersa tormenta trucidauit. Reliqui uero Franci eorum socii per fugam lapsi, Ligere transgressi usque Vasconos transfugerunt ; quam plurimi uero in exilio damnati ultra non conparuerunt.

[a] 4b[2] ; comitatum exercitum 4a
[b] 4a *adds* in
[c] thesaurus 4a ; thesauros *all other MSS*

how the Franks were falling out with each other, he took counsel with the great number of friends he had summoned to assist him, and left the monastery of Luxeuil to return to Francia with a mighty force of followers. Approaching the river Oise, he found the sentries asleep at Pont-Saint-Maxence [1] and killed them. Then he crossed the river and killed those of his enemies that he found lying in ambush thereabouts. The mayor of the palace, Leudesius, escaped, decamping with the royal treasure. [2] Continuing his flight, he abandoned the villa of Baizieux, [3] where Ebroin arrived in time to seize the treasure that he found there. Then Ebroin left Baizieux and reached the villa of Crécy in Ponthieu. [4] He there deceived Leudesius by making a false promise that they should arrange a meeting and, after taking oaths to each other, should part friends. But as usual Ebroin acted treacherously. He laid an ambush for his godfather Leudesius and slew him. King Theuderic was restored to his throne and Ebroin himself speedily resumed control of affairs. He ordered the blessed Bishop Leudegar [5] to be executed after the cruellest tortures and slew his brother Gaerinus, also after refined tortures. Their remaining Frankish friends escaped by flight across the Loire into Gascony. Many were condemned to exile and were never seen again.

---

[1] near Compiègne (Oise)
[2] *Lib. Hist. Franc.* chap. 45 makes it clear that Leudesius fled with Theuderic.
[3] near Corbie (Somme)
[4] near Abbeville (Somme)
[5] cf. *Passio Leudegarii*, ed. Krusch, *M.G.H. Script. Rer. Mero.* v

3

In [a] Auster quoque mortuo Vulfoaldo duce Martinus dux et Pippinus filius Anseghysilo [1] quondam Franco nobile dominabantur, defunctis regibus. Conmissis inuicem principibus Ebroino, Martino adque Pippino aduersus Theudericum regem excitantur ad bellum. Commoto exercitu ad locum cui uocabulum est Lucofao [2] interim commissi ad praelium iniunt ; ibique magno certamine demicantes plurima pars [b] populi ex utrisque partibus corruit. Deuicti cum sociis Martinus atque Pippinus in fugam lapsi sunt ; persecutusque eos Ebroinus maxima parte de illa regione uastauit. Martinus ideoque Lauduno Clauato ingressus infra muros ipsius urbes muniuit. Persecutusque eum Ebroinus ueniens Erchrego uilla,[3] ad Laudunum Clauatum [c] nuncios dirigit Aglibertum ac Reolum Remensis urbis episcopum, ut fide promissa in incertum super uacuas capsas sacramenta falsa dederunt. Qua in re illae credens eos, a Lauduno Clauato egressus cum sodalibus ac sociis ad Erchrego [d] ueniens, illic cum suis omnibus interfectus est.

4

Ebroinus [e] quoque magis atque profusius crudeliter Francos obpremebat, donec tandem aliquando Ermenfredo [f] Franco minas parat, rebus propriis tollere disponit. Consilio cum suis patrato, nocte collecta manu sociorum per noctem super eum consurgens Ebroinum

---

[a] *chap. 97*, 5
[b] 4b^2 ; pras 4a. *See chap. 13, above.*
[c] 4b^2 ; Clauato 4a   [d] 4c^2 ; Ercheco 4a
[e] *chap. 98*, 5   [f] 4c$^{1, 2}$; Ermfredo 4a

3

After the death of Wulfoald and the disappearance of the
kings, Duke Martin and Pippin, son of the deceased
Ansegisel,[1] a Frank of noble stock, ruled over Austrasia.
But these two rulers, Martin and Pippin, fell out with
Ebroin. They stirred up war against King Theuderic,
and they led their force to a place called Bois-du-Fays,[2]
where they fought. Most of the followers of both sides
were engaged in what proved a great battle. Martin and
Pippin nd their supporters were beaten and put to flight.
Ebroin followed them up and laid waste most of that
region. Martin thereupon entered Laon, barricading
himself within the city walls. But Ebroin was behind
him, and when he reached the villa of Ecry[3] he sent
Aglibert and Bishop Reolus of Rheims as his representatives to Laon, where they gave undertakings but swore
falsely upon reliquaries that, unknown to him, were
empty. Yet Martin trusted them over this and left Laon
with his friends and supporters to go to Ecry. And there,
with all his companions they killed him.

4

Now Ebroin oppressed the Franks with ever-increasing
cruelty, until the day came when he was threatening to
rob a Frank named Ermenfred of his possessions. But
Ermenfred consulted his friends about this, and one
night collecting a band of them, burst in upon Ebroin

---

[1] Pippin II of Herstal ; his mother, Begga, was daughter of Pippin I.
Martin may have been duke of Champagne (Ewig) and uncle of Pippin
(Krusch).
[2] near Rethel (Ardennes)
[3] or Ercry, now Asfeld (Ardennes)

interfecit ; quo peremto ad Pippinum ducem [1] in Auster cum muneribus suis peruenit. Quo facto Franci, accepto consilio, Waratonem inlustrum uirum in loco eius honorem maiorem domatus constituerunt. [2] Idcirco praefatus Warato obsedis a Pippino duce [a] accipiens pace inuicem patrata. Erat id temporis memorato Waratone filius ualde efficax adque industrius, eruditus in consilio, qui uice patris cura palatii gerebat, nomine Ghislemarus, qui ob nimiam caliditatem ac sagacitatem patrem ab honore proprio subplantauit. Cui sanctus Audoinus episcopus increpabat sepius ac subinde ut ad pacem uel patris indulgentiam remearet ; qui audire rennuit et in duricia [b] cordis permansit. Fuerunt igitur inter Pippino et praefato Ghislemaro discordie multae et bella ciuilia plurima. Nam ad castro Namuco contra hostem Pippini ducis Ghislemaris consurgens, fraudulenter falso iuramento dato quam plures eorum nobilis uiris occidit. Inde uero reuersus, ob subplantationem patris uel alia malitia non modica quam fallaciter perpetrauerat a Deo percussus praedictus Ghislemaris, ut dignus erat iniquissimum fudit spiritum. Illoque mortuo pater eius Warato honorem pristinum maiorum domatus sui recepit. Eo [c] tempore beatus Audoinus episcopus plenus uirtutibus migrauit ad Dominum. [3]

5

In illo itidem tempore Warato praefatus maiorum domus obiit. Eratque ei matrona nobilis et strenua nomine

---

[a] 4b² ; ducae 4a   [b] 4b² ; duritiam 4a   [c] chap. 99, 5

[1] Pippin II is *Dux Austrasiorum*, a lesser office than the mayoralty of the Austrasian palace, held by Pippin I.
[2] 680. On the date of Ebroin's death and Waratto's succession, see R. L. Poole, *Studies in Chronology and History*, p. 61.

and killed him.   After Ebroin's murder, Ermenfred made his way, laden with presents, to Duke [1] Pippin in Austrasia.   Then the Franks met in council and chose the illustrious Waratto to be mayor of the palace in place of Ebroin.[2]   The same Waratto received sureties from Duke Pippin and in his turn swore peace with him.   But Waratto's son, Ghislemar, by this time had grown up into a very practical man of affairs and was experienced at court and ran the palace in his father's name.   A little too cunning and clever, he displaced his father from his rightful honour.   The blessed Bishop Ouen repeatedly admonished him to be reconciled to his father and ask his pardon ; but he refused to listen and persisted in his hardness of heart.   Thus there was deep discord and constant vendetta between Pippin and the aforesaid Ghislemar.   It came to the point when Ghislemar attacked Duke Pippin's force at the stronghold of Namur, wickedly swore false oaths and then slew many of his nobly-born warriors.   After which venture the same wicked Ghislemar was stricken by God, and died, as he deserved, in grievous sin in return for the supplanting of his father and other great wickedness he had wrought. After his death his father Waratto resumed his former position as mayor of the palace.   It was at this time that the blessed Bishop Ouen, that great worker of miracles, went to his rest.[3]

5

Now, too, died Waratto, mayor of the palace.   He had had a noble and vigorous wife named Anseflidis, and

---

[3] 684

Ansfledis, cuiusque gener nomine Bercharius honorem maiorum domatus palatii suscepit. Eratque statura paruus, intellecto modicus, leuis atque citatus, Francorum amicitia atque consilia sepe contempnens. Haec indignantes Franci Audoramnus, Reolus et alii multi relinquentes Bercharium ad Pippinum per obsides coniungunt, amicitias copulant, super Bercharium uel reliqua parte Francorum concitant.

Pippinus [a] commoto exercito hostile ab Auster consurgens contra Theudericum regem et Bercharium properans ad bellum, coniuncti in oppido Virmandense in loco qui dicitur Textricio [1] bellum mutuo gesserunt. Praeualente Pippino cum Austrasiis Theudericus rex cum Berchario fugam iniit ; Pippinus uictor extitit persecutusque eos ea regione subiugauit. Sequente tempore idem Bercharius ab adolatoribus falsis amicis interfectus est instigante Ansflede matrona socrui sua. Post haec autem Pippinus Theuderico rege accipiens cum thesauris et domum palatii omnia peragens in Auster remeauit. Eratque ei uxor nobilis et prudentissima nomine Plectrudis ; genuitque ex ea filios duos, nomen senioris Drocus, nomen uero iunioris Grimoaldus.

6

Mortuus [b] est autem Theudericus rex : regnauit autem annos XVII. [2] Chlodoueum filium eius paruulum elegerunt in regnum. Non post multos enim annos praedictus rex Chlodoueus egrotans mortuus est ; regnauit autem annos IIII. [3] Childebertus frater eius

[a] chap. 100, 5
[b] chap. 101, 5

her son-in-law, Berchar, became mayor of the palace. He was a little fellow of small ability, light-minded and impetuous. Frequently he slighted his Frankish friends and ignored their counsel. This angered Audoramnus, Reolus and many more of the Franks. So they abandoned Berchar and joined Pippin by sending him pledges, and swore friendship with him. They urged an attack upon Berchar and the Franks that remained with him.

Pippin then raised his warbands and set out with speed from Austrasia to do battle with King Theuderic and Berchar. They met near Saint-Quentin at a place called Tertry,[1] and there they fought. Pippin and his Austrasians were the victors : King Theuderic and Berchar were put to flight. The victorious Pippin gave chase and subjugated the region. Shortly afterwards the same Berchar was slain by false and flattering friends at the instigation of his mother-in-law, the lady Anseflidis. Then Pippin secured King Theuderic and his treasure, made all arrangements about the administration of the palace and returned to Austrasia. By his noble and most intelligent wife, Plectrudis, he had two sons, the elder called Drogo and the younger Grimoald.

6

King Theuderic died after a reign of seventeen years[2] and his little son Clovis was chosen to succeed him as king. But it was not long before King Clovis fell ill and died, having reigned four years.[3] His brother Childebert

---

[1] or Testri-sur-Omignon, near Saint-Quentin (Somme) ; 688
[2] 690-1   [3] 691-5

in regnum resedit. Drocus uero a Pippino genitore suo eruditus ducatum Campaninse accepit. Grimoaldus iunior cum Childeberto rege maior domus palatii super Francos electus est, fuitque uir mitissimus, omni bonitate et mansuetudine repletus, largus in elemosinis et in orationibus promptus.

Pippinus[a] contra Radbodem ducem gentilem Frigionum gentis aduersus alterutrum bellum intulerunt castro Duristate[1] illinc belligerantes inuicem. Pippinus uictor extitit, fugatoque Radbode duce cum Frigiones qui euaserant idem Pippinus cum multa spolia et praeda reuersus est. Post haec Drocus filius Pippino a ualida febre correptus, mortuus est et sepultus est in basilica beati Arnulfi confessoris Mettis urbe.[b] Grimoaldus quoque ex quadam concubina genuit filium nomine Theudoaldo.

Igitur[c] praefatus Pippinus aliam duxit uxorem nobilem et eligantem nomine Chalpaida,[2] ex qua genuit filium uocauitque nomen eius lingue proprietate Carlo ; creuitque puer, eligans atque egregius effectus est.[3]

7

Mortuus[d] est autem his diebus Childebertus rex[4] et sepultus Cauciaeco[5] in basilica sancti Stephani martyris: regnauit autem annos XVI. Dagobertus[6] filius eius sedem regni patris sui accepit. Igitur Grimoaldus filiam Radbodi ducem Frigionum duxit uxorem. Egrotante quoque Pippino Iobuilla super Mosam fluuium[7] cum ad eum uisitandum idem Grimoaldus

---

[a] chap. 102, 5   [b] 4a repeats sepultus est.
[c] chap. 103, 5   [d] chap. 104, 5
[1] Wyk-te-Duerstede on the Leck, S.E. of Utrecht

succeeded him. Drogo, meanwhile, brought up by Pippin his father, was given the duchy of Champagne, while his younger brother Grimoald became mayor of the palace to King Childebert, over the Franks. He was the mildest of men, full of kindness and gentleness ; and he was generous in almsgiving and constant in prayer.

Pippin and the pagan Radbod, duke of the Frisians, went to war and had a battle at the stronghold of Duurstede.[1] Pippin, the victor, returned with much spoil and booty, while Duke Radbod fled the field with such Frisians as escaped. Then Drogo, Pippin's son, died of a fever. He was buried in the church of the blessed confessor Arnulf at Metz. Grimoald, for his part, had a son named Theudoald by some mistress or other.

The aforesaid Pippin took a second wife, the noble and lovely Alpaida.[2] She gave him a son, and they called him in his own language Charles. And the child grew, and a proper child he undoubtedly was.[3]

7

It was now that King Childebert died,[4] and was buried at Choisy [5] in the church of the holy martyr Stephen. He had reigned sixteen years. His successor as king was his son Dagobert.[6] Grimoald married the daughter of Duke Radbod of the Frisians. It happened that Pippin fell ill at Jupille on the Meuse,[7] and this same

---

[2] Probably the mother of count Childebrand, under whose patronage this part of the continuation was written (cf. cont. chap. 34 below).
[3] cf. Luke i. 80 ; ii. 40 ; this alone would betray the continuator's feelings towards the Carolingians. If *elegans* has reference to Hebrews xi. 23 a comparison of Charles with Moses is implied.   [4] 711
[5] Choisy-au-Bac (Oise)   [6] Dagobert III   [7] near Liège

uenisset, cum ad orationem in basilica sancti Landeberti martyris [1] processisset a crudelissimo uiro impio Rantgario nomine interfectus est. Post haec Theudoaldo filio eius paruulo in loco ipsius cum praedicto rege Dagoberto maiorum domato palatii accepit.

8

Insecuto quoque tempore idem Pippinus dux egrotans mortuus est [2] : rexitque populum Francorum annos xxvii s. Reliquit superstitem Carlo filio suo.[3] Post obitum quoque eius Plectrudis matrona praefata suo consilio atque regimine cuncta sese agebat. Demum Franci mutuo in sedicionem uersi, consilio inutile accepto commisso acie in Cocia silua,[4] contra Theudoaldum et leudis Pippino quondam atque Grimoaldo inierunt certamen, corruitque ibi non modicus exercitus. Theudoaldus itaque a sodalibus suis per fugam lapsus euasit. Magna et ualida turbatio et persecutio extitit apud gentem Francorum.

Eodem [a] tempore tunc elegerunt in honorem maiorum domatum quodam Franco nomine Ragamfredo ; commotoque exercitu hostile usque Mosam fluuium properant cuncta uastantes. Cum Radbode duce foedus inierunt. His diebus Carlus dux a praefata femine Plectrude sub custodia detentus Dei auxilio liberatus est.

---

[a] *chap. 105*, 5
[1] at Liège
    16 December 714

Grimoald, when he came to visit him, was cruelly murdered by an impious wretch named Rantgar while on his way to prayer in the church of Saint Lambert, martyr.[1] His little son Theudoald was then made mayor of the palace to King Dagobert in his stead.

8

Some time after this, Duke Pippin fell ill and died.[2] He had ruled over the Franks for twenty-seven and one-half years. His son Charles survived him.[3] After his death his widow, the before-mentioned lady Plectrudis, took everything under her control. The end of it was that the Franks plotted a revolt. They took the foolish course of going to war with Theudoald and the erstwhile followers of Pippin and Grimoald. They came to blows in the Forêt de Cuise,[4] and the forces engaged were considerable. Theudoald fled from his companions and escaped. Great indeed was the consternation that ensued among the harried Franks.

They now chose as mayor of the palace a certain Frank named Ragamfred ; and raising a force they hastened to the Meuse, destroying everything in their path. They made a treaty with Duke Radbod. At this time Duke Charles was put in confinement by the aforesaid Plectrudis, but by God's help was set free.

---

[3] His surname *Martellus* is not attested before the ninth century. It is presumably based on Judas Maccabeus (=Hammer). See Ewig, *Das Königtum*, p. 44.

[4] Compiègne, 26 September 715 (cf. Levison, *Aus Rheinischer und Fränkischer Frühzeit*, p. 344)

9

Itidem [a] tempore Dagobertus rex obiit : regnauit
itaque annos v. Franci vero Chilpericum quendam
regem constituerunt.[b][1] Iterato quidem tempore, commoto exercito contra memoratum Carlum dirigunt ;
ex alia parte idem cum hoste Frigionum uenturo
Radbode [c] duce inuitant. Contra quem praedictus uir
Carlus cum exercitu suo consurgens certamen inuicem
inierunt, sed non modicum ibi perpessus est damnum
de uiris strenuis atque nobilibus, cernensque lesum
exercitum terga uertit. Chilpericus post haec uel
Raganfredus adunata hostile plebe Arduennam siluam
transeunt, ab alia parte prestolante Radbodo duce cum
exercitu suo ; actenus ad Coloniam urbem super Renum
fluuium peruenerunt, regiones illas pariter uastantes.
Munera multa et thesauros a praefata Plectrude
acceptum reuersus est ; sed in uia in loco qui dicitur
Amblaua [2] ab exercitu Carlo grande perpessus est
dispendium.

10

Succedente tempore Carlus commoto exercito contra
Chilpericum et Ragamfredum direxit. Bellum inierunt
die dominica in quadraginsimo xii Kl. Aprl. in loco
nuncupante Vinceco in pago Camaracense [3] ; nimia
cede inuicem conlesi sunt. Chilpericus uel Ragamfredus
deuicti in fugam lapsi terga uertentes euaserunt ;
quos Carlus persecutus usque Parisius ciuitate

[a] chap. 106, 5
[b] 4b[2] ; constituunt 4a
[c] 5a, following L. H. F. ; Radbodo 4a, b

[1] 715. Chilperic II, allegedly son of Childeric II, had been a monk
under the name of Daniel (Lib. Hist. Franc. chap. 52).

9

Now King Dagobert died, after a reign of five years ; and the Franks chose one Chilperic as king.[1] At the same time they assembled their army and set out against the said Charles ; and they invited Duke Radbod to come from the other direction with his army of Frisians. The warrior Charles went with his army to meet Radbod, and in the ensuing battle there was no small loss of brave and noble men. When Charles saw how his army had suffered, he retreated. Chilperic and Ragamfred now called together their forces and crossed the Forest of the Ardennes. Meanwhile on the other side Duke Radbod awaited them with his army. So they reached the city of Cologne on the Rhine. Together they laid waste that region. When they had received many gifts and much treasure from the said Plectrudis, they set out for home ; but on the way, at a place called Amblève,[2] Charles attacked them and inflicted heavy losses upon them.

10

Thereafter Charles summoned his army and marched against Chilperic and Ragamfred. A battle was fought on 21 March, a Sunday in Lent, at a place called Vinchy in the Cambrésis [3] ; and there were great losses on both sides. Chilperic and Ragamfred were beaten and escaped by flight. Hot in pursuit, Charles hurried to the city of Paris. Then he returned to Cologne and

---

[2] near Malmédy. Charles finally defeated Radbod in 718, but of this defeat Alcuin, in his *Life* of St Willibrord, is our only witness (ed. Levison, *M.G.H. Script. Rer. Mero.* VII, p. 127).

[3] 717 (cf. Levison, *Aus Rheinischer und Fränkischer Frühzeit,* p. 344) ; either Vincy (Aisne) or Vinchy 9 km south of Cambrai.

properauit. Deinde *a* Colonia urbe reuersus ipsam ciuitatem coepit. Reserata praefata Plectrude thesauros patris sui reddidit et cuncta suo dominio restituit ; regem sibi constituit nomine Chlothario.[1] Chilpericus itaque et Ragamfredus legationem ad Eodonem [2] dirigunt, eius auxilium postulantes rogant, regnum et munera tradunt. Ille quoque hoste Vasconorum commota ad eos ueniens pariter aduersus Carlum perrexerunt. At ille constanter intrepidus eis occurrere properat. Eudo territus quod resistere non ualeret, aufugit. Carlus insecutus eum usque Parisius Sequana fluuio transito usque Aurilianinse urbe peraccessit, et uix euadens, terminos regionis sue penetrauit, Chilperico rege secum cum thesauris sublatis euexit. Chlotharius itaque rex defunctus discessit.[3] Carlus per missos suos ab Eudone duce idemque praedicto Chilperico rege recepit. Veniensque urbe Nouiomo post non multum tempus cursum uite et regnum amisit *b* et mortuus est ; regnauitque annos VI.[4] Quo mortuo, Theuderico rege statuerunt in sedem regni, qui nunc locum solii regalis obtinet *c* annis uitae simul prestolatis.[5]

II

His ita euulsis Carlus princeps [6] insecutus idem Ragamfredo Andegauis ciuitatem obsedit ; uastata eadem regione, cum plurima spolia remeauit.

a chap. 107, 5
b 4b² ; ammisit 4a
c 4b² ; obtenit 4a

[1] 718. Chlotar IV, perhaps a son of Theuderic III ; presumably intended to rule over Austrasia only (see the views of E. Ewig in *Sankt Bonifatius Gedenkgabe* (Fulda 1954), p. 417).

took that city. At this point Plectrudis opened his father's treasure and surrendered it to him, together with control over everything. He himself chose a king, by the name of Chlotar.[1] So Chilperic and Ragamfred sent an embassy to Eudo,[2] to seek his help. They offered him the kingdom, with gifts as well. He raised a Gascon army and came to them ; and together they now proceeded against Charles, who hastened to meet them quite unperturbed and full of courage. Eudo was terrified when he saw that resistance was useless, and he fled. Charles followed him as far as Paris and, crossing the Seine, reached the city of Orleans. But he just escaped, and made his way into the confines of his own land, bearing with him King Chilperic and the treasure he had taken. King Chlotar now died.[3] Charles sent an embassy to Duke Eudo and received from him the said Chilperic. The latter then came to the city of Noyon where he soon afterwards died, thus bringing his reign to its close. He reigned six years.[4] After his death they raised King Theuderic to the throne, who still reigns over us and looks forward to years of life.[5]

11

Afterwards Prince [6] Charles pursued Ragamfred, laid siege to the city of Angers, laid waste the neighbourhood and then returned home with rich booty.

---

[2] Duke of Aquitaine   [3] 719
[4] 721. His successor Theuderic IV, also taken from the cloister, was son of Dagobert III.
[5] (Died 737.) *Lib. Hist. Franc.* stops at this point.
[6] i.e. mayor of the palace

Per [a] idem tempus [1] rebellantibus Saxonis eis Carlus princeps ueniens praeoccupauit ac debellauit uictorque reuertetur.

12

Succiduis diebus uoluto anni circulo,[2] coacto agmine multitudine Renum fluuium transiit Alamannosque et Suauos lustrat, usque Danubium peraccessit illoque transmeato fines Baguarinsis occupauit. Subacta regione illa thesauris multis cum matrona quandam nomine Beletrude [3] et nepta sua Sunnichilde [4] regreditur.

13

Per idem tempus Eodone duce a iure foederis recedente, quo conperto per internuntios Carlus princeps commoto exercito Liger fluuium transiens, ipso duce Eodone fugato praeda multa sublata bis eo anno ab his hostibus populata iterum remeatur ad propria. Eodo namque dux cernens se superatum atque derisum, gentem perfidam Saracinorum ad auxilium contra Carlum principem et gentem Francorum excitauit. Egressique cum rege suo Abdirama nomine Garonnam [b] transeunt, Burdigalensem urbem peruenerunt, ecclesiis igne concrematis, populis consumptis usque Pectauis profecti sunt [5]; basilica sancti Hilarii igne concremata, quod dici dolor est, ad domum beatissimi Martini euertendam destinant. Contra quos Carlus princeps audacter aciem

---

[a] *chap. 108*, 5   [b] 4c[2] ; Geronna 4a

[1] 724   [2] 725
[3] Wife of Duke Grimoald of Bavaria and widow of his brother Theudebald

The Saxons had risen in rebellion at that very time [1] ; so Charles attacked and defeated them. Then he went home victorious.

12

A year passed,[2] and Charles crossed the Rhine in force, punished the Alamans and Swabians, reached the Danube and crossed into Bavarian territory. When he had subjugated this land he returned home with great treasure, and also with a certain lady Beletrudis [3] and her niece Sunnichildis.[4]

13

It was at the same time that Duke Eudo broke the treaty ; and when news of this was brought to him, Prince Charles crossed the Loire with his army, put Duke Eudo to flight and came back with the rich booty he had collected in his two expeditions of that year. When Duke Eudo saw that he was beaten and an object of scorn, he summoned to his assistance against Prince Charles and his Franks the unbelieving Saracen people. So they rose up under their king 'Abd ar-Rahman and crossed the Garonne to the city of Bordeaux, where they burnt down the churches and slew the inhabitants. From thence they advanced on Poitiers [5] ; and here, I am sorry to say, they burnt the church of the blessed Hilary. Next they were directing their advance towards the like destruction of the house of the blessed Martin ; but taking boldness as his counsellor Prince Charles set the

---

[4] Later wife or mistress of Charles and the mother of his son Grifo
[5] cf. *Vita Pardulfi*, ed. Levison, *M.G.H. Script. Rer. Mero.* VII, p. 33

instruit, super eosque belligerator inruit. Christo auxiliante tentoria eorum subuertit, ad proelium stragem con-
terendam accurrit interfectoque rege eorum Abdirama
prostrauit, exercitum proterens, dimicauit atque deuicit[1];
sicque uictor de hostibus triumphauit.

14

Praecedente [a] alioquin anno sequente [2] egregius bellator
Carlus princeps regionem Burgundie sagaciter penetrauit, fines regni illius leudibus suis probatissimis uiris
industriis ad resistendas gentes rebelles et infideles
statuit,[3] pace patrata Lugdono Gallia suis fidelibus
tradidit. Firmata foedera iudiciaria reuersus est uictor
fiducialiter agens.

15

In illis quippe diebus Eodo dux mortuus est.[4] Haec
audiens praefatus princeps Carlus inito consilio procerum
suorum denuo Ligere fluuio transiit, usque Garonnam [b]
uel urbem Burdigalensem uel castro Blauia ueniens
occupauit illamque regionem coepit hac subiugauit cum
urbibus ac suburbana castrorum. Victor cum pace
remeauit opitulante Christo rege regum et domino
dominorum. Amen.

[a] chap. 109, 5
[b] Geronnam 4a ; Garonnam all other MSS

[1] Although its importance has sometimes been over-estimated, the
battle of Poitiers (October 732) was still the first military reverse of the
Arabs in the West and led to their evacuation of Aquitaine. Bede lived to
hear of it (Hist. Eccl. Book v, chap. 23). Charles' penetration into Burgundy
(see following chap.) is one direct consequence.   [2] 733

[3] Further information about Carolingian treatment of the Burgundian
church may be found in the Gesta Epis. Autisiodorensium (ed. G. Waitz,
M.G.H. Scriptores, xiii) and the Vita Eucherii (ed. W. Levison, M.G.H.
Script. Rer. Mero. vii).   [4] 735

battle in array against them and came upon them like a mighty man of war. With Christ's help he overran their tents, following hard after them in the battle to grind them small in their overthrow, and when 'Abd ar-Rahman perished in the battle he utterly destroyed their armies, scattering them like stubble before the fury of his onslaught; and in the power of Christ he utterly destroyed them.[1]   So did he triumph over all his enemies in this his glorious day of victory!

14

In the course of the following year,[2] that dauntless warrior Prince Charles swiftly penetrated into the land of Burgundy and established men of well-proven ability and valour within the boundaries of that kingdom, to curb disaffection as well as pagan penetration among the people.[3]   Once order had been secured he handed over the region of the Lyonnais to his followers. Having regularised his grants by charter he came home, his victories consolidated by the honesty of such administrative dealings.

15

Duke Eudo died at this time.[4]   Learning this, Prince Charles consulted with his chieftains, crossed the Loire and went to the city of Bordeaux and to the stronghold of Blaye on the Garonne. Then he proceeded to occupy the whole area, including the cities and strongholds. Then he returned in peace, victorious through Christ his helper, Who is King of kings and Lord of lords. Amen.

16

Curricula annorum actenus repperiuntur : Ab Adam uel initio saeculi usque diluuio ann. IICCXLII ; a diluuio usque ad Abraham ann. DCCCCXLII ; ab Abraham usque ad Moysen ann. DV ; a Moysen usque ad Salomonem ann. CCCCLXXVIIII ; a Salomone usque ad reedificationem templi temporibus Darii regis Persarum ann. DXII ; a restaurationem templi usque ad aduentum[1] domini nostri Iesu Christi ann. DXLVIII. Certe ab initio mundi usque ad passionem domini nostri Iesu Christi sunt anni VCCXXVIII et a passione Domini usque isto anno praesente, qui est in cyclo Victorii ann. CLXXVII, Kl. Ian. die dominica, ann. DCCXXXV ; et ut istum miliarium impleatur, restant ann. LXIII.[a]

17

Itemque,[2] quod superius praetermissimus, gentem dirissimam maritimam Frigionum nimis crudeliter rebellantem praefatus princeps audacter nauale euectione praeparat ; certatim alto mare ingressus nauium copia adunata Vnistrachia [b] et Austrachia insulas Frigionum penetrauit, super Bordine fluuio [3] castra ponens. Bubonem gentilem ducem illorum fraodolentum consiliarium interfecit, exercitum Frigionum prostrauit, fana eorum idolatria contriuit atque conbussit igne ; cum magna spolia et praeda uictor reuersus est in regnum Francorum.

[a] LXV 4a
[b] *correctly* Wistrachia *Krusch*

[1] More correctly, to our Lord's death. Krusch detects here the work of an interpolator whose chronology was based on the Incarnation, and who was also responsible for inserting the year 735 in the following sentence, where 736 would be correct.

16

The number of years that have gone is reckoned thus :—
From Adam or the beginning of the world to the Flood,
2242 years ; from the Flood to Abraham, 942 years ;
from Abraham to Moses, 505 years ; from Moses to
Solomon, 479 years ; from Solomon to the rebuilding
of the Temple in the days of Darius, King of the
Persians, 512 years ; from the rebuilding of the Temple
to the coming [1] of our Lord Jesus Christ, 548 years ;
thus from the beginning of the world to the Passion of
Our Lord Jesus Christ is 5228 years, and from the Lord's
Passion to the present year, which is the 177th year in
the cycle of Victorius, Sunday, 1 January, is 735 years.
Thus we lack 63 years to complete this millennium.

17

At this point [2] I must relate what I left out earlier on.
That wild seafaring race, the Frisians, broke out again
in fierce rebellion and our glorious prince, acting decisively as always, prepared a naval expedition, took to
the high seas with a great fleet and penetrated to the
Frisian islands of Westergo and Ostergo. He set his
base on the banks of the river Boorn.[3] He slew Bubo,
the heathen chieftain who had been leading the Frisians
into treachery, and shattered their army. He ground to
pieces the sanctuaries of their gods and burned them
with fire ; and then returned victorious to Francia, laden
with spoils and plunder.

---

[2] 734
[3] The same places occur in Willibad's *Vita Bonifatii*, ed. Levison, *Script. Rer. Germ. in usum scholarum*, 1905, p. 49.

18

Idcirco [1] sagacissimus uir Carlus dux commoto exercitu, partibus Burgundie dirigit Lugdunum Gallie urbem maiores natu atque praefectus eiusdem prouintie sua dicione rei publice subiugauit, usque Marsiliensem urbem uel Arelatum [a] suis iudicibus [2] constituit, cum magnis thesauris et muneribus in Francorum regnum remeauit in sedem principatus sui.

19

Itemque [3] rebellantibus Saxonis paganissimis [b] qui ultra Renum fluuium consistunt, strenuus uir Carlus hoste commoto Francorum in loco ubi Lippia fluuius Renum amnem ingreditur [4] sagace intentione transmeauit, maxima ex parte regione illa dirissima cede uastauit, gentemque illam seuissimam ex parte tributaria esse praecepit atque quam plures hospitibus [c] ab eis accepit ; sicque opitulante [d] Domino uictor remeauit ad propria.

20

Denuo [5] rebellante gente ualida Ismahelitarum quos modo Sarracinos corrupto uocabulo nuncupant inrumpentesque Rodanum fluuium, insidiantibus infidelis[e] hominibus sub dolo et fraude Mauronto [6] quidem cum

[a] 4c[1, 2] ; Arlatum 4a, b[2]   [b] 4b[2] ; paganissimos 4a
[c] sc. obsidibus *Krusch*   [d] 4b[2] ; oppitulante 4a
[e] 4b[2] ; infideles 4a

[1] 736
[2] sc. counts. This presumably means, as Zöllner has pointed out (*Die politische Stellung*, p. 94), that the traditional prefecture and patriciate of Provence were abolished.
[3] 738

18

Charles, that shrewdest of commanders, now [1] went with his army into the land of Burgundy against the city of Lyons. He subjected to his rule the chief men and officials of that province and placed his judges [2] over the whole region as far as Marseilles and Arles. Then he returned to the Frankish kingdom and the seat of his power with gifts and much treasure.

19

When [3] the Saxons, detestable pagans who live beyond the Rhine, rose in rebellion the warrior Charles set out with a Frankish army. He quickly crossed the Rhine at the place where the Lippe flows into it,[4] laid waste most of that region with frightful thoroughness and thus far he taught the men of that region of savages the lesson of paying their taxes, took from them many hostages and came home a conqueror, the good Lord being still his helper.

20

Once more [5] the mighty race of Ishmael, who are now known by the outlandish name of Saracens, rebelled and burst across the river Rhône. With the base, craven collaboration of the heretical Maurontus [6] and his friends,

---

[4] near Wesel

[5] 737. St Boniface's letter to the abbess Bugga (Tangl, No. 27) about Saracen attacks *apud Romanos* may well refer to this situation in southern Gaul.

[6] Referred to in chap. 21, below, as *dux* ; but this does not mean that he was a patrician (cf. Ganshof, ' Les avatars d'un domaine de l'église de Marseille à la fin du viie et au viiie siècle,' *Studi in onore di Gino Luzzatto*, 1949, p. 60).

sociis suis, Auennionem urbem munitissimam ac montuosam ipsi Sarracini collecto hostile agmine ingrediuntur, illisque rebellantibus, ea regione uastata. Ad contra uir egregius Carlus dux germanum suum uirum inlustrium [a] Childebrando [1] ducem cum reliquis ducibus et comitibus illis partibus cum apparatu hostile diriget. Quique praepropere [b] ad eandem urbem peruenientes tentoria instruunt, undique ipsud oppidum et suburbana praeoccupant, munitissimam ciuitatem obsedunt, aciem instruunt, donec insecutus uir belligerator Carlus praedictam urbem adgreditur, muros circumdat, castra ponit, obsidionem coaceruat. In modum Hiericho [2] cum strepitu hostium et sonitum tubarum, cum machinis et restium funibus super muros et edium moenia inruunt, urbem munitissimam ingredientes succendunt, hostes inimicos suorum capiunt, interficientes trucidant atque prosternent et in sua dicione efficaciter restituunt. Victor igitur atque bellator insignis [c] Carlus intrepidus Rodanum fluuium cum exercitu suo transiit, Gotorum fines penetrauit, usque Narbonensem Galliam peraccessit, ipsam urbem celeberrimam atque metropolim eorum obsedit, super Adice fluuio munitionem in girum in modum arietum instruxit, regem Sarracinorum nomine Athima [3] cum satellitibus suis ibidem reclusit castraque metatus est undique. Haec audientes maiores natu et principes Sarracinorum, qui commorabantur eo tempore in regione [d] Spaniarum, coadunato exercito hostium, cum

[a] industrium *all MSS*
[b] ? quampropere (*Mr Douglas' conjecture*)
[c] 4c[1, 2] ; insignes 4a, b[2]   [d] 4b[2] ; regionem 4a

[1] *vir inluster* sometimes signifies rank in Frankish Latin. For Childebrand, a big property-owner in Burgundy, cf. chap. 34, below.
[2] Joshua vi. 20

the Saracens attacked in force the city of Avignon strongly fortified on her rock; and they laid waste the countryside wherever resistance was offered. But our noble Duke Charles sent against them his illustrious [1] brother Duke Childebrand, who proceeded to that region in warlike array with the remaining dukes and counts. Childebrand lost no time in bivouacking in the approaches and surrounding countryside of this excellently provisioned city and in setting about his preparations for the forthcoming engagement until the arrival of Charles, the great commander, who forthwith shut up the city, erected siegeworks and tightened the blockade. Then as once before Jericho,[2] the armies gave a great shout, the trumpets brayed and the men rushed in to the assault with battering rams and rope ladders to get over walls and buildings ; and they took thát strong city and burned it with fire and they took captive their enemies, smiting without mercy and destroying them and they recovered complete mastery of the city. Victorious, therefore, Charles, the dauntless, mighty warrior, crossed the Rhône with his men and plunged into Gothic territory as far as the Narbonnaise. He invested its famous capital, Narbonne itself. He threw up lines on the banks of the Aude in which he installed offensive armament of the battering type. He then continued his lines in a wide sweep round the Saracen emir 'Abd ar-Rahman [3] and his viziers, investing them so. He added carefully constructed works at intervals. When news of this reached them, the chief lords and princes of the Saracens who were still in Spain collected an army out of their united manpower to fight a pitched battle, and set out bravely

---

[3] Iussef ibn 'Abd ar-Rahmān ? (Krusch)

R

alio rege Amormacha nomine aduersus Carlum uiriliter armati consurgunt, praeparantur ad proelium. Contra quos praefatus uir Carlus dux triumphator,[a] super fluuium Byrra et uale Corbaria [1] palatio occurrit. Illisque mutuo confligentibus Sarracini deuicti atque prostrati, cernentes regem eorum interfectum in fugam lapsi terga uerterunt ; qui euaserant cupientes nauale euectione euadere, in stagnum maris natantes, namque sibimet mutuo conatu insiliunt.[b] Mox Franci cum nauibus et iaculis armaturiis super eos insiliunt [b] suffocantesque in aquis interimunt. Sicque Franci triumphantes de hostibus praeda magna et spolia capiunt, capta multitudine captiuorum, cum duce uictore regionem Goticam depopulant. Vrbes famosissimas Nemausum, Agatem hac Biterris, funditus muros et moenia destruens igne subposito concremauit, suburbana et castra illius regionis [c] uastauit. Deuicto aduersariorum agmine, Christo in omnibus praesule et caput salutis uictorie, salubriter remeauit in regionem suam in terra Francorum solium principatus sui.

21

Denuo curriculo anni illius mense secundo [2] praedictum germanum suum cum plurimis [d] ducibus atque comitibus commoto exercitu partibus Prouintie dirigit.[e] Auennionem urbem uenientes, Carlus properans per-

---

[a] 4b² ; 4a *adds* occurrit
[b] 4b² ; insiluunt 4a
[c] 4b² ; regiones 4a
[d] 4b² ; pluribus 4a
[e] diriget 4a ; dirigit *all other MSS*

in arms to meet Charles under another emir, Omar-ibn-Chaled. Our unconquerable Duke Charles made all haste to meet them upon the banks of the Berre, at the palace in the valley of the Corbières.[1] They fought a hard battle, and the Saracens were routed and overwhelmed, and when they saw that their emir had fallen they broke and ran. The survivors, with some idea of escaping in boats, swam out into the sea-lagoons. They fought among themselves in their struggle to get aboard. The Franks were quickly after them in boats with whatever weapons came to hand and pushed them down and drowned them in the water. This was how the Franks reached the decisive victory, took great spoil and booty and a host of prisoners. And then, under the command of their conquering duke they laid waste the Gothic region. The famous cities of Nîmes, Agde and Béziers were burnt, and their walls and buildings he razed to the ground. Their suburbs and the strongholds of that area were destroyed. When, with Christ's help, who alone gives victory and salvation, his enemies were destroyed, Charles returned without hurt to the land of the Franks and to the seat of his power.

21

Later on in the course of this happy year [2] Charles despatched an army under his above-named brother and many dukes and counts with orders to march on Provence. As they reached the city of Avignon Charles himself

---

[1] Aude. The *palatium* was allegedly built by the Visigothic King Athaulf. The swamp would have been the Étang de Leucate and the neighbouring marshland.

[2] Either *illius mense* is interpolated or, as Krusch prefers, we may read *menso* and take *secundo* adverbially.

accessit cunctamque regionem usque litus maris magni
sue dominationi restituit, fugato duce Mauronto in-
penetrabilibus, tutissimis rupibus, maritimis munitioni-
bus.[1] Praefatus princeps Carlus cuncta sibimet adquisita
regna uictor regressus est, nullo contra eum rebellante.
Reuersusque in regione Francorum, egrotare coepit in
uilla Vermbria super Isra fluuium.[2]

22

Eo [a] etenim tempore [3] bis a Roma sede sancti Petri
apostoli beatus papa Gregorius [4] claues uenerandi
sepulchri cum uinculo [b] sancti Petri [5] et muneribus
magnis et infinitis legationem, quod antea nullis auditis
aut uisis temporibus fuit, memorato principi destinauit,
eo pacto patrato, ut a partibus imperatoris recederet
et Romano consulto [6] praefato principe Carlo sanciret.
Ipse itaque princeps mirifico atque magnifico honore
ipsam legationem recepit, munera praetiosa contulit
atque cum magno praemio cum suis sodalibus missa,
Grimone abbati Corbeinsis monasterio et Sigoberto
recluso basilicae sancti Dionisii martyris, itemque Roma
limina sancti Petri et sancti Pauli destinauit.

---

[a] *chap. 110*, 5
[b] 4b² ; uincula 4a

[1] Although he mistranslated this passage, T. Hodgkin gives a fine
summary of Charles' operations in the Midi (*Italy and Her Invaders*, vol. vii,
book viii, chap. 3).
[2] near Senlis (Oise)
[3] 739
[4] Gregory III
[5] cf. the pope's letter to Charles Martel, preserved in the *Codex Carolinus*

caught them up in haste ; and he restored the whole country, down to the Mediterranean, to his rule. Duke Maurontus sought refuge in the impenetrable rocky fastnesses out to sea.[1] When Prince Charles had added to himself all the countries round about, so that none rebelled against him, he came back victorious to Frankish territory. But his health began to decline at the villa of Verberie on the Oise.[2]

22

At this time [3] the blessed Pope Gregory [4] twice sent an embassy from the seat of the holy apostle Peter at Rome to Prince Charles, with the keys of the tomb of the saint, a link from his chains [5] and many rich presents. Such things had never been seen or heard of before. The pope proposed a bargain whereby he should desert the imperial cause and, with the approval of the Roman people,[6] join that of the said Prince Charles. The prince received the embassy with extraordinary honours and made it costly gifts. He then sent Grimo, abbot of Corbie, Sigebert, a monk of the cloister of the holy martyr Denis and others of his entourage with fine presents to the threshold of Saint Peter and Saint Paul at Rome.

(ed. Gundlach, *M.G.H. Epist. Mero. et Karo. Aevi*, I, pp. 478-9). An earlier recipient of a similar gift was Oswiu's queen (Bede, *Hist. Ecc.* III, chap. 29). ' Chain-filings ' is an alternative translation. The ' holy sepulchre ' is St Peter's. There are many references in Pope Gregory I's correspondence to such gifts. I am indebted to Mr Charles Rosser for help in this matter.

[6] cf. Ganshof, ' Note sur les origines byzantines du titre Patricius Romanorum,' *Mélanges H. Grégoire*, II (1950), pp. 272-3, who argues, against Krusch, that *consultus* is not a mistake for *consulatus*.

23

Igitur memoratus princeps, consilio obtimatum suorum expetito filiis suis regna diuidit. Idcirco primogenito suo Carlomanno nomine Auster, Suauia, que nunc Alamannia dicetur, atque Toringia sublimauit ; alterius uero [a] filio iuniore Pippino [1] nomine Burgundiam, Neuster et Prouintiam praemisit.

24

Eo anno Pippinus dux, commoto exercito, cum auunculo suo Childebrando duce et multitudine primatum et agminum satellitum plurimorum Burgundia dirigunt, fines regionum praeoccupant. Interim, quod dici dolor et meror est, sollicitatur ruina, in sole et luna et stellis noua signa apparuerunt,[2] seu et paschalis [b] ordo sacratissimus turbatus fuit. Carlus nimpe princeps Parisius basilicam sancti Dionisii martyris multa munera ditauit, ueniensque Cariciaco uilla palatii super Isra fluuium,[3] ualide febre correptus obiit in pace, cuncta in giro regna adquisita. Rexit [4] autem utraque [c] regna an. xxv s. Transiit itaque xi Kl. Noub.[5] sepultusque est Parisius basilica sancti Dionisii martyris.[d]

---

[a] 4b[2] *adds* secundo
[b] 4c[1, 2] ; paschales 4a
[c] 4c[2] ; utrasque 4a, 4b[2]
[d] *MSS of group V, with their separate capitulation, end at this point.*
[1] the future Pippin III

23

Our prince then, on the advice of his magnates, divided the kingdoms between his sons. He raised the elder, Carloman, to the dignity of ruler over Austrasia, Swabia (now known as Alamannia) and Thuringia. His younger son, Pippin,[1] he set over Burgundy, Neustria and Provence.

24

In this year Duke Pippin raised an army and set out for Burgundy with his uncle, Duke Childebrand, and many noblemen and a great company of followers ; and they took over control of that land. But meanwhile, it grieves me deeply to relate, there appeared harbingers of misfortune, signs in the sun, and the moon and in the stars,[2] and the date of the most holy order of celebration of Easter was the subject of debate. Sure enough, Prince Charles, having bestowed rich gifts on the church of the blessed martyr Denis at Paris, fell ill of a fever on arriving at the palace of Quierzy on the Oise [3] ; and there he died in the peace of Holy Church. His dominion was over all the lands round about, and he had ruled [4] over the two kingdoms for twenty-five and one-half years. He died on 22 October [5] and was buried at Paris in the church of the blessed martyr Denis.

---

[2] 740 ; cf. Luke xxi. 25

[3] Aisne

[4] Not in the technical sense ; but there had been no king since the death of Theuderic IV in 737.

[5] 741, but just possibly on 15 October. (cf. Levison, *Aus Rheinischer und Fränkischer Frühzeit*, p. 343).

25

Chiltrudis quoque filia eius, faciente consilio nefario nouerce [1] sue fraudulenter per manus sodalium suorum Renum transiit et ad Odilonem ducem Bagoariis peruenit ; ille uero eam ad coniugium copulauit contra uoluntatem uel consilium fratrum suorum. Interea [2] rebellantibus Wascones in regione Aquitaniae [a] cum Chunoaldo duce filio Eudone quondam, Carlomannus atque Pippinus germani principes congregato exercito Liger alueum Aurilianis urbem transeunt, Romanos proterunt, usque Beturgas urbem accedunt, suburbana ipsius igne conburent, Chunoaldo duce persequentes fugant cuncta uastantes, Lucca [3] castrum dirigunt atque funditus subuertunt, custodes illius castri capiunt [4] ; etenim uictores existunt. Praedam sibi diuidentes habitatores eiusdem loci secum captiuos duxerunt. Inde reuersi circa tempus autumni eodem [b] anno iterum exercitum admouerunt ultra Renum contra Alamannos sederuntque castra metati super fluuium Danuvii in loco nuncupante . . .,[5] usquequo habitatores Alamanni se uictos uidentes obsides donant, iura promittunt, munera offerunt et pacem petentes eorum se dicione submittunt.

---

[a] 4c[2] ; Aquitania 4a, 4b[2]
[b] 4c[1, 2] ; eadem 4a, 4b[2]
[1] Sunnichildis ; see cont. chap. 12, above
[2] 742

25

His daughter, Chiltrudis, now did what her wicked step-mother [1] told her : with friends' help she went secretly over the Rhine to Duke Odilo of the Bavarians, who married her against the wishes and without the per-mission of her brothers. Meanwhile [2] the Gascons of Aquitaine rose in rebellion under Duke Chunoald, son of the late Eudo. Thereupon the princely brothers Carloman and Pippin united their forces and crossed the Loire at the city of Orleans. Overwhelming the Romans they made for Bourges, the outskirts of which they set on fire ; and as they pursued the fleeing Duke Chunoald they laid waste as they went. Their next objective, the stronghold of Loches,[3] fell and was razed to the ground, the garrison being taken prisoner.[4] Their victory was complete. Then they divided out the booty among themselves and took off the local inhabitants to captivity. Having got home about the autumn of the same year, they set out again with an army across the Rhine to fight the Alamans. They made their camp on the banks of the Danube at a place called . . . .[5] The Alamans belonging to those parts saw that they were beaten, and so they gave hostages, promised to observe their conquerors' laws, presented gifts, begged for terms and submitted to Frankish overlordship.

---

[3] Indre-et-Loire
[4] cf. *Annales Regni Francorum, sub anno* 742 (ed. Kurze, *Script. Rer. Germ. in usum scholarum.*)
[5] The name seems to have been deliberately removed.

26

Inde reuersi anno secundo [1] regni eorum cognatus eorum Odilo dux Bagoariorum contra ipsos rebellionem excitat. Conpulsi sunt generalem cum Francis in Bagoaria admoueri exercito uenientesque super fluuium qui dicitur Lech sederunt super ripam fluminis uterque exercitus, hinc inde se mutuo uidentes usque ad quindecim diebus. [2] Qui tantundem prouocati inrisionibus gentes illius, indignatione commoti periculo se dederunt per loca deserta et palustria, ubi pons [a] transiunde nullatenus adherat; nocteque inruentes diuisis exercitibus eos inprouisos occupauerunt, commissoque proelio praedictus dux Odilo ceso exercitu suo uix cum paucis turpiter ultra Igne fluuium fugiendo euasit. His triumphis peractis non sine dispendio multorum, tamen feliciter uictores ad propria remeauerunt.

27

Euoluto triennio [3] iterum Carlomannus confinium Saxonorum [b] ipsis rebellantibus cum exercitu inrupit ibique captis habitatoribus qui suo regno adfinis esse uidebantur absque belli discrimine [c] feliciter adquisiuit, et plurimos eorum Christo duce baptizatis sacramenta consecrati fuerunt. Per idem tempore rebellante

---

[a] *Krusch's conjecture* ; mons *all MSS*
[b] Saxanorum 4a ; Saxonòrum *all other MSS*
[c] 4c[1, 2]; discrimini 4a, b[2]

[1] 743. In this year also they placed on the throne the last Merovingian, Childeric III, who ruled till 751. He is known only from legal instruments (Pertz, *M.G.H. Dipl.* i, prints two) ; no narrative source mentions him.

26

When they got back—it was the second year of their rule[1] —their brother-in-law, Odilo, duke of the Bavarians, rose in revolt. Thus they had no option but to direct the whole Frankish army towards Bavaria. Reaching the Lech, the two forces camped on its banks and observed one another for a whole fortnight.[2] Finally, stung by the tribesmen's taunts the Franks were shamed into making their way through the marshy terrain, heedless of danger, in a place where there was no vestige of a causeway. They had divided their forces, and now at night fell upon the unsuspecting Bavarians. In the ensuing fight Duke Odilo's army was slaughtered ; and he himself had difficulty in slinking away with a handful of men beyond the river Inn. After which glories the victors made for home, triumphant despite heavy losses.

27

During their third year,[3] Carloman again invaded Saxon marcher territory, where there was trouble. Fortunately, the Saxons who lived on the Frankish frontier submitted without a fight and were enslaved ; and most of them, Christ being our leader, received baptism, and the sacraments began to be provided them. Theudebald,

---

The insoluble problem of when exactly Childeric was tonsured and relegated to the abbey of Saint Bertin is fully discussed by Krusch, *M.G.H. Script. Rer. Mero.* VII, pp. 508 ff.

[2] At Apfeldorf, near Epfach. The Metz annalist records how Pippin taunted the papal legate, who was in Odilo's company at the time (*Annales Mettenses Priores, sub anno* 743, ed. B. de Simson, *M.G.H. Script. Rer. Germ.* 1905, p. 35).

[3] 744. St Boniface presumably took part in the subsequent conversions.

Theudobaldo filium Godafredi [a] duce,[1] Pippinus cum
uirtute exercitus sui ab obsidione Alpium [2] turpiter ex-
pulit fugientem, reuocatoque sibi eiusdem loci ducato
uictor ad propria remeauit.

28

Inde reuersi praecelsi germani, sequente anno [3] prouocati coturno Wasconorum, iterum usque ad Ligerem
fluuium pariter adunati uenerunt.   Quod uidentes
Vascones praeoccupauerunt pacem petentes et uoluntatem Pippini in omnibus exequentes, muneratum eum,
a finibus suis ut rediret [b] precibus obtinuerunt.

29

His ita transactis, sequente anno [4] dum Alamanni
contra Carlomanno eorum fide fefellissent, ipse cum
magno furore cum exercitu in eorum patria peraccessit
et plurimos eorum qui contra ipso rebelles existebant
gladio trucidauit.[5]

30

His itaque gestis, sequente curriculo annorum [6] Carlomannus deuotionis causa inextinctu succensus, regnum
una cum filio suo Drogone [c] manibus germani sui

[a] 4b² ; Godafredo 4a
[b] 4b² ; rideret 4a
[c] 4c¹, ² ; Drohone 4a, b²

[1] Of Alamannia, whose connection with the Merovingian dynasty and
championing of their cause against the Arnulfings is argued by L. Levillain,
' Les Nibelungen historiques,' 1938, p. 42. Not only Theudebald (the
bearer of a Merovingian family name) but his brothers Huoching and

son of Duke Godafred,[1] chose this moment to revolt. Pippin with the pick of his forces winkled him out from his Alpine fastness [2] and put him to ignominious flight and so brought the duchy to heel before returning triumphant.

28

In the year following their return,[3] the famous pair of brothers once more made an expedition to the Loire; for the Gascons were provoking them. When they saw this, the Gascons lost no time in making overtures of peace, submitted in every particular to Pippin's orders, and besought him with gifts and supplications to leave their land.

29

The year after these happenings,[4] Carloman went in great wrath with his army to the territory of the Alamans, who had broken their oath of fidelity to him. Most of those who had rebelled were put to the sword.[5]

30

In the course of the year following this,[6] Carloman, burning for the contemplative life, handed over his rule together with his son Drogo to his brother Pippin and

---

Lantfrid I, and the latter's son, Lantfrid II, rose against Arnulfing domination.

[2] The Vosges, or, more probably, the Swabian Alps
[3] 745   [4] 746
[5] At Cannstatt, in Württemberg
[6] 747, after August 15

Pippini [a] committens, ad limina beatorum apostolorum Petri et Pauli Romam ob monachyrio ordine perseueraturus aduenit. Qua successione Pippinus roboratur in regno.

31

Eodem anno [1] Saxones more consueto fidem quam germano suo [2] promiserant mentire conati sunt. Qua de causa adento [b] exercitu eos praeuenire conpulsus est ; cui etiam reges Winidorum seu Frigionum ad auxiliandum uno animo conuenerunt. Quod uidentes Saxones consueto timore conpulsi, multi ex eis iam trucidati et in captiuitate missi, regiones eorum igneque crematis pacem petentes, iure Francorum sese ut antiquitus mos fuerat subdiderunt et ea tributa [3] quae Chlothario quondam prestiterant plenissima solutione ab eo tempore deinceps esse reddituros promiserunt. Ex quibus plurima multitudo uidentes se contra impetum Francorum rebellare non posse, propriis uiribus destituti petierunt sibi Christianitatis [c] sacramenta conferre.

32

Quo peracto tempore [4] Baiorii consilio nefandorum [5] iterum eorum fide fefellunt et contra praefato principe eorum fide mentiti sunt. Qua de re commoto exercito cum magno agmine apparatu eorum patrias peraccessit. Ipsi uero terrore conpulsi ultra fluuium Igni cum

[a] 4c[1, 2] ; germano suo Pippino 4a, b[2]
[b] *for* attento, *sc.* directo, *Krusch*
[c] 4c[1, 2] ; christianitate 4a

went to the threshold of the blessed apostles Peter and Paul in Rome, in order to become a monk. This succession strengthened Pippin's rule.

31

That same year,[1] the Saxons behaved in their accustomed way by breaking the oath of obedience that they had sworn to his brother.[2] So Pippin had no option but to raise an army and forestall them, the kings of the Wends and of the Frisians coming gladly to his assistance. Seeing this, the Saxons as usual fell victims to fear ; and they sued for terms when already many of them had been killed and taken off into slavery and their lands burnt. They submitted to Frankish control in the ancient manner and promised henceforth to pay in full the tribute,[3] which they had once owed to Chlotar. Most of them asked to have the sacraments made available when it became clear that it was impossible to rebel against the Franks, reduced, as they were, to impotence.

32

It was not long [4] before the Bavarians once again broke faith and, acting on bad advice,[5] cast off their allegiance to the aforesaid prince, who accordingly summoned his forces and marched in great strength upon their land. Terror-stricken, they fled with their

---

[1] 747-8
[2] cf. cont. chap. 27, above
[3] 500 cows, annually (cf. chap. 74, above)
[4] 749
[5] That of the Carolingian Grifo, whose death is recorded in cont. chap. 35, below.

uxoribus ac liberis eorum fugientes, et memoratus princeps super ripam Igni castra metatus, nauale proelium praeparauit qualiter eos ad internitionem persequeretur. Quod uidentes Baiorii *a* eorum uiribus se auxiliare non posse, legatos cum munera multa transmittunt et in eius dicione se subdant et sacramenta uel obsides donant, ut ne ulterius rebelles existant. Ipse uero duce Christo cum magno triumpho in Frantia ad propria sede feliciter remeauit et quieuit terra a proeliis annis duobus.

33

Quo tempore una cum consilio et consensu omnium Francorum missa relatione ad sede apostolica [1] auctoritate praecepta praecelsus Pippinus electione totius Francorum in sedem regni cum consecratione episcoporum et subiectione principum una cum regina Bertradane,[2] ut antiquitus ordo deposcit,[3] sublimatur in regno.[4]

34

Vsque *b* nunc inluster uir Childebrandus comes auunculus [5] praedicto rege Pippino hanc historiam uel gesta

---

a 4b[2] ; Bagoarii 4a

b *4a alone has this important chapter, but not in capitals as printed in Krusch.*

[1] cf. the so-called *Clausula de unctione Pippini*, which confirms this (ed. Arndt and Krusch, *M.G.H. Script. Rer. Mero.* I, p. 465). The huge literature on this subject is evaluated, and the authenticity of the *Clausula* defended, in Wattenbach-Levison, *Deutschlands Geschichtsquellen*, II, p. 163.

[2] His family, and not just Pippin personally, is raised to kingship (cf. Kern, *Gottesgnadentum u. Widerstandsrecht*, ed. Buchner, 1954, p. 78) in place of the Merovingians.

[3] The order, that is, required by St Augustine (*De Civ. Dei*, 19, 13).

wives and children beyond the river Inn. The said prince placed his headquarters on the banks of the Inn, where he made preparations to annihilate them in an engagement by boats. The Bavarians observed this, and knew that they could not resist such power. So they despatched a mission to him with plenty of presents, submitted to his overlordship and undertook by oath and with hostages not to rebel again. Christ being his helper, he then went home in great triumph to Francia, his task fulfilled. For two years the land had peace.

33

It now happened that with the consent and advice of all the Franks the most excellent Pippin submitted a proposition to the Apostolic See,[1] and having first obtained its sanction, was made king, and Bertrada queen.[2] In accordance with that order anciently required,[3] he was chosen king by all the Franks, consecrated by the bishops and received the homage of the great men.[4]

34

Up to this point, the illustrious Count Childebrand, uncle [5] of the said King Pippin, took great pains to have

---

See Heinrich Büttner's comment in *Das Königtum*, p. 160. *Secundum morem Francorum* (*Ann. Regni Franc., sub anno* 750, ed. F. Kurze, *Script. Rer. Germ. in usum scholarum*, Hanover 1895).

[4] November, 751. Pippin was the first Frankish king to be consecrated with chrism. St Boniface's last public act may have been to take the leading part in this consecration (*Ann. Regni Franc., sub anno* 750, loc. cit.).

[5] Childebrand and Charles Martel were sons of the same mother, Alpaida (cf. cont. chap. 6, above), of the house of Nibelung (Levillain, ' Les Nibelungen historiques,' 1937, p. 340).

S

Francorum diligentissime scribere procurauit. Abhinc ab inlustre uiro Nibelungo, filium ipsius Childebrando itemque comite, succedat auctoritas.

35

His transactis sequente anno [1] iterum Saxones eorum fidem quod praefato regi [a] dudum promiserant solito more iterum rebelles contra ipso existunt. Vnde et Pippinus rex ira commotus commoto omni exercitu Francorum, iterum Reno [b] transacto Saxonia cum magno apparatu ueniens,[2] ibique eorum patria maxime igne concremauit et captiuos tam uiros [c] quam feminas [d] cum multa praeda ibidem fecisset et plurimos Saxones ibidem prostrauisset. Quod uidentes [e] Saxones, penitentia commoti cum solito timore clementia regis petunt ut pacem eis concederet et sacramenta,[3] atque tributa multa maiora quam antea promisserant redderent et numquam ultra iam rebelles existerent; rex Pippinus Christo propitio cum magno triumpho iterum ad Renum [f] ad castro cuius nomen est Bonna ueniens. Dum haec ageretur, nuntius ueniens ad prefatum regem [g] ex partibus Burgundie quod germanus ipsius regis [h] nomine Gripho, quod dudum in Vasconia ad Waiofario principe confugium fecerat, a [i] Theudoeno comite Viennense [5] seu et Frederico Vltraiurano comite dum partibus Langobardie peteret et insidias contra ipso praedicto rege pararet Maurienna urbem super fluuium Arboris [4] interfectus est. Nam et ipsi [j] superscripti comites in eo proelio pariter interfecti sunt.

[a] 4c[1, 2] ; rege 4a, b[2]   [b] 4b[2] ; Renum 4a   [c] 4c[2] ; uiris 4a, b[2]
[d] 4a ; feminis 4b[2]   [e] 4c[2] ; conuidentes 4a, b[2]   [f] 4b[2] ; Reno 4a
[g] 4c[1, 2] ; praefato rege 4a, b[2]   [h] 4c[1, 2] ; rege 4a, b[2]
[i] 4c[1, 2] ; ad 4a, b[2]   [j] 4c[1, 2] ; ipse 4a

his history or 'geste' of the Franks recorded. What follows is by authority of the illustrious Count Nibelung, Childebrand's son.

35

In the year following these events,[1] the Saxons broke their oath of fealty to the said king and rose against him in the usual way. King Pippin was furious. He summoned the entire Frankish host and again crossed the Rhine to reach Saxony in great strength.[2] Once there, he fired their land far and wide. Men and women were taken prisoner, and great was the plunder. Many a Saxon fell there. The Saxons were grief-stricken when they saw this and, frightened as always, sought the king's pardon and the restoration of his peace and the sacraments,[3] and would pay much heavier tribute than they had formerly promised and would never again rise against him. King Pippin then returned, through Christ's mercy, in great triumph to the stronghold called Bonn on the Rhine. Meanwhile, news reached the king from Burgundy that his brother Grifo, who had recently fled to Waiofar, lord of Gascony, had been slain in the town of Saint-Jean-de-Maurienne on the river Arc[4] by Counts Theudoenus of Vienne[5] and Frederic of Trans-jura. He was on his way to Lombardy to stir up trouble against the said king. It so happened that the two counts mentioned were also killed in the fight.

---

[1] 753   [2] cf. the account in *Ann. Regni Franc.*, *sub anno* 753
[3] Frankish missions among the Saxons probably start from about this time.
[4] Savoie
[5] Probably brother of Thierry of Autun, son-in-law of Charles Martel (Ewig, *Cahiers de Civilisation Méd.*, 1, 1958, p. 49).

36

Per Ardinna silua ipse rex ueniens et Theudone uilla publica [1] super Mosella resedisset, nuntius ad eum ueniens quod Stephanus papa partibus Rome cum magno apparatu et multa munera iam monte Ioue transmeato ad eius properaret aduentum. Haec audiens rex, cum gaudio et laetitia et ingenti [a] cura recipere eum praecepit et filio suo Carlo [2] ei obuius ire praecepit, qui usque ad Ponteugone uillam publicam [3] ad eius praesentiam adducere deberet. Ibique Stephanus papa Romensis [4] ad praesentiam [b] regis ueniens et multis muneribus tam ipso rege quam et Francis largitus est, auxilium petens contra gente Langobardorum et eorum rege Aistulfo, ut per eius adiutorium eorum obpressionibus uel fraudulentia de manibus eorum liberaret et tributa uel munera quod contra legis ordine a Romanis [c] requirabant facere desisterent. Tunc Pippinus rex praefato Stephano papa apud Parisius ciuitate monasterio sancti Dionisii martyris cum ingenti cura et multa diligentia hiemare praecepit. [5] Legationem ad Aistulfo rege Langobardorum mittens, petens ei ut propter reuerentia beatissimorum apostolorum Petri et Pauli partibus Romae hostiliter non ambularet, et superstitiosas ac impias uel contra legis ordine causas, quod antea Romani numquam fecerant, propter eius petitionem [d] facere non deberent.

---

[a] 4c[1, 2] ; ingente 4a, b[2]   [b] 4c[1, 2] ; praesentia 4a, b[2]
[c] 4b[2] ; ad Romanos 4a   [d] 4b[2] ; petitione 4a

[1] *villa publica* is always a villa of the royal fisc in Frankish sources (cf. J. W. Thompson, *The Dissolution of the Carolingian Fisc in the ninth century*, 1935, p. 3, n. 9).
[2] The future Charlemagne, then twelve years old
[3] Marne. 6 January 754.
[4] The use of *romensis*, both here and earlier in the chronicle, suggests a

36

The king crossed the Forest of the Ardennes and took up residence at the royal villa [1] of Diedenhofen on the Moselle, where he received news that Pope Stephen was on his way from Rome with a great cortège and many gifts ; he had already crossed the Great St Bernard and was hastening to meet him. Hearing this, the king gave orders that he was to be received with glad rejoicing and every mark of attention ; and he told his son Charles [2] to go and meet him and escort him to his presence at the royal villa of Ponthion.[3] Here Stephen, Pope of Rome,[4] came into the king's presence and showered rich gifts upon him and his Franks, and asked for his help against the Lombards and their king, Aistulf, so that he might thereby be freed from their oppressions and their double-dealing. An end might thus be put to the tributes or gifts which, contrary to every right, they had been demanding of the Romans. King Pippin then gave instructions that Pope Stephen was to be entertained over winter at the Parisian monastery of the blessed martyr Denis with every possible care and attention.[5] He further sent an embassy to Aistulf, King of the Lombards, requesting him out of respect for the most blessed apostles Peter and Paul not to violate Roman territory with troop movements and to accede to his request by no longer making wicked heretical demands that were flat against process of law and had never before been admitted by Romans.

---

liturgical connection between Rome and Francia (see Kassius Hallinger in *Sankt Bonifatius Gedenkgabe*, p. 345).

[5] Unlike the Roman sources, the Continuator says nothing about Stephen II's subsequent re-anointing of the king in Saint-Denis (28 July), nor of his producing, at about this time, the famous forgery known as the Donation of Constantine, to justify his claims in Italy.

37

Cumque praedictus rex Pippinus quod per legatos suos petierat non inpetrasset et Aistulfus hoc facere contempsit, euoluto anno, praefatus rex ad K. Mar.[1] omnes Francos, sicut mos Francorum est, Bernaco uilla publica [2] ad se uenire praecepit. Initoque consilio cum proceribus suis eo tempore quo solent reges ad bella procedere,[3] cum Stephano papa uel reliquas nationes qui in suo regno commorabantur, et Francorum agmina partibus Langobardie cum omni multitudine per Lugduno [a] Gallie et Vienna pergentes usque Maurienna peruenerunt.[4] Aistulfus rex Langobardorum haec audiens, commoto omni exercitu Langobardorum usque ad clusas quae [b] cognominatur ualle Seusana ueniens, ibi cum omni exercitu suo castra metatus est et cum telis et machinis et multo apparatu quod nequiter contra rem publicam et sedem Romanam apostolicam admiserat nefarie nitebatur defendere. Et superscriptus rex Pippinus cum Maurienna cum exercitu suo resedisset, et propter angustia uallium montes rupesque exercitus praedicto rege minime transire potuisset, pauci tamen montibus angustisque locis exrumpentibus usque in ualle Seusana peruenerunt. Haec cernens Aistulfus rex Langobardorum omnes Langobardos armare praecepit et cum omni exercitu suo super eos audaciter uenit. Haec cernentes Franci non suis auxiliis nec suis uiribus liberare se putabant sed Deum inuocant et beati Petri apostoli adiutorem rogant, commissoque proelio fortiter inter se demicantes ; Aistulfus rex Langobar-

---

[a] 4b[2] ; Lugdono 4a   [b] 4b[2] ; qui 4a

[1] 754   [2] Aisne   [3] cf. 2 Samuel xi. 1 (Vulg. 2 Kings xi. 1)
[4] See R. L. Poole, ' The See of Maurienne and the valley of Susa ' (*Studies in Chronology and History*) on the creation of the diocese.

37

All the same, King Pippin failed to achieve his object by means of his ambassadors. Aistulf disdained to take notice of his message. So at the end of the year the king summoned all his Franks to meet him on 1 March [1] (the customary Frankish date) at the royal villa of Berny-Rivière [2] ; and there he took counsel with his great men. About the time when kings go forth to battle,[3] he set out for Lombardy with Pope Stephen and all the peoples who dwelt in his kingdom and his Frankish troops. The host passed through the Lyonnais and Vienne and reached Saint-Jean-de-Maurienne.[4] King Aistulf of the Lombards got word of this, summoned the entire Lombard army and made for the defile known as the valley of Susa. There with all his force he established his base, and prepared to defend himself with the weapons, machines of war and mass of stores that he had most wickedly got ready for resisting both the Empire and the Apostolic Roman See. King Pippin and his men had taken up their quarters at Saint-Jean-de-Maurienne. It was impossible for his main army to cross through the narrow passes or over the rocky heights ; but a small party succeeded in breaking through the difficult mountain passes into the valley of Susa. On receipt of this news, the Lombard King Aistulf called all the Lombards to arms and with considerable boldness advanced upon the Franks with his whole force. The Franks realized that neither their number nor their efforts would deliver them, so they called upon God and besought the help of the blessed apostle Peter. Then began the battle, and on both sides the fighting was

dorum Iesum cernens exercitum suum terga uertit et pene omnem exercitum suum quod secum adduxerat, tam ducibus quam *a* comitibus uel omnes maiores natu gentis Langobardorum, in eo proelio omnes ammisit et ipse quodam monte rupis uix lapsus euasit, Ticinum urbem suam cum paucis uenit. Igitur precelsus rex Pippinus patrata Deo adiuuante uictoria, cum omni exercitu uel multitudine agmina Francorum usque ad Ticinum accessit. Castra metatus est undique, omnia quae in giro fuit uastans partibus Italie maxime igne concremauit, totam regionem illam uastauit, castra Langobardorum omnia diripuit et multos thesauros tam auri quam argenti uel alia quam plura ornamenta et eorum tentoria [1] omnia capuit *b* et cepit. Hec cernens Aistulfus rex Langobardorum, quod nullatenus se euadere potuisset, pacem per sacerdotes et obtimates Francorum petens, dictiones superdicto rege Pippino faciens et quicquid contra Romanam ecclesiam uel sedem apostolicam contra legis ordine fecerat plenissima solutione emendaret ; sacramenta et obsides ibidem donat, ut numquam a Francorum dictione *c* se abstraheret et ulterius ad sedem apostolicam Romanam et rem publicam hostiliter numquam accederet. Praefatus rex Pippinus, clemens ut erat, misericordia motus uitam ei et regnum concessit et multa munera Aistulfus rex partibus praedicto regi *d* donat ; nam et obtimates Francorum multa munera largitus est. His itaque gestis Pippinus rex praedicto Stephano papa cum optimatibus *e* suis et multa munera partibus Rome cum magno honore direxit et in sedem apostolicam incolomem ubi prius

---

a *add* 4c[1, 2]
b *cf.* capuisset *chap. 46*
c 4b[2] ; ditiones 4a
d 4c[1, 2] ; rege 4a, b[2]
e 4c[1, 2] ; obtimatis 4a

fierce. But when King Aistulf saw what losses his army was suffering he turned and fled. In this battle he lost nearly the whole of the force he had collected, together with the dukes and counts and all the great men of the Lombard people. He himself only just escaped over the mountains, to reach Pavia with a handful of men. Thus, with God's help, the noble King Pippin had the victory ; and he advanced with his whole army and the numerous columns of the Franks to Pavia, where he pitched camp. Far and wide in all directions he ravaged and burnt the lands of Italy until he had devastated all that region, pulled down all the Lombard strongholds and captured and taken in charge a great treasure of gold and silver as well as a mass of equipment and all their tents.[1] The Lombard King Aistulf now saw that he could no longer escape his fate ; so he begged for terms through the Frankish bishops and magnates, submitting himself to King Pippin's discretion and promising that he would make full amends for whatever wrong he had done to the Roman Church and the Apostolic See. He further gave hostages and a solemn undertaking never to withdraw from Frankish overlordship, and never again to enter with troops within the territories of the Holy See or the Empire. Merciful, as always, King Pippin was moved as an act of grace to grant him his life and crown. King Aistulf made him rich presents, and on the Frankish magnates also he lavished presents. Afterwards, King Pippin despatched Pope Stephen to Rome, with many gifts and with much deference, and escorted by his nobility. He restored the Pope to his

---

[1] *Tentoria* are also mantlets or siege-shelters but this fits the context less well.

fuerat restituit. His transactis Pippinus rex cum omni exercitu suo uel multis thesauris *a* hac multa munera Deo adiuuante reuersus est ad propria.

38

Sequente anno Aistulfus rex Langobardorum fidem suam quod contra rege Pippino promiserat peccatis facientibus fefellit. Iterum [1] ad Romam cum exercitu suo ueniens finibus Romanorum preuagans atque regionem illam uastans, ad ecclesiam sancti Petri ueniens et domos quas *b* ibidem repperit maxime igne concremauit. Hec Pippinus rex cum per internuncios hoc audisset nimium furore et in ira motus, commoto iterum omni exercitu Francorum per Burgundiam, per Caualonnum urbem et inde per Ianuam usque ad Mauriennam *c* ueniens. Rex Aistulfus cum hoc repperisset, iterum ad clusas exercitum Langobardorum mittens qui rege Pippino et Francis *d* resisterent et partibus Aetalie intrare non sinirent. Rex Pippinus cum exercitu suo monte Ciniso transacto usque ad clusas ubi Langobardi eum resistere nitebantur perueniens, et statim Franci solito more ut edocti erant per montes et rupes erumpentes *e* in regno Aistulfo cum multa ira et furore intrant, Langobardos quos ibi repperiunt interficiunt ; reliqui qui remanserant uix fuga lapsi euaserunt. Rex Pippinus cum nepote suo *f* Tascilone Baiouariorum duce [2] partibus Italiae usque

a 4b² ; thesaris 4a, *and hereafter*
b 4c² ; quos 4a, b²
c 4b² ; Maurienna 4a
d 4c² ; Francos 4a, b²
e 4b² ; erumpentibus 4a
f 4b² ; nepotem suum 4a

Apostolic See with his former powers unimpaired. Thereafter with God's help King Pippin returned home with his army, laden with great treasure and many gifts.

38

In the following year, Aistulf, King of the Lombards, wickedly broke the oath of fidelity he had sworn to King Pippin. Once again [1] he appeared before Rome with his army, marauding and laying waste Roman marcher territory. He reached the church of the blessed Peter and burnt to the ground whatever houses he found in the vicinity. When this was reported to King Pippin he was consumed with anger, and in fury once more summoned the entire Frankish army and made his way through Burgundy, the town of Chalon and then Geneva to Saint-Jean-de-Maurienne. At this news, King Aistulf again brought up the Lombard army to the passes, there to halt King Pippin and his Franks and to deny them entry into Italy. King Pippin's army crossed Mont Cenis and arrived at the defile where the Lombards made an attempt to resist them. But without pausing the Franks surged as before across the rocky heights—for now they had learnt their lesson—and burst in fury upon the kingdom of Aistulf, slaughtering whatever Lombards they found still in their path. The remainder of those who had waited for them fled in confusion, only just making good their escape. King Pippin now once again advanced into Italy as far as Pavia with his nephew Tassilo, duke of the Bavarians.[2] He utterly devastated

[1] 1 January 756
[2] son of Duke Odilo and of Chiltrudis, sister of Pippin III (cf. cont. chap. 25, above)

ad Ticinum iterum accessit et totam regionem illam fortiter deuastans et circa muros Ticini utraque parte fixit tentoria, ita ut nullus exinde euadere potuisset. Haec Aistulfus rex Langobardorum cernens et iam nullam spem se euadendi speraret, iterum per subplicationem sacerdotum et optimatum [a] Francorum ueniam et pacem praedicto rege subplicans, et sacramenta quod contra praefato rege dudum dederat hac contra sedem apostolicam rem nefariam fecerat, omnia per iudicio Francorum uel sacerdotum plenissima solutione emendaret. Igitur rex Pippinus solito more iterum misericordia motus ad petitionem optimatum suorum [b] uitam et regnum iterato concessit. Aistulfus rex per iudicio Francorum uel sacerdotum thesaurum quod in Ticino erat, id est tertiam partem, praedicto rege tradidit et alia multa munera maiora quam antea dederat partibus rege Pippino dedit. Sacramenta iterum uel obsides donat, ut amplius numquam contra rege Pippino uel proceris Francorum rebellis contumax esse non debeat et tributa quod Langobardi ad regem [c] Francorum a longo tempore dederant [d][1] annis singulis per missos suos desoluere deberent. Praecelsus [e] rex Pippinus uictor cum magnis thesauris et multa munera absque bellis euentu cum omni exercitu suo inleso ad propriam sedem regni sui remeauit incolumis. Et quieuit terra a proeliis annis duobus.[2]

39

Post haec Aistulfus rex Langobardorum dum uenationem in quadam silua [f] exerceret, diuino iudicio de

[a] 4c[1, 2] ; obtimates 4a, b[2]   [b] 4c[1, 2] ; obtimatibus suis 4a, b[2]
[c] 4c[1, 2] ; rege 4a, b[2]   [d] 4b[2] ; dederunt 4a
[e] Praecellus 4a ; praecelsus *all other MSS*

the whole region, and encamped round the walls of Pavia so that none should escape from the city. King Aistulf of the Lombards observed what was happening and, appreciating that no hope of escape now remained, again implored the king's pardon and peace through the Frankish bishops and nobles. He swore that, in accordance with the findings of the Frankish nobles and bishops, he would make fullest amends for the previous undertakings that he had broken and for the damage he had caused to the Apostolic See. Again King Pippin was moved, as he always was, by compassion; and he acceded to his nobles' wishes and again granted him his life and crown. By judgement of the Frankish nobles and bishops King Aistulf had to yield King Pippin one third of his treasure in Pavia and, in addition, give him many more gifts than on the previous occasion. Aistulf further bound himself by oath and by surrender of hostages never again to rebel against Pippin and the Frankish nobility; and every year he would send representatives with the tribute that the Lombards had long paid to the King of the Franks.[1] The great King Pippin then returned home to his kingdom with victory and a heap of treasure and gifts, without a battle and with his army intact and untouched by war. And for two years the land had rest from wars.[2]

39

Somewhat later, King Aistulf of the Lombards was out hunting in the woods when, by divine judgement, he

---

[f] 4c[2]; quodam siluam 4a

[1] cf. chap. 45, above   [2] cf. end of cont. chap. 32, above

equo quo sedebat super quandam [a] arborem proiectus uitam et regnum crudeliter digna morte ammisit. Langobardi una cum consensu praedicto rege Pippino et consilio procerum suorum Desiderio in sedem regni instituunt.[1]

40

Dum haec ageretur [b] rex Pippinus legationem Constantinopolim ad Constantino imperatore [2] pro amicitiis causa et salutem patrie sue mittens, similiter et Constantinus imperator legationem praefato rege cum multa munera mittens et amicitias et fidem per legatos eorum uicissim [c] inter se promittunt. Nescio quo faciente, postea amicitias quas inter se mutuo promisserant nullatenus sortita est effectu.

41

His itaque gestis et duobus annis cum terra cessasset a preliis,[3] praedictus rex Pippinus legationem ad Waiofario Aquitanico principe mittens, petens ei per legatos suos ut res ecclesiarum de regno ipsius quae [d] in Aquitania sitae erant redderet et sub inmunitatis [e] nomine, sicut ab antea fuerant, conseruatas esse deberent et iudices hac exactores supra predictas res ecclesiarum, quod a longo tempore factum non fuerat, mittere non deberet[4]; et Gotos praedicto rege quod dudum Waiofarius contra legis ordine occiserat ei soluere deberet et homines suos

[a] 4c² ; quondam 4a, b²   [b] 4a, b² ; agerentur 4c²
[c] 4b² ; uicinsim 4a   [d] 4c² ; qui . . . . sitas 4a
[e] 4c¹, ² ; immunitates 4a

[1] March, 757
[2] Constantine V Copronymus   [3] 760

was thrown from his horse against a tree and, as he had richly deserved, lost both life and crown in a painful death. King Pippin assenting, the Lombards unanimously took the advice of their nobles and chose Desiderius to be their king.[1]

40

In the meantime, for the sake of good relations and since it was in the national interest, King Pippin sent a mission to the Emperor Constantine [2] at Constantinople. The Emperor Constantine likewise sent an embassy with many gifts to the king ; and through their representatives each swore friendship and fidelity to the other. What happened then is unknown to me, but this mutual amity that they embarked upon was not predestined to success.

41

It was after this, when there had been no war for two years,[3] that King Pippin sent an embassy to Waiofar, lord of Aquitaine, asking him to restore the ecclesiastical properties of his kingdom situated in Aquitaine, to conserve them under the title of immunities in the traditional manner, and not to send officials and tax-collectors into these properties contrary to established usage.[4] Finally, he asked Waiofar to pay him the blood-price for the Goths whom, not long before, he had illegally killed and to surrender to him those of his men

---

[4] Evidence from the Austrasian churches of Rheims, Trier and Verdun suggests that this restoration was realized soon after 768 (cf. E. Ewig, 'L'Aquitaine et les pays rhénans,' *Cahiers de Civilisation Médiévale*, Poitiers 1958, p. 50).

quos [a] de regno Francorum ad ipso Waiofario principe confugium fecerant reddere deberet. Haec omnia Waiofarius, quod praedictus rex per legatos suos ei mandauerat, hoc totum facere contempsit. Igitur Pippinus rex inuitus coactus [b] undique contraxit exercitum et partibus Aquitanie per pago Trecassino usque Autisiodero urbem accessit. Inde ad Ligerem fluuium cum omni exercitu Francorum ad Masua uico [1] in pago Autisioderinse Ligerem fluuium transmeauit, per pago Bitoriuo usque Aruernico accessit, regionem illam peruagans et maximam partem Aquitanie igne concremauit. Waiofarius princeps Aquitanie per legatos suos pacem supplicans [2] sacramenta uel obsides ibidem donat, ut [c] omnes iustitias quas [d] praefatus rex Pippinus per legatos suos ei mandauerat in placito instituto facere deberet. Rex Pippinus cum omni exercitu suo inleso reuersus est ad propria.

42

Euoluto anno, id est anno decimo regni ipsius,[3] omnes obtimates Francorum ad Dura [4] in pago Riguerinse ad campo Madio [5] pro salutem patrie et utilitatem Francorum tractandum placito instituto ad se uenire praecepit. Dum haec ageretur Waiofarius inito iniquo consilio contra Pippino rege Francorum insidias parat : exercitum suum cum Vniberto comite Bitoriuo et Bladino comite Aruernico, qui dudum ante anno superiore ad praedicto rege Pippino cum Bertelanno

---

[a] 4a ; quod 4b²   [b] coactatus 4a ; coactus *all other MSS*
[c] 4c¹, ² ; et 4a, b²   [d] 4c² ; quos 4a, b²

[1] Nièvre ; and not Mesvres (Loire), as in J. W. Thompson, *The Dissolution of the Carolingian Fisc*, p. 80.

that had fled from the Frankish kingdom to find refuge with prince Waiofar. The latter spurned every single request transmitted to him from the king. Unwillingly, therefore, and because no choice was left him, King Pippin raised a general force and marched towards the borders of Aquitaine through the district of Troyes to the town of Auxerre; thence he continued with the whole Frankish army to the Loire, crossed the river at Mesves [1] in the district of Auxerre, and proceeded through the district of Berry to the Auvergne. He ranged over this area and left most of Aquitaine burning. Waiofar, lord of Aquitaine, then sent an embassy begging terms.[2] He gave oaths and hostages and undertook to restore, at a court of enquiry, all the rights that King Pippin's messengers had demanded. King Pippin and all his men returned home without casualties.

42

In the tenth year of his reign (that is, a year later) [3] King Pippin summoned all the Frankish nobility to come to him to a Mayfield [5] at Düren [4] in Ripuarian territory, to consider in assembly matters of national safety and welfare. Meanwhile, Waiofar in his wickedness started plotting against Pippin, King of the Franks. He made an alliance with Chunibert count of Bourges and Bladinus count of the Auvergne, whom in the previous year he had sent with Bishop Bertelannus of Bourges to

---

[2] For details see *Ann. Regni Franc.*, *sub anno* 760, loc. cit.

[3] 761

[4] between Cologne and Aachen

[5] An early case of the substitution of the Mayfield for the old Marchfield. For its meaning, see L. Levillain, ' Campus Martius,' pp. 62-8. cf. cont. chap. 48, below and chap. 90, above.

T

episcopo Bitorice ciuitatis missus fuerat et animum regis ad iracundiam nimium prouocasset, cum reliquis comitibus clam hostiliter usque Cauallonnum omnem exercitum suum transmisit et totam regionem illam, id est Agustidunensium usque ad Cauallonnum igne concremauit et suburbana Cauallonnum urbis quicquid ibidem repperierunt omnia uastauerunt. Meltiaco [1] uillam publicam incendio cremauerunt ; cum multa spolia et praeda nullo resistente remeauerunt ad propria. Cum haec Pippino rege nuntiatum fuisset, quod Waiofarius maximam partem regni sui uastasset et sacramenta quod ei dederat fefellisset, nimium in ira commotus iubet omnes Francos ut hostiliter placito instituto ad Ligerem uenissent. Commotoque exercito cum omne multitudine iterum usque ad Trecas accessit, inde per Autisioderum ad Neuernum urbem [a] ueniens Ligeris fluuium transmeato ad castrum [b] cuius nomen est Burbone [2] in pago Bitoriuo peruenit. Cumque in giro castra posuisset, subito a Francis captus atque succensus est et homines Waiofarii quos [c] ibidem inuenit secum duxit. Maximam partem Aquitanie uastans, usque urbem Aruernam cum omni exercitu ueniens, Claremonte castro captum atque succensum bellando cepit et multitudinem hominum, tam uirorum quam feminarum uel infantum plurimi, in ipso incendio cremauerunt. Bladino comite ipsius urbis Aruernico captum atque ligatum ad praesentia regis adduxerunt, et multi Vascones in eo proelio capti atque interfecti sunt. Igitur rex Pippinus, urbem captam hac regionem illam totam uastatam, cum praeda uel spolia multa Deo auxiliante inlesum exercitum iterum remeauit ad propria.

[a] 4c^2 ; urbis 4a, b^2

King Pippin, to the latter's great indignation. With
these and with other counts he secretly moved his entire
army to Chalon, and he set fire to the whole region of
Autun as far as Chalon. They laid waste the approaches
to Chalon and destroyed whatever they found there.
They burnt down the royal villa of Mailly.[1] Then they
went home with great spoils and plunder, there being
no one to stop them. King Pippin was furious when he
was told that Waiofar had plundered a large part of his
kingdom and had broken his oaths that he had sworn to
him. He summoned all Franks to assemble in arms at
the Loire. He then set out with a large force to Troyes
and from there went through Auxerre to the town of
Nevers, where he crossed the Loire and reached the
stronghold of Bourbon [2] in the district of Bourges. The
fortress was closely invested ; and then the Franks
stormed it and set it on fire. Such of Waiofar's men as
were found there he took prisoner. He laid waste a large
part of Aquitaine, advanced with his whole force to the
town of Auvergne and took and burnt the fortress of
Clermont. A great many men, women and children
perished in the flames. Count Bladinus of Auvergne
was taken prisoner and brought in chains to the king's
presence. Many Gascons were taken and slain in that
engagement. And now that the town was taken and
the whole region devastated, King Pippin returned home
a second time, his army, by God's help, unscathed,
laden with much plunder.

---

[b] 4c² ; castro 4a, b²
[c] 4c¹, ² ; Waiofario quod 4a

[1] Saône-et-Loire
[2] Bourbon-l'Archambault (Allier)

43

Factum est autem ut, post quod Pippinus rex urbem Aruernam cepit hac regionem illam totam uastauit, sequente anno, id est anno XI regni ipsius [1] cum uniuersa multitudine gentis Francorum Bitoricas uenit, castra metatusque est undique et omnia quae in giro fuit uastauit.[2] Circumsepsit urbem munitionem fortissimam, ita ut nullus egredi ausus fuisset aut ingredi potuisset,[3] cum machinis et omni genere armorum, circumdedit ea uallo. Multis uulneratis plurisque interfectis fractisque muris cepit urbem et restituit eam dicione sue iure proelii [4] et homines illos quos Waiofarius ad defendendam ipsam ciuitatem dimiserat clementiam sue pietatis absoluit dimissisque reuersi sunt ad propria. Vniberto comite uel reliquos Vascones quos ibidem inuenit sacramentis datis secum adduxit, uxores eorum hac liberos in Frantia ambulare praecepit, muros ipsius Bitorice ciuitatis restaurare iubet, comites suos in ipsa ciuitate ad custodiendum dimisit. Inde cum omni exercitu Francorum usque ad castro qui uocatur Toartius [5] ueniens, cumque in giro castra posuisset, ipse castrus mira celeritate captus atque succensus est et Vascones quos ibidem inuenit una cum ipso comite secum duxit in Frantia. Pippinus rex Christo duce cum omni exercitu Francorum cum multa praeda et spolia iterum reuersus est ad sedem propriam.

44

Facta est autem longa altercatio [6] inter Pippino rege Francorum et Waiofario Aquitanico principe : Pippinus

---

[1] 762
[2] The same words are used in cont. chap. 37, above.

43

It happened that the year after the taking of Auvergne and the devastation of all that region, King Pippin—it was the eleventh year of his reign [1]—came with his whole Frankish army to Bourges, fortified his position there and plundered the countryside round about.[2] He then surrounded the town with a strong fortification, with siege-engines and all manner of weapons so that no one would have dared to leave or enter it,[3] and he also built a rampart. Finally he took the city after many had been wounded and more slain, and the walls breached. He restored it to his rule by right of conquest,[4] but of his goodness showed mercy to the men left there as garrison by Waiofar, and dismissed them to go off home. Count Chunibert and such Gascons as he found there had to swear fealty to him and remain in his company : their wives and children were told to set off on foot for Francia. He ordered the repair of the walls of Bourges and left the city in charge of counts of his own. Then he and the entire Frankish host made for the stronghold of Thouars [5] and encamped round about it. The stronghold was captured with extraordinary speed, and was afterwards burnt. He took back with him to Francia the Gascons whom he found there, together with the count himself. And so, Christ going before him, King Pippin came home again with great spoils.

44

The dispute between King Pippin of the Franks and Waiofar, lord of Aquitaine, lasted a long time.[6] But

---

[3] cf. Joshua vi. 1   [4] cf. 2 Kings xiii. 25 (Vulg. 4 Kings xiii. 25)
[5] Deux-Sèvres   [6] cf. 2 Samuel iii. 1 (Vulg. 2 Kings iii. 1)

rex Deo auxiliante magis ac magis crescens et semper in se ipso robustior, pars [a] autem Waiofarii eius tirannitas decrescens cotidie. Waiofarius princeps semper contra praedicto rege Pippino insidias parare dissimulat, nam Mantione comite consubrino suo partibus Narbone cum reliquis comitibus transmisit, ut custodias quod praedictus rex Narbonam propter gentem Saracenorum ad custodiendum miserat aut ad intrandum aut quando iterum in patria reuertebant capere aut interficere eos potuissent. Factum est ut Australdus comis et Galemanius itemque comis [1] cum pares eorum ad propria reuerterent. Sic Mantio una cum multitudine gente Wasconorum super eos inruit. Fortiter inter se demicantes praedictus Galemanius et Australdus ibidem Mantione cum uniuersos pares suos Deo adiuuante interficiunt. Haec cernentes Wascones terga uerterunt, omnes equites [b] quod ibidem adduxerant ammiserunt ; montes uallesque peruagantes pauci tamen uix fugaciter euaserunt. Ipsi uero cum multa praeda uel equites et spolia cum gaudio reuersi sunt ad propria.

45

Dum his et aliis modis Franci et Wascones semper inter se altercarent, Chilpingus comis Aruernorum collecto undique exercitu in pago Lugdunense in regno Burgundie ad praedandum ambulare nitebatur. Contra quem Adalardus comis Caualonensis et Australdus itemque comis cum pares eorum contra eum uenientes et super fluuium Ligeris fortiter inter se dimicantes,

[a] pros 4a ; pars *all other MSS* ; pras *Krusch*
[b] i.e. equos, *as also in following sentence*

whereas King Pippin with God's help flourished and went from strength to strength, the cause of Waiofar and his wicked rule declined daily. Waiofar continued secretly plotting against King Pippin. He sent his cousin, Count Mantio, with other counts to Narbonne with the object of capturing and killing the garrison, sent by the king to hold Narbonne against the Saracens, either as they entered the city or on their way back home. It so happened that Counts Australdus and Galemanius[1] were making for home with their following when Mantio fell upon them with a crowd of Gascons. There was a stiff fight ; but Australdus and Galemanius succeeded, with God's help, in killing Mantio and all his companions. When they saw this, the Gascons turned tail and fled. They thus lost all the horses they had with them. Up hill and down dale they wandered ; but few indeed managed to make good their escape. The Franks continued home rejoicing, with great booty and many horses and trappings.

45

While the Franks and Gascons continued, one way and another, with their running battle, Count Chilping of Auvergne gathered together a force from the surrounding country and set out on a plundering expedition to the district of Lyons in the kingdom of Burgundy. Count Adalard of Chalon and Count Australdus with their followings took the field against him. There was a fierce engagement on the banks of the Loire and Count Chilping

---

[1] Ewig sees them as ' comtes-gouverneurs ' of the new kind instituted by Charles Martel (*Cahiers*, 1, 1958, p. 50).

statim Chilpingus comis in eo proelio a superscriptis comitibus occisus est et multi qui cum eo uenerant ibidem interfecti sunt. Haec uidentes Wascones terga uerterunt ; uix paucis siluis et paludibus ingressi euaserunt. Ammanugus comis Pictauensis dum Toronico infestando praedaret, et ab homines Vulfardo abbate monasterio beati Martini interfectus est et plures qui apud eum ibidem uenerant cum ipso pariter ceciderunt ; reliqui qui remanserant terga uertentes pauci uix euaserunt. Dum haec ageretur, Remistanius auuncolus Waiofario [1] ad praedictum regem ueniens sacramenta multa et fide praedicto rege Pippino promisit, ut semper fidelis tam praedicto rege quam et filios suos omni tempore esse deberet. Rex uero Pippinus in sua dictione eum recepit et multa munera auri et argenti et preciosa uestimenta, equites et arma eum ditauit.

46

Rex Pippinus castro cui nomen est Argentonus [2] in pago Bitoriuo a fundamento miro opere in pristino statu reparare iussit, comites suos ibidem ad custodiendum mittens, ipso castro Remistanio ad Waiofario resistendum cum medietatem pago Bitoriuo usque ad Care concessit. Videns praedictus Waiofarius princeps Aquitanicus quod castro Claremonte rex bellando ceperat et Bitoricas caput Aquitaniae munitissimam urbem cum machinis capuisset,[a][3] et inpetum eius ferre non potuisset, omnes ciuitates quas in Aquitania prouintia dictioni sue erant, id est Pectauis, Lemouicas, Sanctonis, Petrecors, Equolisma uel reliquis quam plures ciuitates et castella,

---

[a] cf. supra, chap. 37

and many of those with him were instantly slain there by the said counts. The Gascons made off when they saw this, but not many escaped through the woods and marshes. Count Ammanugus of Poitiers, who had gone plundering in Touraine, was killed by the men of Abbot Wulfard of the monastery of the blessed Martin, and many of his companions likewise fell with him. The survivors fled, though not many escaped. Meanwhile, Remistanius, Waiofar's uncle,[1] came to King Pippin and swore to him with many oaths always to be faithful to the king and to his sons. So King Pippin took him under his protection and made him rich presents of gold and silver and costly clothes and horses and arms.

46

King Pippin gave orders for the complete restoration, regardless of cost, of the fortress known as Argenton[2] in the district of Bourges, and sent his counts to look after it. He gave the fortress and half of the district of Bourges, as far as the Cher, to Remistanius in order to offer resistance to Waiofar. When Waiofar, lord of Aquitaine, saw how the king had stormed the fortress of Clermont and had taken the powerful city of Bourges, capital of Aquitaine, with siege-engines,[3] and he had been able to do nothing to stop it, he razed the walls of all the Aquitanian cities in his control—that is, Poitiers, Limoges, Saintes, Périgueux, Angoulême and many other

---

[1] Remistanius was a son of Eudo and thus *patruus*, not *avunculus*, of Waiofar.

[2] Argenton-sur-Creuse (Indre)

[3] cf. cont. chap. 43, above

omnes muros eorum in terra prostrauit, quos postea praecelsus [a] rex Pippinus reparare iubet et homines suos ad ipsas ciuitates custodiendum dimisit. Iterum eo anno cum omni exercito suo predictus rex Pippinus ad sedem propriam reuersus est.

47

Iterum sequente anno [1] commoto omni exercito Francorum, per Trecas, inde ad Autisiodero usque ad Neuernum urbem con omni exercito ueniens, ibique cum Francis et proceribus suis placitum suum campo Madio tenens, postea Ligere transacto Aquitania pergens usque ad Lemodicas accessit, totam regionem illam uastans, uillas publicas quae dictione Waiofario erant totas igne cremare praecepit. Totam regionem illam pene uastatam, monasteria multa depopulata, usque Hisandonem [2] ueniens unde maxima parte Aquitaniae plurimum uinearum erat coepit ac uastauit, unde pene omni Aquitania, tam ecclesias quam monasteria, diuites et pauperes uina habere consuerunt, omnia uastauit et coepit. Dum haec ageretur, Waiofarius cum exercito magno et plurima Wasconorum qui ultra Garonnam [b] commorantur, quem antiquitus uocati sunt Vaceti, super praedicto rege ueniens ; set statim solito more omnes Wascones terga uerterunt, plurimi ibidem a Francis interfecti sunt. Hec cernens rex persequi eum iubet et usque ad noctem eum persequens uix Waiofarius cum paucis qui remanserant fugiendo euasit. In eo

[a] 4b[2] ; praecellus 4a
[b] 4b[1], c[1] ; Geronna 4a

cities and fortified places. The noble King Pippin later had them rebuilt and sent his men there to hold the cities. So again that year King Pippin returned home with his entire army.

47

Next year [1] he again summoned the entire Frankish army and went through Troyes and Auxerre to the town of Nevers. And there he held court at the Mayfield with his Franks and the nobility. He then crossed the Loire into Aquitaine and reached Limoges, laying waste all that region. All royal villas that were held by Waiofar he ordered to be burnt. When most of the region had been devastated and its monasteries emptied, he proceeded to Issoudun,[2] the principal centre of the Aquitanian vineyards ; and this he took and destroyed. He tore up all the vineyards from which almost all Aquitaine, churches and monasteries, rich and poor, used to obtain wine. At this point Waiofar came to meet King Pippin with a big army and a host of those Gascons who live beyond the Garonne and were formerly called Vaceti. But straight away all the Gascons followed their usual practice and not a man of them but turned tail : and very many of them were killed there by the Franks. When the king saw what had happened he ordered that Waiofar should be pursued ; and pursued he was, till nightfall. But he just got away with a handful of men still with him.

---

[1] probably 763
[2] Creuse ; or perhaps Yssandon (Corrèze)

proelio Bladinus comis Aruernorum, quem praedictus rex ceperat [1] et [a] postea ad Waiofarium confugium fecerat, in eo proelio interfectus est. Rex Pippinus obpitulante Deo uictor extitit. Patrata iterum uictoria cum magno triumpho iterum ad Degontio [2] cum omni exercito Francorum ad Ligere ueniens, inde per pagum Agustidunense ad propriam sedem remeauit inuictus. Waiofarius legacionem ad praedicto rege mittens, petens ei quod Betoricas et reliquas ciuitates Aquitanie pro- uincie, quod de manu eius predictus rex abstulerat, ei redderet et postea ipse Waiofarius dictionis sue fa- ceret ; tributa uel munera quod antecessores suos reges Francorum de Aquitan a prouintia exire consueuerant annis singulis partibus praedicto regi [b] Pippino soluere deberet. Sed hoc rex per consilio Francorum et pro- cerum suorum facere contemsit.

48

Euoluto igitur anno [3] commoto omni exercito Francorum uel plurimum nationum [c] quod in regno suo commora- bantur, usque ad Aurilianis ueniens ibi placitum suum campo Madio, quod ipse primus pro campo Martio pro utilitate Francorum instituit,[4] tenens multa munera a Francis uel proceris suis ditatus est.[5] Iterum Ligere transacto totam Aquitaniam pergens usque ad Aginnum ueniens totam regionem illam deuastans. Videntes tam Wascones quam maiores natu Aquitanie necessitate conpulsi plurimi ad eum uenerunt, sacramenta ad eum ibidem donant, dictionis sue faciunt. Ita omnem

[a] *add* 4c[1]
[b] 4b[2] ; rege 4a
[c] 4c[1] ; nationes 4a

In this battle was killed Count Bladinus of Auvergne, who had been arrested by the king [1] and had subsequently fled to Waiofar. King Pippin won the day, God helping him. He set out for home in great triumph, reached Digoin [2] on the Loire with the entire Frankish host, and continued unconquered on his way home through the district of Autun. Waiofar now sent an embassy to the king, begging him to restore Bourges and the other Aquitanian cities which the king had taken from him ; and then he would submit to him. He undertook to send annually to King Pippin whatever tribute and gifts earlier Frankish kings had been accustomed to receive from the province of Aquitaine. However, the king took the advice of the Franks and nobles : he spurned the offer.

48

A year later [3] he summoned to Orleans the whole host of the Franks and the other peoples that dwelt in his kingdom. There he held court at a Mayfield, which he had first substituted for the Marchfield for the convenience of the Franks [4] ; and he received fine gifts from the Franks and his nobles. [5] Then again he crossed the Loire, marched through the length of Aquitaine to Agen and laid waste the whole region. The Gascons and the magnates of Aquitaine now saw that they had no option but to come to him : many there swore oaths to him and became his men. When the whole of

---

[1] cf. cont. chap. 42, above
[2] Saône-et-Loire   [3] 766
[4] cf. cont. chap. 42, above
[5] not bribes but customary gifts

Aquitaniam prouintiam nimium ^{a} uastatam, cum multa praeda hac spolia ^{b} per pago Petregorico et Egolismam, iam pene omni Aquitania adquesita, cum omni exercito Francorum iterum eo anno reuersus est in Frantia cum suis omnibus.

49

Iterum denuo sequente anno [1] commoto omni exercito Francorum, per pago Trecasino, inde ad urbem Autisiodero ueniens, ad castro qui uocatur Gordinis [2] cum regina sua Bertradane iam fiducialiter Ligere transito ad Bitoricas accessit ; palacium sibi edificare iubet. Iterum campo Madio, sicut mos erat, ibidem tenere iubet ; initoque consilio cum proceris suis, prefata regina Bertradane cum reliquis Francis hac comitibus fidelibus suis in praedictas Bitoricas dimisit. Ipse praedictus rex cum reliquis Francis et obtimatibus ^{c} suis persequendum Waiofarium perrexit. Cumque praedictus rex ipsum Waiofarium persequente non repperiret, iam tempus hiems erat, cum omni exercito ad Bitoricas ubi praefata regina Bertradane dimiserat reuersus est.

50

Dum hec ageretur, Remistanius, filius Eudone quondam, fidem suam quod praedicto regi ^{d} Pippino promiserat ^{e} fefellit, et ad Waiofarium iterum ueniens dictioni ^{f} sue faciens. Quod Waiofarius cum magno gaudio eum recepit et adiutorem sibi contra Francos uel praedicto

---

^{a} 4c[1] ; nimiam 4a ^{b} 4b[2] ; spoliam 4a

Aquitaine had been thoroughly devastated and most of it subjugated, he marched back through the district of Périgueux and Angoulême, laden with spoils and plunder ; and thus again that year he returned to Francia with the entire Frankish army and all his followers.

49

Next year [1] he again called together the whole Frankish host and marched through the district of Troyes and the town of Auxerre to the fortress of Gordon,[2] and thence with his Queen Bertrada boldly over the Loire to Bourges. There he had a residence built and, as the custom was, again ordered the holding of a Mayfield. After taking counsel with his nobles, he left Queen Bertrada in Bourges with certain Franks and counts that he trusted. The king himself set out with the remaining Franks and nobles in pursuit of Waiofar. But as he could not catch Waiofar and it was already winter, he returned with his army to Bourges, where he had left Queen Bertrada.

50

Meanwhile Remistanius, son of the late Eudo, broke the oath of fealty that he had sworn to King Pippin. He went back to Waiofar and became his man. Waiofar was delighted to receive him and to make use of his help

---

c 4b² ; obtimatis 4a   d 4b² ; rege 4a
e 4b² ; promisserat 4a   f 4b² ; dictionis 4a

1 767   2 near Sancerre (Cher)

rege eum instituit. Superscriptus *a* Remistanius contra praedicto rege et Francos seu custodias quas ipse rex in ipsas *b* ciuitates dimiserat nimium infestus accessit et Bitoriuo seu et Limoticino quod ipse rex adquisierat, praedando nimium uastauit, ita ut nullus colonus terre ad laborandum tam agris quam uineis colere *c* non audebant. Praedictus rex Pippinus in Betoricas per hiemem *d* totum cum regina sua Bertradane in palatium resedit. Totum exercitum suum per Burgundias ad hiemandum *e* mittens, natale domini nostri Iesu Christi uel sanctam epiphaniam *f*1 ad Betoricas urbem *g* per consilio episcoporum *h* uel sacerdotum uenerabiliter celebrauit.

51

Euoluto igitur eo anno [2] cum in Betoricas resederet, mediante Febroario, omnem exercitum suum quem in Burgundia ad hiemandum miserat ad se uenire praecepit ; initoque consilio contra Remistanium insidias parat. Hermenaldo, Berengario, Childerado et Vniberto [3] comite Bitoriuo cum reliquis comitibus et leudibus *i* suis ad ipsum Remistanium capiendum clam mittens, predictus rex Pippinus cum omni exercitu Francorum iterum ad persequendum Waiofarium ire distinauit. Bertrada regina Aurilianis ueniens et inde nauale euectione per Ligere fluuium usque ad Sellus [4] castro super fluuium ipsius Ligere perueniens. His itaque gestis nunciatum est regi quod missos suos, quos dudum ad Amormuni [5] regi Saracenorum miserat,*j*

---

a 4b² ; superscriptos 4a   *b* 4b² ; ipsis 4a
c scolere *all MSS*   *d* 4c¹ ; hiemen 4a, b²
e 4c¹ ; (h)yemando 4a, b²   *f* 4b² ; epiphania 4a

against the Franks and their king. This same Remistanius attacked the king and the Franks and the garrisons which the king had left in the cities, and he laid waste the districts of Berry and Limoges annexed by the king. He did this so effectively that not a peasant dared work in the fields and vineyards. King Pippin spent the whole winter with Queen Bertrada in his residence at Bourges. He sent the entire army to winter in Burgundy and, attentive to the word of his bishops and royal chaplains, celebrated the twelve days from Christmas to Epiphany[1] with all honour in the town of Bourges.

51

In mid-February of the next year [2] while he was still in Bourges, he ordered the whole army that he had sent to winter in Burgundy to come to him ; and he laid plans for trapping Remistanius. First Hermenald, Berengar, Childerad and Count Chunibert [3] of Bourges were secretly despatched with other counts and magnates to catch Remistanius, while King Pippin himself again set off with the main Frankish army after Waiofar. Queen Bertrada came to Orleans and thence by boat along the Loire to the stronghold of Chantoceaux [4] on the river's bank. News now reached the king that ambassadors whom he had sent to the emir Amormuni [5]

---

[g] 4b² ; orbem 4a
[h] epys., 4a. *y is often preferred by this scribe*
[i] 4b² ; leodibus 4a   [j] 4b² ; misserat 4a
[1] i.e. till 6 January 768
[2] 768
[3] cf. cont. chap. 42, above
[4] Maine-et-Loire
[5] i.e. emir-almunenyn, leader of the faithful. The reigning caliph was Almansor (Abou Djafar).

U

post tres annos ad Marsiliam reuersus fuisset ; legationem predictus Amormuni rex Saracenorum ad
praefato rege cum multis muneribus secum adduxerat.
Quod cum conpertum regi fuisset, missos suos ad eum
direxit, qui eum uenerabiliter reciperent et usque ad
Mettis ciuitatem [a] ad hiemandum ducerent. Igitur
suprascripti comites qui ad Remistanium capiendum
missi fuerant per diuino iudicio et fidem regis capiunt
et legatum ad praesentiam regis cum uxore sua
adduxerunt. Quem statim rex Vniberto et Gislario
comite Betoricas ciuitate ipso Remistanium [b] in patibulo
eum suspendi iussit. Praedictus rex Pippinus usque
ad Garonnam accessit ; ibi Vascones qui ultra Garonna
commorantur, ad eius presentia uenerunt et sacramenta
et obsides praedicto rege donant ut semper fideles
partibus regis hac filiis suis Carlo et Carlomanno omni
tempore esse debeant. Et alii multi [c] quam plures ex
parte Waiofarii ad eum uenientes et dictionis sue
facientes, rex uero Pippinus benigniter eos in sua
dictione recepit. Waiofarius cum paucis per siluam [d]
qui uocatur Edobola in pago Petrocoreco latitans huc
illucque uagatur [e] incertus. Prefatus rex Pippinus ad
Waiofarium capiendum insidias iterum parat. Inde ad
reginam suam [f] ad Sellus ueniens, legationem Saracenorum, quod ad Mettis ad hiemandum miserat, ad Sellus
castro ad se uenire praecepit, et ipsi Saraceni munera
quod Amormuni transmiserat ibidem presentant. Iterum
rex ipsos Saracenos qui ad eum missi fuerant munera
dedit et usque ad Marsilia cum multo honore adducere
praecepit. Saraceni uero nauale euectione per mare
redeunt [g] ad propria.

[a] 4b[2] ; ciuitatis 4a   [b] Remistagnum *all MSS*
[c] 4c[1] ; aliae mult(a)e 4a, b[2]   [d] 4b[2] ; siluis 4a

of the Saracens had returned to Marseilles after an absence of three years, and that they were accompanied by a mission from the Saracen emir Amormuni with many gifts. The king received the report and thereupon sent off representatives to welcome them honourably and to conduct them to winter-quarters in the city of Metz. Furthermore the counts I spoke of above who had been sent out to catch Remistanius were as good as their word ; for, with God's help and inasmuch as he was forsworn, they captured Remistanius and his wife and brought them bound to the king's presence. The king promptly ordered Chunibert and Count Gislarius of Bourges to hang Remistanius on a gibbet in that same city. King Pippin now journeyed to the Garonne, where the Gascons who live beyond the Garonne came to his presence. They gave hostages and swore evermore to remain loyal to the king and to his sons, Charles and Carloman. Many more of Waiofar's supporters came and submitted to his overlordship, King Pippin magnanimously accepting their allegiance. Waiofar and a few followers were in hiding in the Forêt de Ver in the district of Périgueux wandering about, uncertain how to avoid pursuit. Again King Pippin laid schemes to capture Waiofar. First, coming to his queen at Chantoceaux, he summoned the Saracen embassy that had been sent to winter in Metz to meet him in the fortress of Chantoceaux. The Saracens there presented him with the gifts sent by Amormuni, whereupon he gave to the Saracens of that same mission gifts in return, and had them escorted with much honour to Marseilles. There the Saracens took ship and returned to their native country.

---

e 4b² (*corr.*) ; uagatus 4a   *f* 4b² ; ad regina sua 4a
g 4b² ; redunt 4a

52

Praecelsus [a] rex Pippinus iterum de Sellus castro cum paucis ad persequendum Waiofarium eo anno iterum perrexit et usque ad Sanctonis mira celeritate primus cum paucis uenit. Cum hoc Waiofarius audisset solito more terga uertit. Rex Pippinus in quattuor partes comites suos, scaritos et leudibus suis ad persequendum Waiofarium transmisit.[b] Dum hec ageretur, ut adserunt consilio [c] regis factum fuisset, Waiofarius princeps Aquitanie a suis interfectus est. Praefatus rex Pippinus, iam totam Aquitaniam adquesitam, omnes ad eum uenientes dictionis sue sicut antiquitus fuerat faciunt, cum magno triumpho et uictoria Sanctonis, ubi Bertrada regina resedebat, ueniens.

53

Dum Sanctonis praefatus rex uenisset et causas pro salute patriae et utilitate Francorum tractaret, a quedam febre uexatus egrotare cepit [1] ; comites suos ac iudices ibidem constituit. Inde per Pictauis usque ad Turonis urbem ad monasterium beati Martini confessoris accessit ; ibique multa elemosina tam ecclesiis quam monasteriis uel pauperum largitus est et auxilium [d] beati Martini petens, ut pro eius facinora Domini misericordia deprecare dignaretur. Inde promouens cum praedicta regina Bertradane et filios suos Carlo et Carlomanno usque ad Parisius ad monasterium [e] beati Dionisii martiris ueniens ibique moratus est aliquamdiu.[f] Cernensque quod uite periculum euadere non potuisset, omnes proceres suos, ducibus uel comitibus

[a] 4b² ; praecellus 4a   [b] 4b² ; transmissit 4a
[c] 4c¹ ; cosilia 4a   [d] 4b² ; ausilium 4a

52

The noble King Pippin set out again that year from Chantoceaux with a small company to hunt for Waiofar. He travelled with great speed to Saintes, his first destination. Hearing this, Waiofar made off at once, as usual ; whereupon the king despatched his counts with their troops and his own men in four columns to pursue Waiofar. But in the meantime, Waiofar, lord of Aquitaine, was assassinated by his own followers— allegedly with the king's connivance. King Pippin had now won control of the whole of Aquitaine ; all came to him, as in the old days, to become his men. And so, victorious and triumphant, he returned to Saintes, where Queen Bertrada was in residence.

53

While the king was at Saintes, busying himself with affairs of national Frankish importance, he was troubled with a kind of fever and fell ill.[1] He there appointed his counts and judges. Thence he travelled through Poitiers to the monastery of the blessed confessor Martin at the city of Tours, where he made many gifts to churches and monasteries as well as to the poor ; and he sought the help of the blessed Martin as intercessor with the Lord, that He should deign to have mercy on his sins. He went on, with Queen Bertrada and his sons Charles and Carloman, to the monastery of the holy martyr Denis at Paris, and remained there some time. However, when he realised that recovery was impossible, he summoned to him all his great men, the Frankish dukes

---

e 4c[1] ; monasterio 4a, b[2]   *f* 4c[1] ; aliquandiu 4a, b[2]

[1] cf. *Ann. Regni Franc.*, *sub anno* 768, loc. cit.

Francorum, tam episcopis quam sacerdotibus ad se uenire precepit. Ibique una cum consensu Francorum et procerum suorum seu et episcoporum regnum Francorum quod ipse tenuerat equali sorte inter predictis filiis suis Carlo et Carlomanno, dum adhuc ipse uiueret, inter eos diuisit : id est Austrasiorum [1] regnum Carlo seniore filio regem instituit, Carlomanno uero iuniore filio regnum Burgundiae, Prouintiae et Gotiae,[a] Alesasis et Alamania tradidit. Aquitania prouintia quam ipse rex adquesierat inter eos diuisit. His gestis rex Pippinus post paucos dies ut dolus est ad dicendum ultimum diem et uitam simul caruit[2] ; sepelieruntque eum praedicti reges Carlus et Carlomannus filii ipsius regis,[b] in monasterio Sancti Dionisii martiris ut ipse uoluit, cum magno honore. Regnauitque ann. xxv.[3]

54

His transactis, praedicti reges Carlus et Carlomannus unusquisque cum leudibus [c] suis ad propriam sedem regni eorum uenientes, instituto placito initoque consilio cum proceribus eorum mense Septembrio die dominico xiiii Kl. Octobris,[4] Carlus ad Nouionem urbem et Carlomannus ad Saxonis ciuitatem,[d] pariter uno die a proceribus eorum et consecratione [e] sacerdotum sublimati sunt in regno.

[a] 4c[1] ; Burgundia, Prouintia et Gotia 4a
[b] 4b[2] ; reges 4a
[c] 4b[2] ; leodibus 4a
[d] 4b[2] ; ciuitate 4a
     4b[2] ; consecrationem 4a

and counts, bishops and priests. Then, with the approval of the Frankish nobility and the bishops, he divided the kingdom that he himself had inherited, and while he was yet living, equally between his sons Charles and Carloman. He made Charles, the elder, king over the Austrasians,[1] while the younger, Carloman, was given the kingdom of Burgundy, Provence, Septimania, Alsace and Alamannia. Aquitaine, the province which he had himself conquered, he divided between them. A few days later, I grieve to say, King Pippin breathed his last.[2] His sons, King Charles and King Carloman, buried him, as he had wished, with great honour in the monastery of the holy martyr Denis. He had reigned twenty-five years.[3]

54

Afterwards, the two new kings, Charles and Carloman, went with their followings to their respective seats of royal power. They summoned their nobles to meet them in council, and then, both on the same day, Sunday, 18 September,[4] they received consecration by the Church and were raised to their thrones by their great men, Charles at the town of Noyon and Carloman at the city of Soissons.

---

[1] Charles also received Neustria.
[2] 24 September 768
[3] more accurately, twenty-seven years
[4] rightly, 9 October (*Ann. Regni Franc.*, *sub anno* 768, loc. cit.)

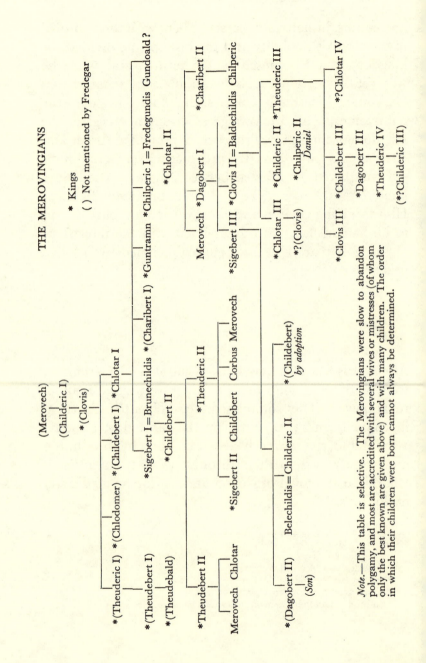

THE MEROVINGIANS

* Kings

( ) Not mentioned by Fredegar

Note.—This table is selective. The Merovingians were slow to abandon polygamy, and most are accredited with several wives or mistresses (of whom only the best known are given above) and with many children. The order in which their children were born cannot always be determined.

THE ARNULFINGS OR CAROLINGIANS

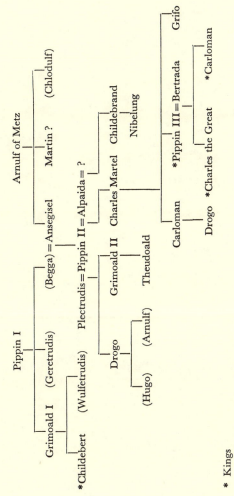

* Kings
( ) Not mentioned by Fredegar

INDEX

INDEX

Persons and places named in the text are indexed under the form given in the translation. An index verborum is omitted as it would have to take account of the complete chronicle if it were to be of value. Reference may be made to the Lexica in the edition of Krusch.

Aar, river, 12
Abbelin, count, 29
' Abd ar-Rahman, ? Iussef Ibn, 94
' Abd ar-Rahman, 90, 91
Abraham, 92
Abundantius, Frankish duke, 62
Adalard, count of Chalon, 113
Adalgisel, duke, 63, 64, 73
Adaloald, Lombard king, 22, 41
Adalulf, Lombard, 42, 43
Adam, x, 92
Aeconius (Hiconius), bishop of Saint-Jean-de-Maurienne, 14
Aega, mayor, 51, 67, 68, 70, 71, 72, 75
Aegulf, abbot of Saint-Denis, 68
Aegyla, patrician, 5, 14
Aetherius, bishop of Lyons, 15
Aetius, Roman patrician, 61
Africa, 51, 69
Agaune, *see* Saint Maurice
Agde, 95
Agen, 47, 116
Agilolf. *See* Ailulf
Agilulf (Ago), Lombard duke, king, 10, 20, 22, 38, 41
Agilulf, Lombard noble, 38
Aglibert, 83
Ago. *See* Agilulf
Aighyna, duke, Saxon noble, 45, 46, 65
Aighyna, Gascon duke, 66
Ailulf, (Agilolf), bishop of Valence 77
Aisne, river, 34
Aistulf, Lombard king, 104, 105, 106, 107, 108, 109
Alamans, Alamannia, xii, xlii, 7, 16n, 29, 30, 57, 75, 90, 97, 98, 100, 121

Albenga, 60
Alboin, Austrasian noble, 33
Alcuin, 88n
Alethius, patrician, 34, 36, 37
Alexander the Great, 54
Alexandria, 69
Almansor, caliph, 118n
Alpaida, wife of Pippin II, xxvi, 86, 102n
Alps, Swabian, 100
Alsace, 29, 36, 121
Alzeco, Bulgar leader, 61
Amalbert, brother of Flaochad, 76, 77
Amalbert, Frankish noble, 81
Amalgar, duke, 48, 62, 65, 77, 78
Amand, Saint, 51n
Amblève, 88
Amiens, 13n
Ammanugus, count of Poitiers, 114
Amormuni, emir, 118, 119
Anaulf, Persian ruler, 7, 8, 9
Andelot, 7, 30
Andernach, 33
Angers, 89
Angoulême, 114, 117
Annales Mettenses Priores, 99n
Annales Regni Francorum, 98n, 102n, 103n, 110n, 120n, 121n
Anno Domini, 92
Anōsharvān. *See* Chosroes I.
Anseflidis, wife of Waratto, 84, 85
Ansegisel, father of Pippin II, 83
Ansoald, 42
Antioch, 8
Antonina, wife of Belisarius, xiii
Aosta, 37, 38
Apfeldorf, 99n
Aquitaine, 48, 89, 98, 109, 110, 111, 114, 115, 116, 117, 120, 121

Arar, river. *See* Saône
Arc, river, 103
Arcis, 12
Ardennes, 31, 39, 62, 88, 104; group of MSS. lvi
Arèle, villa, 16
Argenton, 114
Aridius, bishop of Lyons, 15, 20, 21
Aripert. *See* Charibert, son of Gundoald
Arles, 93
Arnac-Pompadour, monastery of, lii
Arnebert, duke, 44, 45, 48, 65, 66
Arnulf, Saint, bishop of Metz, 32, 43, 44, 49
Arnulfings. *See* Carolingians
Athaulf, Visigoth king, 95n
Atlantic ocean, 13
Aubedo, Frankish legate, 59, 60
Aude, river, 94
Audoenus (Ouen, Saint), bishop of Rouen. *See* Dado
Audolenus, father of Boso, 45
Audoramnus, 85
Augers, court at, 70
Augustine, Saint, 2n, 102n
Australdus, count, 113
Austrasia, Austrasians, xiii, xviii, xxiii, xxiv, xxv, xxvi, xlii, lv, 11, 12, 23, 29, 30, 32, 33, 34, 35, 36, 39, 43, 44, 47, 49, 50, 51, 57, 58, 62, 63, 64, 71, 72, 73, 75, 81, 83, 84, 85, 89n, 97, 121
Austrenus, bishop of Orleans, 16
Autbert, count, xxvi
Authari, Lombard king, 22, 38
Autun, xxvii, 49, 77, 78, 111, 116
Auvergne, 73, 110, 111, 112
Auxerre, 13, 49, 77, 110, 111, 114, 117
Avars, 39, 40, 49, 60, 61 ; *see also* Huns
Avenches (Wifflisburg), xii, xvii, xxii, 29, 30
Avignon, 94, 95
Avitus, bishop, 4

Baizieux, villa, 82
Baldechildis, wife of Clovis II, 80
Barontus, duke, 56, 65

Baudemundus, 51n
Baudulf, 27
Bavarians, 61, 90, 98, 99, 101, 102
Beauvais, 13n
Bede, ix, xiv, liii, lvi, 79n, 91n, 96n
Befulci, 40
Begga, mother of Pippin II, 83n
Belechildis, wife of Childeric II, 81
Beletrudis, Bavarian, 90
Belisarius, xii
Beppelen, duke, 10
Berchar, mayor, 85
Berchildis, wife of Dagobert I, 50
Berengar, count, 118
Berny-Rivière, villa, 105
Berre, river, 95
Berry, 110, 118
Bertefred, 7
Bertelannus, bishop of Bourges, 110
Bertetrudis, wife of Chlotar II, 36, 37, 39
Bertha, stepmother of Godinus, 44, 45
Berthar, count, xix, 27, 28, 31, 32, 78
Berthar of Charpeigne, 43
Bertoald, mayor, 15, 16, 17
Bertrada, queen, wife of Pippin III, 102, 117, 118, 119, 120
Besançon, 27
Béziers, 95
Bible, references to, lxi
    Ecclesiasticus, *sapiens quidam*, 1
    Joshua vi. 1, 112n
    Joshua vi. 20, 94n
    2 Samuel iii. 1, 112n
    2 Samuel xi. 1, 105n
    2 Kings xiii. 25, 112n
    Psalm xxii. 18, 9
    Ecclesiasticus xxiv. 19, 25n
    Luke i. 80, ii. 40, 86n
    Luke xxi. 25, 97n
    Hebrews xi. 23, 86n
Bilichildis, wife of Theudebert II, 22, 23, 30
Bladinus, count of Auvergne, 110, 111, 116
Blaye, 91
Bobbio, monastery of, 29
Bobo, duke, 73, 74
Bodilo, 81
Bois-du-Fays, 83

Bondy, 81*n*
Boniface, Saint, xxvii, xxviii, 93*n*, 99*n*, 102*n*
Bonn, 103
Bonneuil, villa, 37
Boorn, river, 92
Bordeaux, 90, 91
Boso, duke, 5, 9
Boso, son of Audolenus, 45
Bourbon, 111
Bourcheresse, villa, 24*n*
Bourges, 98, 111, 112, 114, 116, 117, 118
Bretons, Brittany, 10, 13, 66
Brodulf, uncle of Charibert II, 46, 47, 48
Brocaria, villa, 24*n*
Brunechildis, queen, xl, 12, 13, 14, 15, 16, 18, 19, 20, 21, 22, 23, 24, 25, 27, 32, 33, 34, 35
Bruyères-le-Châtel, villa, 24
Bubo, Frisian duke, 92
Buchonia, forest of, 73
Bugga, abbess, 93*n*
Buis, 78*n*
Bulgars, 60, 61 ; spelling, xxxii
Burgundy, Burgundians, xviii, xix, xxiii, xxiv, xxvii, lxi, 4, 6, 11, 18, 23*n*, 32, 33, 34, 35, 36, 37, 39, 45, 46, 47, 48, 62, 64, 65, 66, 68, 75, 76, 77, 91, 93, 97, 103, 107, 113, 118, 121
  Annals, xiii, xvii, xx, xxi, xxii
Byzantium (Roman Empire), x, xiii, 15, 49, 51, 52, 55, 58, 60, 68, 69, 105, 106; *see also* Constantinople

Caesar, *de Bello Gallico*, 27*n*
Caesara, empress (? Shīrīn, Sira), 7, 8
Cahors, 47
Cambrésis, 88
camels, 35
Campania, Campanensis, 29
Canche, river, 13*n*
Cannstatt, 100*n*
Cantabria, 21
Carellus, 43*n*
Carloman, son of Charles Martel, 97, 98, 99, 100

Carloman, son of Pippin III, xiv, 119, 120, 121
Carolingians (Arnulfings), xlii, lvi, lix ; glorification of, xviii, xxiv, xxvi, xxvii ; annals, liv
Caspian sea, 54; gates, 54, 55
castra/castrus, xliv
Catalaunian fields, battle of, 61*n*
Caucasus, 54, 55
Cautinus, duke, 14
Chadoin, referendary, 33, 65
chain filings, links, 96*n*
Chainulf, count, 70, 71
Chaira, duke, 65
Chalcedon, 52
Chalon, xviii, xxii, 4, 20, 32, 48, 49, 76, 78, 107, 111; synod of, 15
Châlons-sur-Marne, 34
Chamar, father of Radulf, 64
Champagne, 13, 29, 34, 86
Channel, English, 13, 16
Chantoceaux, 118, 119, 120
Charibert (Aripert), son of Gundoald, 22, 43
Charibert II, 46, 47, 48, 51, 55, 56, 65
Charles Martel, xxvi, xxvii, 86, 87, 88, 89, 90, 91, 92, 93, 94, 95, 96, 97, 102*n*
  meaning of name, 87*n*
Charles the Great, xiv, xxvi, 104, 119, 120, 121
Charoald, Lombard king, 41, 42, 58
Chartres, 45
Chaubedo, son of Berthar, 78
Chenôve, 5*n*
Cher, river, 114
Childebert, son of Theuderic II, 15, 32, 34
Childebert II, 6, 7, 10, 11, 12, 18, 22, 29, 38
Childebert III, son of Theuderic III, 85, 86
Childebrand, count, duke, xxvi, xxvii, xxviii, lvi, 86*n*, 94, 95, 97, 102
Childerad, count, 118
Childeric II, 80, 81, 88*n*
Childeric III, 99*n*
Chilperic I, 3, 5, 35
Chilperic II (Daniel), 88, 89

Chilperic, son of Charibert II, 55
Chilping, count of Auvergne, 113
Chiltrudis, daughter of Charles Martel, 98, 107n
Chindaswinth, king of Spain, 69, 70
Chlotar I, 63, 101
Chlotar II, xi, xviii, xl, xlii, 5, 11, 12, 13, 16, 17, 20, 30, 32, 33, 34, 35, 36, 37, 38, 39, 41, 42, 43, 44, 45, 46, 47, 50
Chlotar III, 80
Chlotar IV, 89
Chlotar, son of Theudebert II, 35
Choisy, 86
Chosroes I (Anōsharvān), 7n, 52, 53
Chramnelen, duke, 65, 77, 78
Chramnulf, 45
chrism, consecration with, 102n, 104n, 121
Christmas, celebration of, 118
Chrodoald, Agilolfing noble, 43, 73
chronicles, problems of composition, xiv
Chrotechildis, wife of Clovis I, 14n
Chuc, mayor, 38
Chunibert, bishop of Cologne, 49, 63, 71, 72
Chunibert, count of Bourges, 110, 112, 118, 119
Chunoald, duke of Aquitaine, 98
Claudius, mayor, 19
Clausula de unctione Pippini, 102n
Cleph, Lombard king, 37
Clermont, 111, 114; College of, in Paris, xlvii
Clichy, villa, 44, 46, 66, 67, 70
Clovis I, xii, 14n
Clovis II, 59, 64, 67, 68, 70, 71, 72, 75, 77, 80
Clovis III, 85
Codex Carolinus, 96n
Colchis. See Ercolia
Cologne, li, 31, 32, 88
    Saint Pantaleon, abbey of, li, lii, lv
Colroy, 23
Columbanus, Saint (see also Vita), 2n, 23-29
comet, 11, 13
Comminges, St-Bertrand-de-, 5
Compiègne, villa, 17, 72, 87n

Constance, Lake, 28n ; monasteries near, lv
Constans II, emperor, 68, 69
Constantine I, donation of, 104n
Constantine III, emperor, 55, 68
Constantine V Copronymus, emperor, 109
Constantinople, 6, 8, 52, 69, 109 ; see also Byzantium
continuations, continuators, authorship of, xxvii
    language of, xliii ff., lviii, lix
    later use of, liv
Corbie, abbey of, xlix, 96
Corbières, valley of, 95
Corbus, son of Theuderic II, 16, 32, 34, 35
Crécy, villa, 82
Crodobert, Alaman duke, 57

Dado (Audoenus, Ouen, Saint, bishop of Rouen), referendary, 66, 81n, 84
Dagobert I, xx, xlii, 39, 43, 44, 45, 47, 48, 50, 51, 54, 55, 56, 57, 58, 59n, 61, 62, 63, 64, 65, 66, 67, 68, 71, 72
Dagobert III, xlviii, 86, 87, 88, 89n
Daniel. See Chilperic II
Danube, river, 90, 98
Dares Phrygius, De Origine Francorum, xxvi, xlvi
Darius, 92
De Cursu Temporum. See Hilarian
De Origine Francorum. See Dares Phrygius
Dentelin, duchy of, xlii, 13, 30, 32, 64
Dervan, duke of the Sorbes, 57
Desiderius, 5
Desiderius, Lombard king, 109
Desiderius, Saint, bishop of Auxerre, 13n
Desiderius, bishop of Vienne, 15, 21
Diedenhofen, villa, 104
Digoin, 116
Dijon, 48, 79
domesticus, 5n
Domnolus, bishop of Vienne, 15
Domnolus, domesticus, 5
Dormelles, 13

Doubs, river, 27
Droctulft, Lombard duke, 38*n*
Drogo, duke, son of Pippin II, 85, 86
Drogo, son of Carloman, 100
Droizy, 12*n*
Düren, 110
Duurstede, 86

Easter, date of celebration, 97
Eborin, constable, 20
Ebrachar, Breton duke, 10
Ebroin, mayor, 80, 81, 82, 83, 84
eclipses, 10, 15
Ecry, villa, 83
Egra, river, 57*n*
Egypt, 69
Einhard, liii, lvi
Épinay-sur-Seine, villa, 67
Époisses, villa, 24
Erchinoald, mayor, xliii, 71, 75, 77, 80, 81
Ercolia (Colchis), 54
Ermenarius, comptroller, 46
Ermenberga, princess of Spain, 20
Ermenfred, 83, 84
Ermenfred, son-in-law of Aega, 70, 71
Ermenric, domesticus, 77
Étampes, 17
Eudila, *dux Vltraioranus*, 34, 36
Eudo, duke of Aquitaine, 89, 90, 91, 98, 114*n*, 117
Eusebius, liii; drawing of, xlix
Eusebius, Byzantine legate, 41
Eustacius, abbot of Luxeuil, 37
Eutyches, heresy of, 55

Falco, assassin, 35*n*
Fara, son of Chrodoald, 73
Faverney, villa, 19
Flaochad, Burgundian mayor, xi, xix, xxiii, 75, 76, 77, 78, 79
Flood, The, 92
Forêt Charbonnière, 13*n*
Forêt de Cuise, 87
Forêt de la Brotonne, 16*n*
Forêt de Ver, 119
Francio, duke, *magister militum*, 21
Franks, Francia, *passim*. Trojan origin of, xi, xii, xx, xxvi

Fredegar, name, xv ff., lxii
  Fredegar-Oudarius, xvi
  Fredegar-Scholasticus, xvi
  identity, xvi, xvii
  language of, xxviii ff., xxxix ff.
  present text, lvi ff.
  present translation, lx
  chronology, lxi
  previous editions, lxii
  translations of, lxiii
  bibliographical note, lxiii ff.
  rusticity, 2*n*
Fredegundis, queen, 5
Frederic, count of Transjura, 103
Fredulf, domesticus, 74
Frisians, Frisia, 86, 88, 92, 101
Friuli, 58*n*

Gaerinus, brother of Leudegar, 82
Galemanius, count, 113
Garonne, river, 90, 91, 115, 119
Gascons (Vaceti), Gascony, xlv, 14, 45, 47, 48, 56, 65, 66, 67, 82, 89, 98, 100, 111, 112, 113, 114, 115, 116, 119
Gauto, Lombard noble, 38
Geneva, xxii, 14, 107
Genialis, duke of Gascons, 14
Genoa, 60
Gesta Epis. Autisiodorensium, 91*n*
Gesta Francorum, 103
Gesta Theuderici Regis, lii
Ghislemar, son of Waratto, 84
Gildas, 12*n*
Gislarius, count of Bourges, 119
glossaries, 2*n*
Godafred, Alaman duke, 100
Godegisel, 14*n*
Goderamnus, of Cologne and Hildesheim, lii
Godinus, son of Warnachar, 44, 45
Gomatrudis, wife of Dagobert I, 44, 49
Gordon, 117
Goths, 9, 109, 121; conversion of, 7
Gozbert, Thuringian duke, 64*n*
Great St Bernard, 104
Gregory, bishop of Antioch, 8, 9
Gregory, bishop of Tours, ix, x, xi, xii, xiv, xvii, xxi, xxiii, xxiv, xxv, xxxviii, xlii, xlvi, li, liii,

Gregory, Bishop of Tours—*cont.*
    lvi, lx, lxii, 1, 2, 3, 4*n*, 5*n*, 6*n*,
    7*n*, 9*n*, 18*n*, 63*n*, 68*n*, 70*n*
Gregory, patrician, 69
Gregory I, pope, 96*n*
Gregory III, pope, 96
Grifo, son of Charles Martel, xxvii,
    90*n*, 101*n*, 103
Grimo, abbot of Corbie, 96
Grimoald I, mayor, son of Pippin I,
    xlii, 72, 73, 75
Grimoald II, mayor, son of Pippin
    II, 85, 86, 87
Grimoald of Bavaria, 22, 90*n*
Gundeberga, Lombard princess, 22,
    41, 42, 43, 59, 60
Gundebert, son of Gundoald, 22
Gundeland, mayor, 38
Gundoald, 5, 6*n*
Gundoald of Bavaria, 22
Guntheuca, 14*n*
Gunthimar, 21*n*
Guntramn Boso, duke, 7, 9
Guntramn, king of Burgundy, xi, 1,
    4, 5, 6, 7, 9, 10, 11, 38
Gyso, count, 77

Hadrian I, pope, xi
Haecpert, scribe, l, lv
Hagar, race of. *See* Saracens
Helena, Saint, drawing of, xlviii
Heraclius I, emperor, xi, 21*n*, 41*n*,
    51, 52, 53, 54, 55
Heraclius, exarch of Carthage,
    51*n*
Hermenald, count, 118
Hermenric, duke, 65
Herpin, count, 29, 36
Herpo, constable, *dux Vltraioranus*,
    33, 35, 36
Hetan, Thuringian duke, 64*n*
Hiconius. *See* Aeconius
Hilarian, *De Cursu Temporum*, xxvi,
    xlvi
Hippolytus. *See Liber Generationis*
Hruodi, duke, 64*n* ; *see also* Radulf
Huns, 61*n* ; *see also* Avars
Hunsrück, 62*n*
Huoching, son of Godafred, 100*n*
Hydatius, chronicle of, xi, xvii,
    xviii, xx, xxii, xxiv, xlvi, lxii, 1

Idarwald, 62*n*
immunities, 109
Ingobad, count, 35
Ingobert, 81
Inn, river, 99, 102
Innowales, count, 73, 74
Ireland, 28
Isaac, patrician, 58
Ishmael, race of. *See* Saracens
Isidore of Seville, xi, xvii, xix, xxi,
    xxii, xxiv, xlvi, 1, 2*n*
Issoudun, 115
Italy, 20, 22, 28 ; *see also* Lombards
iudicium Francorum, 29, 33, 44

Jericho, 94
Jerome, Saint, x, xi, xii, xvii, xviii,
    xx, xxii, xxiv, xxvi, xlvi, 1, 2*n*,
    54*n* ; drawing of, xlix
Jerusalem, 55, 68
Jews, baptism of, 54
John, patriarch of Constantinople,
    7, 9
Joppa, 9
Jordanes, historian, 54*n*
Joshua, 94
Judicael, Breton king, 66
Jupille, 86
Jura, territory, people, East of,
    xviii, 10, 16, 29, 30, 35
justice, Dagobert's, 48
Justinian I, emperor, xii

Khagan, Avar ruler, 39

Laffaux, 12
Landri, mayor, 16, 17
Langres, 30, 48
Lantfrid I, son of Godafred, 100*n*
Lantfrid II, 100*n*
Lanzo, valley of, 38
Laon, 83
Lech, river, 99
Léger, Saint. *See* Leudegar
Lesio. *See* Leudegasius
Leucate, Étang de, 95*n*
Leucone, 81*n*
Leudebert, duke, 65
Leudefred, Alaman duke, 7
Leudegar (Léger) Saint, bishop of
    Autun, 81, 82

Leudegasius (Lesio), bishop of Mainz, 31
Leudegesil, constable, patrician, 5, 6
Leudemund, bishop of Sion, 36, 37
leudes, 4*n*
Leudesius, son of Erchinoald, mayor, 81, 82
Leuthar, Alaman duke, 75
Leuvigild, king of Spain, 6
Lex Ribvaria, 43*n*, 44*n* ; *see also* Ripuaria
Lex Salica, 43*n*, 81*n*
Liber Generationis of Hippolytus, x, xi, xvii, xviii, xx, xxii, xxiv, xxvi, xlvi, xlix, 1
Liber Historiae Francorum, x, xiii, xxv, xxvi, xliii, l, lii, liii, lv, lvi, lx, lxi, 12*n*, 80*n*, 81*n*, 82*n*, 88*n*, 89*n*
Liège, liii, lvi ; *see also* Saint Lambert, Saint Laurence
Limoges, 114, 115, 118
Lippe, river, 93
Livry, forest of, 81
Lobbes, monastery of, liii
Loches, 98
Lognes, bois de, 81*n*
Loire, river, 13, 16, 44, 47, 82, 90, 91, 98, 100, 110, 111, 113, 115, 116, 117, 118
Lombards, Lombardy, xlii, 10, 37, 38, 39, 41, 57, 58, 59, 60, 103, 104, 105, 106, 107, 108, 109 ; *see also* Italy
Lomello, fortress, 42
Lorsch, abbey of, li, liii, liv, lv, lvi
Louet, river, 17
Lucerius, priest, xlvii, xlviii
Luni, 60
Luxeuil, monastery of, xlix, 23, 26, 37, 81, 82
Lyons, Lyonnais, xxii, 76*n*, 91, 93, 105, 113

Mailly, villa, 111
Mainz, 62, 74
Mâlay-le-roi, villa, 37, 68
Manaulf, 78
Manno of Saint-Oyan, li
Mantio, count, 113
manuscripts, survey of, xlvi ff.

Augsburg 223, li, lxii
Berlin 127, xviii ; *Lat. Quart. 266*, liii
Berne 318, l
Brussels 6439/51, liii ; *9361/67*, liii
Giessen univ. 254a, liii
Graz univ. fol. 42/59, lii ; *quart. 33/52*, liii
Heidelberg univ. Palat. Lat. 864, liii, lvi, lix, lxii
Karlsruhe, lii
Leiden Voss. Lat. 5, l ; *Voss. Lat. 20*, lii
Leningrad λ F. Otd. IV, liii
London, British Museum : *Harleian 2767*, li ; *Harleian 3771*, li, lv, lix ; *Harleian 5251*, l, lv
Metz 134, l, lv
Milan S. Ambrogio M. 13, li, lv
Montpellier Schol. med. 158, lii, lxii
Munich Lat. 4352, lii, lix, lxii
Namur Soc. Archéol. 11, liii
Paris, Bibliothèque Nationale : *Lat. 4883 A*, lii ; *Lat. 5921*, liii, lvi, lix, lxii ; *Lat. 9765*, liii, lvi, lix ; *Lat. 10910*, xvii, xlvii ff., lv, lvi, lvii, lxii ; *Lat. 10911*, liii, lvi
Rome, Vatican : *Reg. Lat. 213*, li, lv, lix ; *Reg. Lat. 549*, lii ; *Reg. Lat. 713*, l.
Saint Gall 547, liii, lvi
Saint Omer 706, xv, liii
Troyes 802, li, lv, lxii
Vienna 428, liii ; *473*, liii, lvi ; *482*, li ; *univ. 3334*, lii
Marchfield, 105, 116
Marlenheim, villa, 36
Marseilles, 12, 93, 119
Martin, duke, 83
Martin, Saint, intercessor, 120 ; feast of, 17 ; *see also* Saint Martin, church of
Martina, wife of Heraclius I, 55*n*
Mary, sister of Heraclius I, 55*n*
Maurice, emperor, 6*n*, 8, 9, 15, 38, 41, 51, 52
Maurontus, duke of Provence, 93, 96

Mayfield, 76, 110, 115, 116, 117
Mediterranean, 96
Mehrerau, abbey of, l, li, lv
Melun, xxvi
merchants, Frankish, 39, 56
Merovech, son of Chlotar II, 16, 17, 35
Merovech, son of Theudebert II, 32
Merovech, son of Theuderic II, 20, 32, 34, 35
Merovingians, xxvii
Mesves, 110
meteor, 6
Metz, xxiv, 11, 30, 32, 62, 63, 72, 119
Meuse, river, 86, 87
Midi, xiv, xlv
millennium, 92
Moissac, liv$n$
monothelitism, 55n
Mons Adraldus, xxvi
Mont Cenis, 107
Montmartre, 46
Moselle, river, 62n, 104
Moses, 86n, 92
Mummolus, 5

Naix, 30
Namur, 84
Nantechildis, wife of Dagobert I, 49, 50, 64, 67, 68, 71, 72, 75, 76
Nantes, 28
Narbonne, 94, 113
Neptune, a present for, 52
Neustria, Neustrians, xxv, xlii, 35, 39, 46, 47, 50, 51, 62, 63, 64, 68, 77, 78, 97, 121n
Nevers, 111, 115
Nibelung, count, xxvi, xxvii, xlv, 103 ; family, 102n
Nîmes, 95
Noyon, 89, 121
numerals, roman and arabic, lviii

Oderzo, 60
Odilo, Bavarian duke, 98, 99, 107n
Oise, river, 13, 82, 96, 97
Old Testament, xxviii ; see also Bible

Omar-ibn-Chaled, emir, 95
Orbe, villa, 35
Orleans, 11, 16, 51, 75, 89, 98, 116, 118
Orosius, liii, 54
Orvanne, river, 13
Ostergo, Frisian island, 92
Oswiu's queen, 96n
Otto, son of Uro, 72, 75
Ouen, Saint (Audoenus), bishop of Rouen. See Dado
Ours, Saint, 14

Palladius, bishop of Eauze, 45
Pannonia, 60, 61
Paris, 5, 12, 17, 44, 49, 67, 77, 88, 89, 97
Passio Kiliani, 64n
Passio Leudegarii, 82n
Paternus, Frankish legate, 51
patrician, 5, 6
Patricius Romanorum, title, 96n
Patricius, bishop, 14
Patrick, Saint, 12n
Paul the Deacon, liii, 7n, 8n, 10n, 11n, 13n, 22n, 37n, 41n, 43n, 58n, 59n, 61n
Pavia, 59, 106, 107, 108
Périgueux, 47, 114, 117, 119
Persia, Persians, 7ff., 15, 52, 53
Peter, court physician, 18
Peter, Saint, relics, 96 ; help of, 105; see also Rome
Phocas, emperor, 15, 51, 52
Pippin I (of Landen), mayor, 32, 43, 49, 50, 51, 71, 72
Pippin II (of Herstal), duke, 83, 84, 85, 86, 87
Pippin III (the Short) duke, king, xxvi, xxvii, xxviii, xlii, 97, 98, 99, 100, 101, 102, 103, 104, 105, 106, 107, 108, 109, 110, 111, 112, 113, 114, 115, 116, 117, 118, 120, 121
Pitto, 43
place names, spelling of, lix
plague, 12
Plectrudis, wife of Pippin II, 85, 87, 88, 89
Poitiers, 90, 114, 120 ; battle of, 91n

Pompeius, Lombard noble, 38
Pont-Saint-Maxence, 82
Ponthion, villa, 104
Pope. *See* Gregory I, Gregory III, Stephen II, Theodore I
proper names, spelling of, lix
Protadius, patrician, 16, 17, 18, 19
Provence, 6, 12, 44, 93, 95, 97, 121
puer, 7n
Pyrenees, 22, 47, 65

Quierzy, villa, 18, 97
Quolen, patrician, 12

Radbod, Frisian duke, 86, 87, 88
Rado, mayor, 35
Radulf, (Hruodi), Thuringian duke, xlii, 64, 73, 74
Ragamfred, mayor, 87, 88, 89
Ragamund, 28
Ragnetrudis, mistress of Dagobert I, 50
Ragnoberta, wife of Flaochad, 75
Rantgar, assassin, 87
Rauching, duke, 7
Ravenna, 58
Reccared I, Visigoth king, 6, 7
Reccared II, Visigoth king, 61n
Reccaswinth, Visigoth king, 70
Reichenau, abbey of, l
Remistanius, uncle of Waiofar, 114, 117, 118, 119
Renève, village, 35
Reolus, bishop of Rheims, 83, 85
Reuilly (? Romilly), villa, 49
Rheims, 47 ; *and see* Saint Rémi, church of
Rhine, river, 31, 33, 62, 73, 74, 88, 90, 93, 98, 103
Rhön, 73n
Rhône, river, 93, 94
Ricomer, patrician, 19
Ripuaria, 110 ; *see also Lex Ribvaria*
rito barbaro, 12, 29
Rocco, duke, 20, 34
Roman Empire. *See* Byzantium
Romanus (Gallo-Roman), 16
Rome, Romans, 96, 101, 102, 104, 105, 106, 107 ; duchy of, 69
Romensis, 104
Romilly. *See* Reuilly

Rothari, Lombard king, 59, 60
Rouen, xxv, 13n
Rueil, villa, 5
Rusticius, bishop, 14

Saint Aignan, church of, Orleans, 45
Saint Arnulf, church of, Metz, xlvii, liii, livn, lv, lvi, 86
Saint Bénigne, church of, Dijon, 79
Saint Bertin, abbey of, liii, lvi, 99n
Saint Claude, monastery of, li
Saint Denis, monastery of, Paris, xxv, 45, 67, 80n, 96, 97, 104, 120, 121
Saint Epvre, church of, Toul, 45
Saint Gall, abbey of, l, lvi
Saint Germain, church of, Auxerre, 62n
Saint Germain, abbey of, Paris, xxvi
Saint Hilary, church of, Poitiers, 90
Saint Hubert, monastery of, liii, lvi
Saint-Jean-de-Losne, 48, 79
Saint-Jean-de-Maurienne, 14, 103, 105, 107
Saint Lambert, church of, lii, 87
Saint Laurence, monastery of, Liège, liii
Saint Marcel, church of, Chalon, 4, 10
Saint Martin, church of, Tours, 45, 90, 114, 120
Saint Maurice, church of, Agaune, 4, 68
Saint Médard, church of, Soissons, 45
Saint Pantaleon, abbey of. *See* Cologne
Saint Quentin, 85
Saint Rémi, church of, Rheims, xii, li, lv, 71, 109n
Saint Stephen, church of, Choisy, 86
Saint Ulrich, monastery of, Augsburg, lii
Saint Vaast (Vedast), monastery of, Arras, liii, lvi
Saint Vincent, church of, Paris, xxvi, 47
Saint Wandrille, abbey of, livn
Saintes, 47, 114, 120
Saintois, 23, 29, 73
Salins, 16n

Samo, Wendish king, xlii, 39, 40, 56, 57, 63
Saône (Arar), river, 34, 79
Saracens (Hagar, Ishmael, race of), 54, 55, 68, 69, 90, 91, 93, 94, 95, 113, 119
Saragossa, 62
Savona, 60
Saxons, Saxony, 31, 62, 63, 90, 93, 99, 101, 103
Scotingi, 16
Secundinus, bishop of Lyons, 15
Seine, river, 13, 16, 89 ; territory of, 4
Seltz, 29
Sens, 39n, 49, 77
Senuvia, 5
Septimania, 121
Servatus, Frankish legate, 51
Shīrīn. See Caesara
Sidonius Apollinaris, 2n
Sicharius, Frankish legate, 56, 57
Sichildis, wife of Chlotar II, 44, 45
Sideleuba, 14
Sidoc, bishop of Eauze, 45
Sidonia, 5
Sigebert II, x, 14, 32, 33, 34, 35
Sigebert III, 50, 51, 63, 64, 71, 72, 73, 74, 75
Sigebert, monk of Saint-Denis, 96
Sigismund, 4
Sigoald, duke, 34
Simon, son of Jacob, 9
Sira. See Caesara
Siroes, son of Chosroes, 53n
Sion, 36, 37
Sisebut, king of Spain, 15n, 21, 22n, 28n, 61
Sisenand, king of Spain, 61, 62, 69
Slavs. See Wends
Soissons, xii, 47, 121
Solomon, 92
Solothurn, 14
Soule, river, 66
Sorbes, Slav people, 57
Spain, x, 6, 9, 20, 21, 22, 61, 62, 69, 70, 94
Stephen II, pope, 104, 105, 106, 107
Suintila, king of Spain, 61, 69
Sunnichildis, wife of Charles Martel, 90, 98n

Supputatio Eusebii Hieronimi, x ; see Jerome, Saint
Susa, 37, 38, 105
Swabians, Swabia, 90, 97
Syagrius, count, 6

Taso, Lombard duke, 41, 42, 58
Tassilo, Bavarian duke, 107
Tertry, 85
Testri-sur-Omignon, 85n
Theodore I, pope, xi
Theodoric, Visigoth king, 61n
Theophanes, historian, 53n
Theudebald of Bavaria, 90n
Theudebald, son of Godafred, 99
Theudebert II, 6, 11, 12, 13, 14, 18, 19, 20, 22, 23, 29, 30, 31, 32, 35
Theudelinda, Lombard queen, 22
Theudelinda, wife of Godegisel, 14n
Theuderic II, xviii, 6, 11, 12, 13, 14, 15, 16, 17, 18, 19, 20, 21, 22, 23, 24-29, 30, 31, 32, 33, 34, 35, 65
Theuderic III, 80, 81, 82, 83, 85, 89n
Theuderic IV, xxvn, 89, 97n
Theudfrid, dux Vltraioranus, 10
Theudichildis, wife of Theudebert II, 30
Theudila, daughter of Childebert II, 20, 35
Theudoald, son of Grimoald II, 86, 87
Theudoenus, count of Vienne, 103
Thierry of Autun 103n
Thomas of Jerusalem, 9
Thorismund, Visigoth king, 61
Thouars, 112
Thrace, 69
Thun, lake of, 12
Thurgau, 29
Thuringians, Thuringia, xlii, 11, 31, 33, 57, 62, 63, 64, 73, 74, 97
Ticinum. See Pavia
Toledo, 7
Toul, 30
Toulouse, 47, 48, 62
Tours, Touraine, 114
Tours, Gregory, bishop of. See Gregory
Trier, 43, 109n

Troy. *See* Franks
Troyes, 46, 110, 111, 115, 117
Tulga, king of Spain, 69, 70
Turin, 41
Tuscany, 41, 58

Uncelen, Alaman duke, 7, 18, 19
Unstrut, river, 73
Uro, domesticus, 72
Ursio, 7
uxus, 53

Vaceti. *See* Gascons
Valence, 76*n* ; synod of, 4*n*
Varigotti, 60
Venerandus, Frankish duke, 62
Verberie, villa, 96
Verdun, 109*n*
Victor, Saint, 14
Victorius, cycle of, 92
Vienne, 105
Vilaine, river, 10
villa publica, 24, 104, 115
Vinchy, 88
Vincy. *See* Vinchy
vine-growing, xlv, 115, 118
Vingeanne, river, 35
vir inluster, 94*n*
Vita Amandi, 51*n*
    Ansberti, 65*n*
    Audoini, 66*n*
    Balthildis, 80*n*
    Bonifatii, 92*n*
    Columbani, xlix, lxi, 21*n*, 23-29, 35*n*
    Desiderii, 15*n*, 21*n*, 28*n*, 35*n*
    Eligii, 35*n*, 71*n*, 79*n*
    Eucherii, 91*n*
    Lamberti, 81*n*
    Leudegarii, xxviii*n*
    Pardulfi, 90*n*
    Praejecti, xxviii*n*
    Radegundis, xxviii*n*
    Sigiramni, 79*n*
    Vedastis, xii
    Willibrordi, 88*n*

Vogelsberg, 73*n*
Vosges, 31, 39, 100*n*

Waiofar, lord of Gascony, 103, 109,
    110, 111, 112, 113, 114, 115,
    116, 117, 118, 119, 120
Waldebert, domesticus, 45
Walderic, duke, 65
Walluc, Wendish duke, 61
Wambae, Historia, 35*n*
Wandalmar, chamberlain, *dux Vltra-
    ioranus*, 5, 10, 16
Wandalmar, duke, 65
Wandelbert, duke, 78
Wangen, 29
Waratto, mayor, 84
Warnachar, xviii, 12, 15, 33, 34, 35,
    37, 38, 44, 46
Warni (Thuringians), 11
wax tablet, 33
Wends, 39, 40, 49, 56, 57, 61, 62,
    63, 64, 101
Westergo, Frisian island, 92
Wgost-Uhošťany, Bohemia, 57*n*
Wifflisburg, xii ; *see* Avenches
Willebad, patrician, xix, xxiii, 49,
    65, 76, 77, 78, 79 ; spelling,
    xxxi
Wintrio (Quintrio), duke of Cham-
    pagne, xxxi, 10, 12
Witteric, king of Spain, 20, 21
Wogastisburg, xlii, 57
wolf story, 31
Worms, 33
Wulf, patrician, 19
Wulfard, abbot of Saint Martin,
    Tours, 114
Wulfegundis, wife of Dagobert I, 50
Wulfoald, duke, 81, 83

Yarmūk, battle of the, 55*n*
Yssandon, 115*n*

Zülpich, 31